"Reich's judgment about the means by which this country might recover its advantage could serve as a standard in debate over fundamental issues of politics and economics."
—*The New Yorker*

"One of the most important works of the decade"
—Walter Mondale

"Reich and his book rise out of the muck. . . . [He] goes at economics in a plain way, relatively free of the usual jargon."
—*Book Week*

"Economics still may be 'the dismal science,' but this brimming vision of it is anything but."   —*Working Woman*

"Few books on economics are bold enough to capture one's imagination. This is one."   —Senator Gary Hart

"An important and provocative book . . . Reich succeeds admirably in identifying our economy's underlying problems and the failure of current policies to address them."
—*The Washington Monthly*

"A challenging, thoughtful, and surprisingly readable book. If your favorite politician doesn't have one, send him or her a copy instead of a contribution."   —*St. Petersburg Times*

"An important contribution to a needed debate"
—*Boston Globe*

PENGUIN BOOKS

THE NEXT AMERICAN FRONTIER

Robert B. Reich teaches business and public policy at the John F. Kennedy School of Government at Harvard University. Formerly the director of policy planning for the Federal Trade Commission, he is coauthor with Ira Magaziner of *Minding America's Business*. His articles have appeared in *Foreign Affairs, The New Republic, Harvard Business Review, The Atlantic,* and various scholarly journals. Mr. Reich lives in Cambridge, Massachusetts, with his wife and son.

THE NEXT
AMERICAN
FRONTIER

ROBERT B. REICH

PENGUIN BOOKS

Penguin Books Ltd, Harmondsworth,
Middlesex, England
Penguin Books, 40 West 23rd Street,
New York, New York 10010, U.S.A.
Penguin Books Australia Ltd, Ringwood,
Victoria, Australia
Penguin Books Canada Limited, 2801 John Street,
Markham, Ontario, Canada L3R 1B4
Penguin Books (N.Z.) Ltd, 182–190 Wairau Road,
Auckland 10, New Zealand

First published in the United States of America by
Times Books 1983
First published in Canada by
Fitzhenry & Whiteside, Ltd., 1983
Published in Penguin Books 1984

LIBRARY OF CONGRESS CATALOGING IN PUBLICATION DATA
Reich, Robert B.
The next American frontier.
Originally published: New York: Times Books, 1983.
Includes index.
1. Business and politics—United States—History.
2. United States—Economic policy—1981–
3. Social justice. I. Title.
[JK467.R45 1984] 322'.3'0973 83-23741
ISBN 0 14 00.7040 0

Printed in the United States of America by
R. R. Donnelley & Sons Company, Harrisonburg, Virginia
Set in Videocomp Bembo

FOR CLARE

Acknowledgments

Ideas rarely emerge full-grown but instead are nurtured by conversation, debate, and argument. This book is no exception. I am indebted, first of all, to several of my colleagues here at Harvard's Kennedy School of Government—particularly Richard Neustadt, William Hogan, Mark Moore, Herman Leonard, Stephen Kelman, and Francis Bator—whose careful comments on earlier drafts, coupled with their own thought-provoking research, added immeasurably to whatever strengths the book now possesses. Across the river at the Business School, Joseph Badaracco and Thomas McCraw both helped me comprehend the mysterious ways of business decision making, and management consultants Tom Hout, Edward Morrison, and Ira Magaziner helped keep my sights focused on the real world of competitive strategy. I owe a special thanks to Ira, whose extraordinary knowledge of international business and insights into industrial policy are an invaluable fund on which I continue to draw.

Ezra Vogel, Raymond Vernon, Frank Weil, William Diebold, Jr., Jacques Feuillan, George Lodge, and Michael Pertschuk also have had a substantial influence on my thinking about these matters. The manuscript benefited from the readings and comments of Sidney Blumenthal, David Roe, Marc Lackritz, John Isaacson, and Clare Dalton. My secretary, Mrs. Elizabeth Miele, deserves a large gold medal for extraordinary care, patience, and cheerfulness.

Finally, I am indebted to several outstanding Kennedy School students for their help in tracking down obscure data and computerizing the text: Holly Wong, Molly Conway, Howard Frant, Jim Brenner, and Derek Kirkland. One student deserves special mention. Jack Donahue not only assisted in research but also helped in editing the book and in tightening its arguments. In this case, the student taught the teacher. Research for the book was supported by a grant from the Columbia University Center for Law and Economic Studies.

ROBERT B. REICH

Cambridge, Massachusetts
January 1983

CONTENTS

ORIGINS

Part One

I
TWO CULTURES

1.

Since the late 1960's America's economy has been slowly unraveling. The economic decline has been marked by growing unemployment, mounting business failures, and falling productivity. Since about the same time America's politics have been in chronic disarray. The political decline has been marked by the triumph of narrow interest groups, the demise of broad-based political parties, a succession of one-term presidents, and a series of tax revolts.

These phenomena are related. Economics and politics are threads in the same social fabric. The way people work together to produce goods and services is intimately tied to the way they set and pursue public goals. This link is perhaps stronger today than at any time in America's past because we are moving into an era in which economic progress depends to an unprecedented degree upon collaboration in our workplaces and consensus in our politics.

Our decline has a great deal to do with how we have come to view our roles as economic actors and as citizens and with the mismatch between that view and the changed economic environment we face. This book is about the origins of America's industrial organization and the social values bound up with it, about the economic evolution that is making them both obsolete, and about the change that must occur if we are to regain our momentum.

2.

Americans tend to divide the dimensions of our national life into two broad realms. The first is the realm of government and politics. The second is the realm of business and economics. Our concerns about social justice are restricted to the first realm; our concerns about prosperity, to the second. Issues of participation, equality of opportunity and civil rights, public education and mass transit, social security and welfare, housing, pollution, and crime are seen as aspects of government and politics—the substance of our civic culture. Issues of productivity and economic growth, inflation and unemployment, savings, investment, and trade are seen as aspects of business and economics—the substance of our business culture. Democrats and liberals traditionally lay claim to the first realm; Republicans and conservatives, to the second.

Americans whose principal frame of reference is the civic culture charge business with undermining civic values by compromising politicians with campaign contributions, polluting air and water, and endangering workers and consumers. Americans whose principal frame of reference is the business culture feel that government and politics intrude mischievously on the free market, at best distracting businessmen from the vigorous pursuit of national prosperity, at worst subverting the system of individual enterprise.

Our civic culture embodies a vision of community, premised upon citizenship. Its concern with democratic participation and the sharing of wealth stems from a conviction that such commitments enrich life and affirm the interdependency of individual lives. The profit motive is anathema to this vision because it apparently gives selfishness precedence over the common good. The pursuit of profit cannot be the sole guide to behavior, so this vision holds, because there would then be no firm distinction between productive enterprise and robbery, between voluntary trade and coercion. Unleashed fear and greed would destroy the fabric of community.

The business culture embodies a moral vision of its own—one of individual responsibility and freedom. According to this vision, the market offers a superior organizing principle for society because it promotes the common good while preserving individual autonomy. The market rewards endeavors to the extent that they contribute to others' well-being. Because their efforts enrich them, people willingly apply their talents and energies to the common good—a Frank Sinatra to entertain us or a Thomas Edison to invent for us. Incompetence, carelessness, and laziness are not rewarded. Collectivism is anathema to this vision because it seems to discourage such unforced efforts and to rely instead on more intrusive, less efficient incentives, such as coercion, compassion, or patriotism. Such a society, according to the business culture's moral vision, would offer both less prosperity and less freedom.

In countless ways Americans are called upon to choose between these two sets of central values—social justice or prosperity; government or free market; community or freedom. A debate over environmental pollution becomes a contest between the vision of a restored community flourishing within a scenic and healthy environment and the opposite vision of unfettered entrepreneurs whose ambition and daring would create new products and processes to benefit all. A debate over taxes and government spending becomes a divisive dispute over the relative value of business investment versus such intangibles as education, public health, and income security.

This choice is falsely posed. In advanced industrial nations like the United States, drawing such sharp distinctions between government and market has long ceased to be useful. Government creates the market by defining the terms and boundaries for business activity, guided by public perceptions of governmental responsibility for the overall health of the economy. Business, meanwhile, is taking on tasks that once were the exclusive province of government, involving responsibility for the work communities that are coming to be many Americans' most important social environment. The interwoven organizations of government, business, and labor together determine how America's resources are allocated and employed. Public and private spheres are becoming indistinguishable.

Like the Himalayan mountain called by two different names, depending on the side from which it is viewed, America's public and private sectors are coming to represent but two sides of the same process of economic evolution. The public effects of private business decisions often loom larger than any direct returns to investors. Private investments in coal extraction, for example, have profound implications for the financial viability of utilities, railroads, and mining towns, for soil erosion and water and air quality, for the rate of mine fatalities and black lung disease. The fate of the American auto industry similarly affects the rest of our society. One out of every six jobs in the economy depends on the industry; it uses much of the steel, glass, and machine tools made in the United States and most of the synthetic rubber. Its products shape America's culture and at the same time kill some 50,000 citizens each year on the highways, maim hundreds of thousands more, and shroud entire cities in smog. The level and pattern of investment in steel, chemicals, nuclear energy, drugs, textiles, and electronics also reverberate through our national life, serving some aspects of our well-being while threatening others.

Meanwhile, public investments—in education, job training, road, sewer, and port construction, health care, research, and day care—powerfully shape the prospects for private businesses and determine the direction of America's economic development.

The false choice between civic values and business values is blinding Americans to the real economic choice that must be faced over the next decade and thus is threatening America's future. This real choice is between shielding America from a changing world economy and adapting to engage the new realities of international competition. Only adaptation can lead to renewed prosperity. But as this book seeks to show, adaptation will require that American institutions, both public and private, support the social changes that must accompany economic change. And for this to occur, America must transcend the peculiar distinction traditionally drawn between our civic culture and our business culture.

3.

The cleavage between the business and civic cultures in America is a legacy of the nation's singular history. That history shaped both America's economic and social organizations and the ideology that developed alongside them.

Many of the first settlers came to this continent precisely to escape oppressive governments. The young country's formative political experience involved defying a strong central state in England. The original colonies, many populated by wary social minorities, were anxious to ensure that no one of them would come to dominate the others by gaining control of a powerful government.

During the years when the foundations of America's culture were being fixed, avoiding social conflict was far easier than settling it. The vastness of America's territories enabled generations of Americans to solve social problems by escaping from them, instead of working to change them. So long as the frontier beckoned, the sensible way to settle disputes was not painful negotiation, but simply putting some distance between the disputants. American notions of civic virtue came to center less on cooperating with the neighbors than on leaving them alone.

The ideology of escape from social problems lived on in America long after the nation's physical boundaries set limits to flight. It found expression in nineteenth-century utopian cooperatives and in twentieth-century suburban sprawl. It is still represented in America's vast network of highways and its "love affair" with the automobile. And it continues in our reluctance to acknowledge the end of the era of cheap fossil fuels and to devise strong measures for energy conservation; in our inability to halt the dumping of toxic wastes into aquifers; and within America's wealthy, suburban enclaves, whose residents are almost oblivious to the presence of real poverty in nearby central cities.

Perhaps most important, the economic challenge of America's early periods was straightforward—to exploit the staggering resources of a continental nation. Conquering this first American frontier demanded little but vision, daring, and initiative. Ongoing collaboration was rarely needed. Distribution seemed an almost empty issue. Americans cherished the myth of endless resources and wealth waiting for anyone ready to go after it.

Apart from its role in developing early transportation systems, government was not critical to the first stage of America's economic evolution. The government's functions were few and in general were more social and cultural than economic. This pattern endured in American myth long after it had altered in fact.

As the freewheeling era of mobilization gradually ended around the beginning of this century, America came to face a different set of economic challenges. New, more structured forms of business organization appeared. Efficient mass production required that whole industries informally coordinate their investment and production. Labor unions also organized by industry. Government programs helped support and stabilize this emerging system through regulations, war mobilizations, formal bargaining arenas, and social programs designed to help those who were unemployed or infirm. This was America's era of management (the subject of Part II). Management principles, applied by a new class of specially trained professionals, guided the United States to a prosperity that made it the envy of the world.

But the American ideology remained largely impervious to these changes. Social myths, once formed, proved remarkably durable. Ideology was able to accommodate each change and fit it into the old mythic categories with no fundamental revisions in the underlying notions of how America worked.

As the control of American industry passed from inventors and promoters to trained professionals, these managers adopted the image of the earlier entrepreneurs, despite their sharply different function in America's changed economy. Similarly, as continued progress required government to take on a more active role in the economy, each new program, however important, was seen as somehow unique or temporary, an extraordinary departure from government's strictly limited economic role. (Chapter V reviews some of these programs, dedicated unabashedly to industrial goals.)

For a time America could easily afford to cast professional managers as entrepreneurs and to maintain the fiction that crucial government economic policies were minor exceptions to the rule of noninvolvement. But as detailed below, the advantage that had previously allowed Americans the luxury of attending separately to their business and civic cultures has begun to erode.

4.

Since the close of America's first frontier the nation's civic culture and business culture have competed for ideological dominance, producing a pendulumlike vacillation in Americans' fundamental loyalties. With each swing of the pendulum, the country has adopted the perspective of one of the cultures, at the expense of the other.

The business culture held sway in the 1880's, when mass-production techniques first began to transform the relationship of managers and workers and the modern corporation was born. But the business culture's inability to understand and respond to the civic responsibilities attendant upon large corporate size helped inspire Populist and Progressive activism around the turn of the century, leading to antitrust legislation and the establishment of the Federal Trade Commission, to laws governing hours and working conditions, and to legislation protecting consumers from dangerous drugs and unwholesome meat.

The business culture rebounded during the 1920's, after American business had joined in successful partnership with the government on the War Industries Board and had thereby earned a measure of public trust. But the business culture's subsequent failure to respond to the claims of labor and consumers foreshadowed New Deal programs to protect these groups—legislation establishing a framework for labor-management relations, regulations governing the securities and banking industries, programs of Social Security and public works, and laws further protecting consumers from unsafe foods, drugs, and cosmetics.

The business culture took precedence for a third time in the 1950's and early 1960's. Government fiscal and monetary policies seemingly ensured steady economic growth, and Americans enjoyed the prosperity that business and government, working together, promised to provide. The old, the disabled, and the unemployed could live off the surplus. Indeed, the modern welfare state seemed perfectly compatible with the reigning Keynesian concern with compensating for the economy's tendency to inadequate consumption. The spectacular performance of the American economy during that interval demonstrated that active government intervention had become not just compatible with prosperity but essential to it.

But the business culture once again confronted a new set of emerging public concerns about the environment, health, consumer safety, equal opportunity, and political corruption. A third wave of regulation, beginning in the late 1960's, spawned thirty-five separate regulatory programs, covering everything from unsafe toys and flammable fabrics to unsafe mines and toxic chemicals. A welter of new social programs accompanied this wave of regulation. This third period of civic activism ended with the election of Ronald Reagan.

Over time, the cycle has intensified. Each swing of the ideological pendulum has added momentum to the opposite swing. The culture in the ascendant, as it enacts its one-sided agenda, invariably has disappointed public expectations, discredited its vision, and inspired calls for a change of course. In periods during which the business culture has predominated, economic growth has generated new social problems. But the business culture, basing its claim for legitimacy exclusively upon the promise of economic growth and development, has ignored the need for social change. Thus, each period of civic activism has been preceded by dramatic revelations of public harms or dangers attendant upon business activity —Upton Sinclair's accounts of unsanitary conditions in the meat-packing industry at the turn of the century; Ida Tarbell's ringing indictment of the Standard Oil trust; Louis Brandeis's exposé of the banking industry; more recently, Rachel Carson's stirring account of environmental decay; Jessica Mitford's disclosures about the funeral industry; and Ralph Nader's string of exposés concerning dangerous cars, drugs, and food additives.

Nor were these journalistic efforts (called muckraking before World War I and investigative reporting since the late 1960's) idle warnings. They preceded or accompanied dramatic scandals and disasters linked to business decisions: the Triangle Shirtwaist factory fire; Jay Gould's Wall Street manipulations; the elixir sulfanilamide disaster; fatalities linked with flaws in General Motors' Corvair and Ford's Pinto; scandals over union pension funds and foreign bribes; Allied Chemical's dumping of kepone into the James River; mine cave-ins; leaks from nuclear reactors; asbestosis.

In each period such events and revelations have spurred middle-income citizens into political action. In the Progressive era organizations first sprang up at the local level, promoting environmental protection, consumerism, and better government. During the New Deal middle-income groups formed antibusiness coalitions with urban ethnics, intellectuals, and organized labor. In the most recent period middle-income groups joined with the organized poor on certain issues affecting business and with students and labor on others.

Each period of civic activism has lasted about a decade before the interest of the middle-income groups waned and the civic coalitions, of which they were a central part, began to disintegrate. In the first two periods the immediate cause of the decline was an international crisis, culminating in a military buildup and the outbreak of global hostilities.

The most recent period ended with an international economic crisis and Americans' almost exclusive concern with their threatened prosperity. In all three periods middle-income groups, whose economic survival was suddenly at stake, forsook their civic activities and joined in an unstable coalition with the business culture.

Each period of civic activism has been marked by calls for national economic planning. Each period of business predominance has been marked by calls for less government and for reductions in social spending. Neither set of demands has produced a wholesale restructuring of American society, of course, but they have set the terms of national debate. They have fixed the ideological poles around which public discussion of the proper roles of government and business still oscillates.

5.

This sparring between the business and civic cultures did little damage while the United States was largely isolated and economically unrivaled. The two cultures could set and pursue their agendas independently—even antagonistically—without disastrous consequences so long as the strength of the economy depended on producing large amounts of standardized products primarily for the nation's huge domestic market. In this era of substantial economic autarky, it did not matter that social and economic policies were at odds with each other and that America lacked any mechanism to accelerate economic change or to forge a social consensus that would allow adaptation. The American economy grew not by evolving, but by taking its basic style of production to its limits—ever larger volumes of standardized goods at ever lower unit costs. This required no real alliance but, at most, a truce, between America's business and civic cultures.

This has changed. The reasons are well known, even if their implications are still not widely recognized. First, Western Europe and Japan have fully recovered from World War II and its disruptive aftermath, and America is now one among several mature industrial countries. The second change will prove to be even more important in the sweep of world economic history: Many developing countries—members of the third world—are emerging as industrial powers. Already much of the world's steel, textiles, rubber, ships, and petrochemicals come from countries not long ago dismissed as backward. Economic development in Asia and Latin America is at least as uneven and traumatic as it was in Europe; but the long-term trend is unmistakable, and it is irrevocably altering the dynamics of international competition. Finally, postwar technical and institutional innovations have made finance, physical resources, and finished goods more mobile, so that the world is fast becoming a single, highly competitive marketplace. The details and the subtler implications of these changes are taken up in Chapter VII.

These developments—Europe's and Japan's reconstruction, third world industrialization, and more efficient world trade—should surely be welcome. But together they pose an unprecedented challenge for America. How will the United States adjust to the changing world economy?

One option is to refuse to acknowledge that there has been any fundamental change. We can refrain from any special policies to respond to growing competition and let world market forces take their course. This path leads to predictable results: As other economies progressively become capable of standardized mass production—and as lower wages or favored access to markets or resources let them produce more cheaply than the economy of the United States allows—America would be outcompeted in industry after industry. Its imports would rise, and its exports fall, until a weakening dollar slowed the trend. Companies would close domestic plants and send capital abroad to merge profitably with foreign resources. Workers would be priced out of production jobs until wages fell to meet those of their foreign rivals, with the exception of those jobs—mostly low-paying services—that are naturally immune to foreign competition. By the year 2000 historians would be writing of the exceptional period in the middle of the preceding century when the lack of serious competition gave the United States a transient economic preeminence.

This scenario accords with the natural dynamics of an open world market as international advantage shifts. But we will almost certainly not see such a future. This process of relative decline would be enormously painful, and before it worked itself out, there would be powerful political demands for government action to blunt the onslaught of international competition. Thus, a more likely American response to economic change would be to resist it. As standardized mass production becomes cheaper abroad and the core of the American economy erodes, we can ban or sharply restrict imports. We can pass laws forbidding companies to build foreign plants, and we can restrict the flow of financial capital overseas. America has already taken the first steps down this road. But if we choose this response, other countries will do the same. International trade will slow to a trickle. The world economy will stagnate. Even though protection seems appealing in many individual cases, the internal dynamics of protectionism guarantees that it will quickly become devastatingly universal. And beyond this pragmatic case against a strategy of protection, surrendering to the notion that the United States can prosper only if foreign competition is kept at bay seems repugnant to some very basic American sensibilities.

There is another path open to America. Its basic direction is not mysterious: As the rest of the world progresses, we must also progress if we are to retain our role of economic leadership. Accommodating world development without succumbing to the new competition means that we cannot continue to rely on high-volume, standardized industries after other countries have become better suited for them. Rather, our economic future must be rooted in the only resource that will remain uniquely American: Americans themselves. The industries that will sustain the next stage of America's economic evolution will necessarily be based on a skilled, adaptable, and innovative labor force and on a more flexible, less hierarchical organization of work.

There is no single type of industry that meets these conditions. Some, like advanced fiber optics, are well-known high-technology industries. Others are as superficially old-fashioned as pesticides custom-blended for specific ecologies. Chapter VII describes the features that define these industries as a group (collectively characterized as flexible-system production).

The industries in which the United States can retain a competitive edge will be based not on huge volume and standardization, but on producing relatively smaller batches of more specialized, higher-valued products— goods that are precision-engineered, that are custom-tailored to serve individual markets, or that embody rapidly evolving technologies. Such products will be found in high-value segments of more traditional industries (specialty steel and chemicals, computer-controlled machine tools, advanced automobile components) as well as in new high-technology industries (semiconductors, fiber optics, lasers, biotechnology, and robotics).

If a substantial share of business and labor can successfully make the shift to products and processes based on a durable American advantage, we can confidently face a future of open adaptation to the evolving international economy. America can prosper in a prospering world.

But we are as yet ill-prepared for such adaptation. Responding rapidly and effectively to new international competition requires far-reaching economic and social changes, and America is not organized for changes of this magnitude. For the nation to find a new leading role in the changing world economy, our economic organizations will have to evolve. Rather than seek stability for mass production, business, labor, and government must adapt to a new, flexible system of production, geared to instability. Later chapters trace some of the directions this adaptation will likely take. The common feature of these changes is that they all have an important public dimension. For America's next stage of economic evolution, the government's role in industry must become not so much more extensive as more open, more explicit, and more strategic. This is not because public officials are somehow wiser or more far-seeing than private managers, but because renewed national prosperity depends on certain social investments that executives (judged by the profits of their separate firms) cannot be expected to undertake and on a broader economic perspective than private managers can attend to. Yet the radical separation between America's business culture and its civic culture blocks them both from recognizing and responding to these new needs. The myth of the two cultures is retarding the next stage of America's economic and social progress. Adaptation must involve both the business and civic cultures, but we have no institutions for bridging that gap and orchestrating adjustment. It is thus not surprising that the difficulty of adjustment has inspired efforts to evade the new challenges of the changing world economy.

Unable to shift easily to more flexible, skill-intensive production, America's business leaders have tried to maintain short-term profits through various legal and financial maneuvers—the paper entrepreneurialism described in Chapter VIII. Such efforts—while often spectacularly lucrative in the short run—merely rearrange industrial assets without changing the underlying process or organization of production. Business leaders have also joined in coalition with organized labor to obtain protection from imports in the form of tariffs, quotas, and subsidies.

Chapter IX shows how government assistance has been sought to avoid international competition rather than to meet it. The third predictable manifestation of America's slowness to adapt is that an ever larger proportion of the labor force finds itself locked into dead-end jobs. Chapter X discusses how this is occurring and how social policies have so far failed to prepare Americans to participate in the dynamic segments of the world economy.

6.

The industrialized countries of Europe (with the exception of Great Britain) and Japan took paths to industrialization radically different from America's. While the United States began its development with an almost empty continent, these other nations began with the remnants of a feudal system. For them, economic progress was of necessity less a matter of marshaling resources than of transforming society—dismantling and restructuring an existing social order. The recent devastations of war forced Japan and much of Western Europe to reconstruct their economies and societies once again; no such fundamental reconstruction was ever required of Americans.

These other industrialized nations have therefore been forced by their histories to appreciate the link between their civic and business cultures. Their governments were the instruments by which the rising middle class of merchants and manufacturers struggled to overcome the encrustations of feudalism—the rigid structures of economic privilege, rank, and tradition which had blocked economic change. Traditions of legitimate government involvement in orchestrating economic change were firmly established. Industrialization in these countries came later and was more wrenching, often more violent than it was in America. Their national markets, moreover, were smaller, and old craft guilds slowed economic change, with the result that mass production never took as firm a root in these nations as in the United States. The traumatic process has left these countries with a deep sense of the unity of economic and social change and bequeathed to several of them a more adaptable economic structure.

The Japanese and these Europeans draw no sharp distinction between their business and civic cultures. In contrast with the United States— where many socially aware citizens are ignorant of or even bored by the details of economics and production—many Japanese and continental

Europeans have a lively awareness of industry. The average Japanese citizen is familiar with the size, quality of management, and product lines of Japan's major companies: Company handbooks equivalent to *Moody's* in the United States are issued quarterly in large numbers and at a low price. Popular weekly magazines are devoted to gossip and scandals concerning companies. The two leading Japanese daily newspapers—each with a circulation four times greater than the largest American daily— are filled with detailed business news.

These societies almost naturally connect economic development with social change. Government, business, and labor negotiate to devise public policies and business strategies that will propel their societies and economies forward. There is open, intense bargaining over wages and prices, social services, and patterns of savings and investment. This bargaining helps ensure that the gains and losses of economic change are shared in such a way that no group feels a disproportionate burden and that none experiences a disproportionate windfall.

Social investments in citizens' health, education, and welfare are typically seen as comparable to and no less important than private investments in business plant and equipment. Both are viewed as integral to the continued well-being of the nation. After-tax distribution of income in these nations is more equal than it is in America—with their poorest citizens receiving a much larger share of the national income, and their wealthiest a much smaller share.[1] Workers in these nations have much more job security than American workers, more government-sponsored training and retraining, more generous unemployment assistance, and health benefits that are distributed more widely.[2] In all these ways these nations understand that industrial development is dependent on social adaptation. Their business cultures and civic cultures complement each other.

The success of modern Japan, in particular, seems to contradict Max Weber, the German sociologist, who attributed the West's economic progress to the demise of traditional relationships like guilds, parishes, and clans and to the simultaneous rise of individualism. Japan's emphasis on community, consensus, and long-term security for its workers—based squarely on traditional communal relationships—appears to have spurred its citizens to greater feats of production than has the rugged individualism of modern America.

It is no coincidence that since 1970 many of these other nations have been more successful than America in adjusting to the new realities of international competition. Between 1973 and 1981, America's average annual increase in productivity lagged behind West Germany, France, Holland, Belgium, Italy, Denmark, Sweden, Japan, and even Britain.[3] While international comparisons are always imprecise, in several respects the American living standard is now below that of several other industrialized countries.[4] Unemployment is higher.[5] The life expectancy of the average American is lower than that of the average citizen in fourteen other industrialized nations.[6] Our levels of pollution are higher than those of eight other industrialized countries.[7]

It is, of course, true that many of these nations are more homogeneous than America. The United States cannot simply contrive social cohesion. Our melting-pot culture inevitably will suffer from tensions that these other nations can avoid. It is also true that these nations have endured economic contractions during the past few years, similar to the contraction that has plagued America. The world is now too interdependent for economic difficulties or successes to be easily contained within the borders of a single nation, so that the issue of America's place and prospects among industrialized nations is, of course, a relative one. But that is precisely the cause for concern, for by almost every measure of social well-being, America's relative position is declining. Even when the worst of the current worldwide recession is over, the structural problems in the American economy will remain. Unless addressed, America's relative decline will continue.

The recent progress achieved by Japan and several European countries, and America's relative decline, require no convoluted explanations. For largely historical reasons these countries are organized for economic adaptation. And for largely historical reasons America is not.

7.

No view of the government's proper role in the economy can claim legitimacy in America unless it carries with it the promise of prosperity. In the quarter century following World War II, liberalism did just that. For more than twenty years, between the mid-1940's and the late 1960's, an uneasy truce prevailed between America's business culture and its civic culture. Liberalism successfully married the modern welfare state—the embodiment of the civic culture—to principles of Keynesian demand management of the economy. Steps toward social justice fitted hand in glove with economic growth because both depended upon a strong central government to organize a substantial portion of the national economic activity.

The result has been the emergence of two parallel sets of bureaucracies —one public, the other private. The public bureaucracies were responsible for America's civic concerns: for public health, education, job training, welfare, public transportation, housing, and environmental and safety regulation. The private, corporate bureaucracies were responsible for the nation's business concerns: for investment, productivity, and economic growth. The two operated in parallel isolation, interacting only in strictly limited, often almost incidental ways.

That truce was broken, first by a new wave of civic activism and then, beginning in 1970, by a precipitous economic decline. In the face of that decline liberalism has been all but silent. Civic values have once again been subordinated to business values. The ideology of the civic culture has been replaced by a new version of the business culture's ideology, which promises prosperity at the acknowledged cost of social justice. This business ideology calls for government measures to raise the level of savings and reduce consumption, so that resources may be devoted to investment without fueling inflation. Although differing in particulars, these proposals typically call for across-the-board income tax cuts coupled with tax reductions on savings and investments; limits on government spending, particularly for huge and growing programs like Social Security, Medicare, and welfare; and a relaxation of regulations pertaining to health, safety, and the environment.

These proposals would result in a sharply less equitable distribution of income and—less obviously but no less certainly—of public goods, like clean air, clean water, opportunities for outdoor recreation, safe products, and safe working environments. Any across-the-board reduction in income taxes disproportionately benefits upper-income groups, who now pay the most taxes. This regressivity will be worsened by cuts in Social Security, Medicare, and welfare, upon which the poor and elderly are particularly dependent. Similarly, proposals to relax regulations promoting health, safety, and environmental quality will transform clean air, clean water, outdoor recreation, safe products, and safe working conditions into private commodities available only to those who can afford to buy them by living in exclusive neighborhoods, using bottled water, vacationing in pristine environments, and turning down hazardous jobs.

However troubling these proposals may be to the national conscience, their promise of economic growth and productivity has given them political appeal. By abandoning its own promise of prosperity, liberalism has ceded the very ideal that once rallied the American majority around its social vision. Without that promise, liberalism's call for social justice is redolent of charity, to be balanced against the more compelling goals of growth and productivity—a moral luxury to be indulged in when and to the extent we can afford it. At worst, it has degenerated into demands for preserving economic relationships as they were when times were better: erecting tariffs and quotas against foreign imports, regulating factory closings and relocations, limiting direct investment abroad, and investing public funds in dying industries. Without the promise of prosperity the liberal agenda has become a paean to the status quo.

Liberalism and the civic values that underlie it no longer can base its connection between prosperity and social justice on simple notions of aggregate demand management. The business culture is correct when it turns to the supply side of the economic ledger and asks what conditions will generate growth and productivity. It is the business culture's answer, not its question, that is wrong.

In advanced industrial countries, productivity and economic growth are coming to depend not so much on the overall level of investment as on how investment is used. The pace of economic evolution is forcing some basic social changes. Within complex industrial systems there are so many potential bottlenecks and crucial linkages, so many transactions to be coordinated within and among public and private bureaucracies, and, therefore, so much room for either productive collaboration or crass manipulation that the quantity of raw resources available for investment is coming to be less important than how the investment is directed and absorbed. Put simply, the organization of an advanced economy can either encourage productivity—by providing people with skills and knowledge and by inspiring high morale and motivation in the work force—or discourage productivity by doing just the opposite.

The way people are organized is becoming a critical determinant of productivity. But it is difficult even to recognize the underlying patterns of organization, and harder still to change them. We understand when a factory is not producing at full capacity, but it is far more difficult to perceive the unused potential in people. We keep precise accounts of underused industrial plants, but we tend to ignore underused people and to dismiss the possibilities of tapping this potential by reorganizing work. This failure of perception is as true for the macroorganization of the economy as a whole as it is for the microorganization of the firm: When we use unemployment to battle inflation, we do not recognize the toll it takes on America's future productivity. When we trim our collective expenditures on education, training, health, nutrition, and similar intangibles, we do not see its cost in terms of America's future economic growth.

Policies that spread the benefits and burdens of economic change more equitably among our citizens are superior to those that widen the gap between rich and poor. The case for social justice is becoming less dependent on moral arguments, however powerful they may be. People who feel themselves to be respected members of the economic and social system are more apt to work productively within it than are those who feel that the dice are loaded against them. The bitterness and alienation of ghetto youth should be evidence enough. But beyond this obvious, negative point is the fact that America's place in the evolving world economy will increasingly depend on its workers' skills, vigor, initiative, and capacity for collaboration and adaptation. Our future wealth lies in our human capital. The kinds of policies we need may be termed social justice or investments in America's future; regardless of the label, they represent the next stage of America's economic and social advance.

The central theme of this book is that in the emerging era of productivity, social justice is not incompatible with economic growth, but essential to it. A social organization premised on equity, security, and participation will generate greater productivity than one premised on greed and fear. Collaboration and collective adaptation are coming to be more important to an industrialized nation's well-being than are personal daring and ambition. And at an even more fundamental level, the goals of prosperity and social justice cannot validly be separated. America's well-being is a function of the quality of life enjoyed by all our citizens; it is only indirectly a function of abstract rates of investment and economic growth. Social concerns are the ends that economics seeks to serve. It is perverse to relegate them even implicitly to a separate and subordinate status.

America has a choice: It can adapt itself to the new economic realities by altering its organizations, or it can fail to adapt and thereby continue its present decline. Adaptation will be difficult. America's current patterns of organization were once so successful that they have endured long after they have outlived their usefulness. To change the way we conduct our businesses and our government implies a more general change of customs, attitudes, and values which are parts of our cultural heritage. This more fundamental change is emotionally difficult. It becomes even more difficult as economic decline sets in because then change threatens the economic security of people who are desperately trying to hold onto what they have. A new consensus is difficult to achieve when each person seeks to preserve his standard of living but finds that he can only do so at the expense of someone else. But failure to adapt will rend the social fabric irreparably. Adaptation is America's challenge. It is America's next frontier.

II
THE ERA OF
MOBILIZATION

1.

Over the course of the past century American industry perfected a wholly new organization of production, geared to manufacturing very large quantities of relatively simple, standardized products. The key was long production runs with each step along the way made simple and routine. Sometimes the long runs were on an assembly line carrying materials continuously from one stage to the next; sometimes the process involved very large batches of chemical compounds; sometimes it was based on continuous-process machines that automatically turned out parts or whole products. But however the principles were embodied, this new organization of production moved materials through the manufacturing process at an unprecedented velocity. As the scale of production increased, the cost of producing each unit plummeted.

More than America's treasure of natural resources, more than its energetic backyard inventors and tinkerers, more even than its abundance of qualified workers—this organization of high-volume, standardized production was responsible for generating startling increases in productivity and unparalleled national prosperity.

American society gradually came to structure itself around this core production process. The model of machine production shaped not only business enterprises but also government, labor unions, the professions, and ultimately the way Americans came to view themselves.

Since much of our story concerns the organization that grew up around this core production process and what it implied for American society in general, it is important to understand its origins. Its appeal derived not solely from the prodigious efficiency it promised but also from its tendency to eliminate arbitrary and capricious rule within the large institutions that came to dominate American life. The managerial organization brought order and stability precisely at the point when these qualities were essential to the next stage of America's economic growth and social progress.

The first era of American productivity spanned roughly fifty years, from 1870 to 1920. During the first three decades of the period America underwent an economic expansion unparalleled in world history. In 1860 the annual value of the nation's manufactured products totaled $1.8 billion. By 1900 it had grown to $11 billion, in constant dollars. The annual increase in total productivity, which had hovered around three-tenths of 1 percent for most of the nineteenth century, suddenly surged in the last decades to nearly six times that rate. Then, almost as suddenly as the surge had begun, it slowed. During the first two decades of the twentieth century the rate of increase in output per worker declined by 50 percent.[1]

The sharp climb in productivity in this first era (as well as its subsequent decline) resulted from how America organized itself. Inventions were quickly transformed into productive processes, tailored to the special needs and opportunities of the nation. Laborers accustomed to hard work swarmed into America's cities from farms and from overseas, supplying the new factories with a disciplined work force. New railroad and telegraph systems provided industrialists with efficient means of supplying their factories and coordinating the distribution of their wares. The extraordinary mobility of capital, labor, and materials in late-nineteenth-century America rapidly transformed inventions into new methods of production and new products.

But the organization on which this mobility was founded could not respond to the new demands that industrialization placed upon it. The organizational fluidity that had allowed entrepreneurs to summon quickly the nation's resources had become, by the first decades of the new century, a fundamental weakness; once summoned, America's human and capital resources had no coherent structure in which to fit themselves. The nation's nascent private enterprises and government institutions were simply too decentralized, piecemeal, idiosyncratic, and unreliable to handle a suddenly complex industrial society.

This tension—between the advantages of a loose network of government, business, and social organizations that let people and capital be easily "unglued" and put to more productive uses and the need for coherent and reliable institutions to stabilize the economic and social environment for high-volume production—formed the central dilemma of the first era.

2.

The inventions that initiated the era were Great Britain's legacy to America. The first sustained process of industrialization had begun in Britain a hundred years before. At the heart of the British Industrial Revolution had been a desperate quest for alternatives to rapidly diminishing timber resources. Britain turned to iron as a substitute building material and to coal as a substitute fuel. Coal and iron in turn inspired new inventions, like the steam engine, which then spread to other nations that had not yet exhausted their own timber.[2]

Inventions bred new inventiveness, as each new process or machine provoked additional insights and inspired further refinements. Abraham Darby's coke-smelting process, introduced in the 1750's, led by 1784 to Henry Cort's puddling and rolling process for the large-scale production of refined iron and subsequently to a wide variety of ironmaking furnaces. Hargreaves's jenny, for spinning cotton (1764), was but a step along the way to Arkwright's water frame (1769), Crompton's mule (1779), a collection of other machines for carding, roving, roller printing, and bleaching cotton, leading in turn to Roberts' automatic mule (1825).

The output of many commodities—particularly coal, iron, and textiles

—reached unprecedented levels. The productivity of a British spinning worker, for example, increased 300-fold between 1750 and 1825.[3] By the time of the Crystal Palace Exhibition of 1851 Britain's ability to innovate, to recognize and solve technical problems had transformed it into the "workshop of the world." The transformation had increased the real incomes of all its citizens, even the less advantaged (except perhaps the Irish).

Cheap British goods flooded Europe and North America, forcing every other economy to adjust to the change. Some adjusted by seeking niches in which the British did not yet compete. Others sought to specialize in selling Britain raw materials or intermediate goods. Many tried to compete with Britain head-on by adopting British inventions and combining them with local labor or raw materials that were cheaper than British resources.

Despite Parliament's efforts to maintain Britain's industrial lead by prohibiting the export of machinery and blueprints and the emigration of skilled artisans, British inventions soon found their way to Holland, France, Germany, America, and beyond. Industrial spies smuggled out machines and drawings. Scientific journals published detailed blueprints. British mechanics, machine builders, and skilled craftsmen fanned out over the rest of the globe, carrying knowledge in their heads and hands.

If it was to maintain its lead, Britain had little choice but to continue to increase its productivity. But there was a limit to its capacity for improvement. Its Industrial Revolution had been founded on invention. Yet the greatest potential for further productivity increases lay less in technology alone than in the organization of production—through the application of these inventions to large-scale manufacturing. Invention could take Britain to the threshold of high-volume production, but no farther.

Britain simply was not as well organized for high-volume production as were others. Its potential domestic market for standardized goods was relatively small, so that it could not achieve the massive economies of scale available to other nations whose emerging railroads and telegraph lines would provide them with large national markets and who would impose tariffs and quotas to keep out foreign goods. Britain's rigid class structure constrained many of its potential entrepreneurs. The work force as a whole was not mobile enough to supply the concentrations of labor needed for high-volume production. Nor, finally, could Britain easily transform the organization of its work force from craft industry to high-volume production. Notwithstanding all the new machinery at their disposal, workers in most of Britain continued to function as independent contractors, using equipment and workshops that they owned or rented, gaining their training through apprenticeship within a craft, and leaving the lower-skilled tasks to women and children in their families.[4]

The Crystal Palace Exhibition of 1851, therefore, marked the beginning of the end. The rapid flow of its inventions to regions with lower wages, larger markets, and more mobile resources enabled other nations to catch up to Britain in productivity and, ultimately, in wealth. During the next half century Great Britain lost the lead in most segments of the coal, steel, and textile industries and failed to develop strength in the emerging industries of automobiles, electrical apparatus, and chemicals. Few could have predicted in the mid-nineteenth century, however, that Britain's real heir would be America.

3.

America's first era of productivity drew upon British inventiveness. American industry increasingly substituted machine tools for craftsmen, interchangeable parts for hand tools, and coal for wood, water, and animal energy. The process of rapid substitution, once begun, knew no bounds; by the end of the 1880's the center of America's economic activity was already shifting from coal and steam, textiles, and machine tools to new industries that elaborated and extended upon these basic technologies—to steel, electricity, organic chemicals, and the internal-combustion engine.

In the half century spanning 1870 and 1920 a major invention made its appearance in America, on average, every fifteen months. Most of these inventions were based on British discoveries; American innovators merely applied these discoveries to specific products and processes. Many of these applied inventions became the building blocks of new industries. By the time Charles Duryea, Ransom Olds, Elwood Haynes, Henry Ford, and other tinkering mechanics had begun playing with the idea of "horseless carriages" in the early 1890's, for example, all the fundamental inventions necessary to realize the idea had already been developed.

Other inventions spawned entire industries on their own. In the 1870's came the typewriter, telephone, and Edison's electric light bulb and phonograph; in the 1880's, aluminum and vulcanized rubber; in the 1890's, the wireless; in the first decade of the new century, the electric washing machine and the airplane. Indeed, most of the products that were to dominate U.S. industry for the next fifty years were modifications of technologies developed during this period.

Still other inventions improved the productivity of existing industries, creating machines and processes that allowed production on a scale never before imagined. A cigarette-making machine, developed in 1881, was so productive that fifteen of them satisfied America's entire annual demand for cigarettes. In 1884 George Eastman invented a continuous-process method for making photographic negatives by using a gelatin emulsion on film, instead of glass plates. In the same decade Procter & Gamble developed a new machine for mass-producing Ivory soap, and Diamond Match began using a machine that produced and boxed matches by the billions. In 1899 the newly invented rotating kiln produced cheap and uniform portland cement. In 1903 Michael Owens perfected a method for drawing glass from furnaces mechanically and then forming bottles molded by compressed air; the process revolutionized the glass container industry. Frederick Winslow Taylor (whom we shall hear more of later) and his collaborator at the Bethlehem steelworks introduced high-speed carbon tool steel in 1906, an innovation that more than doubled the productivity of machine tools by giving them a much harder cutting edge than before. The same year the open-hearth method of steel production replaced the far less efficient Bessemer process. And the newly invented Northrop loom automatically ejected empty bobbins from the shuttle and inserted fresh ones in the instant that the shuttle was at rest between trips across the loom, thereby vastly increasing the efficiency of weaving.

Yet none of these inventions could increase productivity on its own. Each needed to be embedded within a new system of production and distribution. Unlike Britain's earlier Industrial Revolution, which had merely given workers new tools and cheaper sources of energy that enabled them to perform more efficiently essentially the same tasks they had been doing before, the innovations of the latter decades of the nineteenth century could be exploited only through large-scale systems of factories, specialized equipment, reliable sources of materials and channels of distribution, and a new organization of work.

The successful transformation of invention into production thus required a new form of organization. And the organization that emerged was a large-scale version of the invention at its center. There were no preexisting models of high-volume production on which to draw, and those who mobilized resources had to understand the new technologies intimately so that they could effectively structure an organization around the process. Thus, inventors naturally took upon themselves the job of organizing the resources necessary to complete their grand designs. "My work here is done, my light is perfected," mused Thomas Edison, after his experiments had borne fruit. "I am now going into the practical production of it."[5] While an Englishman named Joseph Swan had as strong a claim to the invention of the electric light bulb itself, only the American Edison was able to parlay it into an industrial empire.

Inventions that were imported from overseas were often redesigned to suit the emerging American system of high-volume production. This process of adaptation was fueled by competition: American producers who modified foreign machinery to suit their specific manufacturing needs often found that they had a competitive advantage over others who sought simply to replicate the foreign process. Between 1864 and 1871, for example, ten steel companies in America began making steel by the British-invented Bessemer process. Initially all but one of them had imported British steelworkers to set up their operations, and for the first few years the companies that relied on British labor were profitable. But by the end of the 1870's the Cambria Company—which had adapted the Bessemer process to its own resources and market conditions—had gained a commanding lead over all its competitors. The president of Cambria explained his company's success by noting that the technology had been adapted without preconceptions. "We started the convertor plant without a single man who had ever seen the outside of a Bessemer plant. We thus had willing pupils with no prejudices and no reminiscences of what they had done in the old country."[6]

The adaptation of new technologies to new production processes radically transformed many American industries. Mechanical industries that processed tobacco, grain products, soap, and canned foodstuffs, for example, substantially increased their output through continuous-process machinery; Pillsbury Flour, American Tobacco, and Quaker Oats, among others, established dominant positions by applying such production processes.

Industries that distilled and refined petroleum, sugar, animal and vegetable fats, alcohol, and chemicals reaped enormous savings from new heat and chemical technologies, giant furnaces, whirling centrifuges, converters, and rolling and finishing equipment. Standard Oil, American Sugar Refining, and Carnegie Steel, among others, gained unprecedented efficiencies from such large-batch technologies.

Metalworking industries benefited from more efficient machine tools and a wider variety of raw and semifinished materials; International Harvester and Singer Sewing Machine were among the firms that profitably applied these innovations.

The linkage of invention and production was not unique to America, of course. It was a global phenomenon, spurred both by the international reach of many of the new technologies and by the new mobility of human and capital resources in nations that were then undergoing political consolidation, like Japan and Germany. Inventor-promoters circled the globe. Alfred Nobel, the Swedish inventor of dynamite, opened an explosives factory in Hamburg in 1866. The following year Isaac Merritt Singer opened the first overseas sewing machine factory in Glasgow. Werner von Siemens, who invented the forerunner of today's teleprinter, organized the stringing of telegraph lines across Europe in the 1870's. In the first decades of the new century the Krupps and I. G. Farben organized steel and chemical operations. Even in Japan, after the last of the Tokugawa shoguns had formally relinquished authority to the young emperor Meiji in 1868, an emerging group of inventor-promoters built lasting business enterprises: Iwasaki Yatarō, founder of the Mitsubishi group; Yasuda Zenjirō, founder of a group of companies bearing his name; and Minomura Rizaemon, of Mitsui.

America, however, was singularly well suited to the high-volume production of standard goods. Capital and labor were uniquely mobile. The country was large; its material resources were unfathomed; its energy sources were cheap and plentiful; its potential market was almost beyond imagination. The railroad tracks and telegraph lines that rapidly spread across the continent enhanced these opportunities.

America's inventor-promoters were able to mobilize capital with relative ease. Since the Civil War, during which a large group of northern investors financed the Union mobilization, American capital markets had become increasingly extensive and efficient. After the war this market expanded rapidly, financing railroad, banking, mining, and manufacturing ventures. By 1900 an estimated 4.4 million stockholders had interests in American corporations; by 1917 the number had doubled.[7]

The capital assets of U.S. firms grew in tandem. While in 1860 total investment in manufacturing plants amounted to no more than $1 billion, by 1900 investment in plants had increased to $12 billion (valued in 1860 dollars). Capital invested per worker, meanwhile, grew from about $700 in 1870 to $2,000 at the turn of the century. Capital invested in manufacturing as a whole increased from $2.7 billion in 1879 to $8.2 billion in 1899 and on to $20.8 billion by 1914.[8]

As American capital became more mobile, so did American workers. Laborers poured into the cities from the farm and from the immigrant steamer, in search of work and better pay. In 1870 more than two-thirds of America's workers were engaged in occupations other than manufacturing—agriculture, forestry, or fishing. Ten years later these pursuits claimed only 50 percent of the work force. By 1910 only one-third of the work force was still farming, logging, or fishing for a living. The number of wage earners in manufacturing grew from 1.3 million in 1860 to 5.3 million in 1890.[9]

The cities exploded. In 1870, 1 out of every 5 Americans lived in a city with 8,000 or more inhabitants. By 1900 the proportion was 1 of 3. By 1920 fully half the population of America was living in cities. New York City's population increased fourfold between 1860 and 1910. Midwestern cities grew even faster. Chicago had 109,260 inhabitants in 1860. By 1910 it was the nation's second largest city, with 2.2 million people, a twentyfold increase. St. Louis, Cleveland, and Detroit grew almost as rapidly.[10]

The cities changed in culture as well as in size. During the 1870's, 280,000 immigrants arrived in the United States each year. By the first decade of the twentieth century the yearly average had risen to 1 million. Largely as a result of this influx, the nation's population doubled between 1870 and 1900. By the turn of the century a quarter of all adult males in America had been born abroad.

Before 1890 many immigrants had traveled to the Midwest to start their own farms. But increasingly they remained in the cities, forming an army of available manufacturing labor. In 1873 four out of every five children in the Detroit schools were of foreign parentage. Three out of every four inhabitants of Chicago were foreign-born at the turn of the century. By 1910 at least one-third of the population of most American cities had been born abroad.[11]

Immigrants constituted the majority of workers in many of America's new manufacturing industries. A 1908 government study found that only one-fifth of the wage earners in twenty-one principal branches of industry were native white Americans. Almost three-fifths were foreign-born. In the car-building and repair industry, 71 percent of the male employees were children of foreign-born.[12]

The flood of immigrants was a boon to American industry. Their large numbers created intense competition for jobs, and ended the upward movement of real wages. And because many of these immigrants were in the habit of working long and hard, and had a relatively decent level of nutrition, they were dependable and disciplined.

America's railroad and telegraph networks perfectly complemented its industrialization. The country had 23 miles of railroad track in 1830. By 1890 it had 208,152 miles. The telegraph developed in tandem. Invented in 1844, it was used commercially by 1847. By 1890 long-distance facilities were in full operation.[13]

Fast, regular, and reliable transportation and communication were essential to high-volume, standardized production. In order to sustain the high fixed costs of large-scale machinery, America's new industries depended on a constant flow of production within the factory. But such a flow depended in turn on a predictable stream of materials and products through the economy. Manufacturers could not afford either the cost of maintaining huge inventories at each end of their production process or the risk of being suddenly out of materials or merchandise. The railroad and telegraph reduced these risks and costs by letting manufacturers schedule the shipments they needed and sell their wares directly to wholesalers. The railroad and telegraph lubricated the flow of goods into and out of the new enterprises.

The extraordinary mobility of America's capital and labor and the new reliability with which goods could be scheduled and transported together formed the necessary conditions for high-volume, standardized production. In the last decades of the nineteenth century America's organization of efficient capital markets, open immigration, and reliable rail and telegraph systems permitted productive resources to be mobilized on a larger scale than the world had ever before witnessed.

4.

But these strengths became weaknesses once the mobilization was complete. First, America's highly responsive and freewheeling capital and labor markets enabled so many manufacturers to establish operations so rapidly that productive capacity soon overran the nation's ability to consume at prices high enough to cover the fixed costs of production. Ruinous price competition set in. Secondly, the technology of high-volume production placed such a large work force in one location that problems of supervision, coordination, and control strained the average company's ability to manage, resulting in wasted effort and labor unrest. And thirdly, the relatively sudden explosion in the number of urban dwellers and factory workers soon overburdened the government's limited capacity to ensure a minimum level of public health and safety. In short, the very speed of the mobilization swamped the nation's ability to cope with its less welcome side effects. Having successfully mobilized its resources for high-volume production, America found itself without the institutional means of coordinating and controlling the process.

America's inventor-promoters were innovative and ambitious, but they were not "managers" in the modern sense of the term. They did not concern themselves with the administrative tasks of organization—with developing standard operating procedures for coordinating their enterprises and accounting and cost controls for monitoring their subordinates. Apart from the burgeoning railroad and telegraph companies, Americans had had no experience with large organizations in either government or business. The need for detailed systems of coordination and supervision went unrecognized. Instead, business leadership was assumed to require simple strength of character: the Protestant virtues of prudence, punctuality, and perseverance.

To Americans of the late nineteenth century, success was more the product of the proper attitudes than of any special knowledge or skill. The reformist lawyer Orison Swett Marden exhorted America to new feats of personal strength in his best-selling book, *Pushing to the Front, or*

Success Under Difficulties (1894), followed by *The Victorious Attitude, Architects of Fate,* and *The Secret of Achievement.* President William McKinley and the industrialist Charles Schwab publicly endorsed Marden's work. Americans named their children after him.[14]

The emerging leaders of American business proclaimed themselves self-made men and lauded the Christian mission of business enterprise. Economic growth, and the strength of character that underlay it, were styled as the salvation of the nation. Industrialists like Cornelius Vanderbilt, Andrew Carnegie, John D. Rockefeller, and Pierre du Pont and financiers like J. P. Morgan, Andrew Mellon, Jay Gould, and James Fisk amassed huge fortunes in the process of mobilizing America's capital and human resources. The consistency of their adherence to Christian principle may be debatable, but not their determination.

It is interesting to note, parenthetically, that a similar apotheosis of business culture occurred about this time in Japan. Business leaders were considered the heirs of much of the feudal samurai's role as benefactors of the community and servants of the state. But whereas in America similar sentiments failed to penetrate very deeply into the national consciousness—possibly because of the deep American antipathy to vested economic power and to aristocracy in whatever guise or because the American entrepreneur's veneer of civic virtue was generally revealed to be somewhat thin—in Japan the ideal seemed to have held genuine meaning. Confucianism stressed the duties of altruism and community service over profit, and both the new business leaders and the public appeared to accept this teaching at full value. When Iwasaki Yatarō, the founder of Mitsubishi, died in 1885, his funeral was attended by 50,000 mourners.[15]

Apart from its religious and altruistic gloss, America's emphasis on personal determination and strength of character was entirely consistent with the job of transforming invention into high-volume production. Entrepreneurial energies, often mixing creativity with ruthlessness, were critical to the task of mobilizing vast resources. But an ideology glorifying solitary personal initiative gradually became inconsistent with the needs of an emerging economy grown suddenly more complex. Three new and interrelated problems loomed large during the first decades of the new century. None could be solved by personal initiative alone. Each needed a system of management.

The first problem, paradoxically, was overproduction. The explosion in productive capacity that marked the first decades of America's industrialization soon outpaced the nation's ability to distribute, market, and consume all the new output. Firms had energetically built up capacity, despite the fact that their rivals were doing the same. As supply burgeoned, producers anxious to sell enough to recover the cost of their new factories turned to cutthroat competition. Prices declined. The wholesale price index, which had stood at 193 in 1864, had dropped to 82 by 1890. A major depression jolted the economy in the summer of 1893, impoverishing entire agricultural areas, closing thousands of banks, and throwing more than one-fourth of the unskilled urban work force out of jobs.[16]

It soon became apparent to the inventor-promoters of the era that they needed to protect themselves against overproduction. Their first strategy was the crude one of simply seeking agreements within the industry to hold back production. Such cartelization was being employed in Germany with some success in maintaining prices. But in Germany a large public bureaucracy monitored and enforced the cartel agreements against rebellious price-cutters. Having played a significant role in that nation's industrialization, the German government possessed the bureaucratic machinery, and public legitimacy, necessary to manage the cartels. By contrast, without any preexistent government organization to monitor capacity and prices, the agreements forged by American manufacturers rarely held together. Moreover, large segments of the U.S. public (including commodity farmers, small wholesalers, and retailers) viewed them as illegitimate. The political animus which these agreements aroused culminated in passage of the 1890 Sherman Antitrust Act, which rendered them illegal.

With collusion among separate firms prohibited, American manufacturers sought to control supply by merging their enterprises. Through merger, capacity could be restricted, and efficiency improved. Production could be concentrated in the most efficient plants, others could be closed, and supply and distribution bottlenecks could be overcome. In 1896, 26 independent firms disappeared through merger. In the following year the number increased to 69. One year later 303 firms were acquired. By 1899 the number was up to 1,207. Between 1898 and 1902 approximately one-third of the manufacturing capital stock of the entire nation was consolidated.[17] The first giants of modern American business emerged from this radical implosion: International Harvester, Alcoa Aluminum, U.S. Steel, General Electric, National Biscuit Company, United Fruit Company, American Telephone & Telegraph Company, and Standard Oil. A few years later General Motors joined the group.

Arguably, the new giant companies that survived succeeded because merger had made them more efficient. Through consolidation they had gained economies of scale in manufacturing and distribution. Merged companies in industries that lacked such potential for scale efficiencies— such as U.S. Leather, National Wall Paper, and National Starch—failed to survive.

But economic efficiency was no answer to the political questions that were raised about the legitimacy of these giants. The enterprises that survived consolidation were plagued for decades by public controversy over their size and concomitant political and economic power. Despite their technical efficiency, they seemed strangely impervious to market forces. Lacking any explicit relationship to government, they also appeared to be unaccountable to the public. Indeed, on occasion, they seemed capable of subverting democratic processes. Ida Tarbell's muckracking *History of the Standard Oil Company* (1904) revealed in stark detail the ruthlessness of John D. Rockefeller and, by implication, of all the entrepreneurs who were gobbling up smaller rivals. In the presidential election of 1912 Woodrow Wilson warned darkly that if large-scale combinations were accepted, their political power would thwart all public attempts to control them. "The masters of the government of the United States are the combined capitalists and manufacturers of the United States. . . . The government of the United States at present is a foster-child of the special interests."[18] Periodically the legitimacy of these giant enterprises would be challenged in court: Both Standard Oil and American Tobacco were soon broken up by Supreme Court decree. U.S. Steel, International Harvester, General Electric, and AT&T all were targets of antitrust prosecution during subsequent decades.

Thus, while the merger wave of the turn of the century had temporarily ended the threat of industrial overcapacity, it had created a new problem for America's emerging enterprises: that of political legitimacy. Nor was the original problem of overcapacity resolved for long. As the fixed costs of high-volume production continued to climb, American companies searched for other ways to coordinate their investment decisions. It gradually became clear, as the new century unfolded, that American firms needed politically acceptable methods of organizing themselves by industry. (Chapter V chronicles how this need was met.)

5.

The second problem facing the inventor-promoters was the managing of people within the new business enterprises. As the scale of production grew larger, greater numbers of workers were needed at the same location, and their efforts needed to be coordinated more precisely. This entailed careful management.

But America had no management tradition. Until the turn of the century American businesses employed relatively few people, and their management structures were simple. Cyrus McCormick began production at his Chicago Harvester works in 1849 with only 123 employees. Despite sales and production that expanded so rapidly that McCormick boasted his works were "the largest factory of its kind in the world," the company employed no more than 3,500 workers on the eve of the Civil War. In 1870 the Pullman Company—then one of America's largest enterprises—had only 200 workers constructing its sleeping cars.[19] Managing such modest establishments was relatively straightforward, and no American company had a separate layer of salaried middle managers standing between owners and shop-floor supervisors. Nearly all top managers were owners, either partners or major stockholders in the enterprise they managed.

Nor did government afford a useful model of administration. Unlike Germany, France, and Japan—whose well-established public bureaucracies provided many new businessmen and entrepreneurs with administrative training—the United States had no government bureaucracy on which to draw. By 1871 only 51,000 American civilians worked for the federal government; 37,000 of these were postal employees, most of them clerks in local post offices.[20]

The transition to managing high-volume production was further complicated by the traditional dominance of skilled craftsmen in the manufacturing process. Prior to 1870 skilled craftsmen typically were not salaried; rather, they contracted directly with enterprise owners and were paid according to the amount they produced. The craftsmen then subcontracted some of their tasks to other skilled and unskilled workers.

Through their knowledge and control over day-to-day manufacturing tasks, these skilled craftsmen had enormous power within the enterprise. That power was enhanced by their organization into craft unions, such as the Amalgamated Association of Iron, Steel, and Tin Workers.

Skilled craftsmen stalled the shift to high-volume production. They naturally resisted the introduction of machines that would render their skills redundant. And because they were organized strictly by craft—rather than by steps in the production process—they were not prepared to take on the tasks of managing, supervising, and coordinating high-volume manufacturing.

The first major move to abolish craft control took place at Andrew Carnegie's Homestead Steel Works. In 1892, after having made some mechanical improvements in the production process, the company demanded wage cuts from the skilled craftsmen whose jobs were affected. The Amalgamated refused, and threatened to strike. Carnegie and his works manager, Henry Clay Frick, viewed this as an opportunity to "bust" the union. They locked out the skilled workers, surrounded the mill with a barbed-wire fence, summoned Pinkerton troops, and declared the mill a "nonunion" shop. Carnegie succeeded. The Homestead strike marked the start of the transition from craft control to managerial control.[21]

But managerial control initially amounted to little more than replacing skilled craftsmen with foremen. The number of foremen in American manufacturing and construction firms swelled fourfold in the decade between 1890 and 1900, from 90,000 to 360,000. These foremen were given total responsibility for specific steps in the production process. So long as each foreman coordinated his production with that of other foremen, he was free to manage his workers in any way he wished. He could hire and fire, promote or demote, or otherwise reward and discipline workers in his charge. Within his sphere of responsibility, he was no less autonomous than the skilled craftsman had been, but with this important difference: While the craftsman's control over his subordinates had been justified by his superior skills, the foreman's power rested solely on his formal position in the organizational hierarchy. The craftsman's task had been to make a product; the foreman's job was to supervise and control workers.

Absolute discretion opened the door to arbitrary and idiosyncratic supervision. The "foreman's empire," as workers termed it, was deeply resented. The power of factory foremen sparked the same questions of legitimacy that greeted the new industrial trusts. Unconstrained by law or custom and little governed by market forces, these new centers of power were responsible to no one and therefore aroused Americans' suspicion and resistance. Indeed, workers' perception of favoritism, prejudice, and unfairness on the shop floor inspired a campaign of union organization and the outbreak of strikes and work stoppages that shook industry in the first decades of the twentieth century.[22]

In Britain and Germany the trade union movement was well under way by the 1860's. But American workers began to organize on a mass basis only in the 1890's, after the great wave of industrial consolidation had begun. Unionism and labor unrest came in the wake of the new giant enterprises. By 1897 American trade unions had 447,000 members; seven years later membership had reached over 2 million. The number of strikes increased dramatically over this period. In the five years between 1893 and 1898 there were 7,029 strikes. In the following five-year period, 1899 to 1904, the number of strikes soared to 15,463.[23] This rise in labor unrest was largely due (in the words of Samuel Gompers, first leader of the American Federation of Labor) to "autocracy in the shop."[24] The Pullman strike of 1894, for example, was the direct result of "[f]avoritism and nepotism" in the plant, according to an independent inquiry undertaken soon afterward.[25] Brutal treatment at the hands of local agents produced widespread strikes and work stoppages in Colorado mines between 1903 and 1913.

Several of America's largest enterprises sought to quell labor unrest by offering their workers a broad range of benefits. General Electric instituted suggestion boxes, health and safety programs, and, by 1912, a worker pension plan. International Harvester's reforms of the period included flush toilets, pure drinking water, and (for workers who refused to join the union or take part in strikes) a pension plan and sickness and accident benefits. Between 1902 and 1915 U.S. Steel provided its workers with a stock subscription plan, a workmen's compensation plan, a pension plan, lunchrooms, and medical facilities. In steelmaking communities, U.S. Steel built churches, schools, social clubs, playgrounds, swimming pools, athletic fields, boardinghouses, and training schools for workers' children. Other companies followed suit. A government study of 1919 revealed that of 431 companies surveyed, 375 had instituted some sort of medical program, 80 had disability plans, 75 had pension plans, and 153 had recreation facilities.[26]

But such worker benefit programs skirted the central issue of arbitrary authority on the shop floor. The strikes continued. Indeed, workers' unrest was most intense in the largest enterprises, precisely where the benefit programs had been pushed the hardest. In 1916 a spontaneous walkout shut down International Harvester's Chicago plant. In 1918 workers went on strike at General Electric's mammoth Lynn, Massachusetts, plant. In 1919, some 367,000 steelworkers went on strike, prompting the governor of Indiana to send troops into Gary to maintain order. After four months of hostilities and the deaths of eighteen workers the union relented. At a subsequent Senate investigation of the causes of the strike workers testified about "abusive" foremen who had laid off workers "for nothing."[27]

The substitution of foremen for craftsmen on the shop floor had allowed the introduction of high-volume machine production, but it had created a new problem. Lacking any mechanism in place for monitoring and guiding the decisions of foremen, the newly consolidated enterprises suddenly found themselves confronted with massive resistance to arbitrary rule. As the enterprises expanded, the resistance hardened. Idiosyncratic decision making by foremen also began to jeopardize the firms' ability to coordinate and synchronize production. Together, labor unrest and breakdowns in coordination began to undermine the new efficiencies of high-volume production. It became clear, as the new century unfolded, that America's emerging enterprises needed more efficient—and more legitimate—methods of managing their operations.

6.

The third set of problems flowing from America's transformation to high-volume production was more general and pervasive. The sudden growth of America's cities, and the crowded conditions in which their new populations lived, spawned a welter of social problems—poor sanitation, epidemics, homelessness, crime, fires, and dereliction. The yearly waves of new immigrants, coupled with the cycles of boom and bust that characterized the last decades of the century, aggravated these conditions. As trains, trams, and new roads linked expanding metropolitan areas to central cities, the middle class began to move to suburban communities. Established neighborhoods eroded. Immigrants clustered in ethnic enclaves. City bosses, like Richard Croker of Tammany Hall and George B. Cox in Cincinnati, gained power. Periodic riots and occasional bombings heightened middle-class fears of urban anarchism, inspiring vigilante leagues and the erection of public armories.

America was not organized to deal with mass poverty and unemployment or with the new necessities of urban life. American institutions had been premised on small communities in which the family, the church, and voluntary charities had taken care of most social ills. Government was simply not geared to delivering social services even-handedly and efficiently on a large scale. The limited social services available in many American cities were dispensed arbitrarily, often offered in exchange for political support. The problem was both ideological and structural. Poverty and disease, no matter how widespread, were still considered matters of personal misfortune rather than manifestations of social dysfunction. The appropriate response, therefore, was assumed to be private charity rather than public program. Public intervention was not even a realistic alternative since (apart from asylums and almshouses) America had no administrative apparatus for caring for large numbers of people.

Meanwhile, rich inventor-promoters, inspired by a blend of religion and noblesse oblige, engaged in a vast array of philanthropic projects. Andrew Carnegie (whose annual income then exceeded $12.5 million and whose total wealth reached $1 billion in 1919 dollars) exhorted other wealthy men to place their "excess" fortunes in the hands of trustees, to use for the public good, rather than to leave it to their undeserving progeny. Carnegie built libraries and educational foundations. John D. Rockefeller poured his "excess" into Baptist colleges and divinity schools. Others founded symphony orchestras, universities, or churches. Many middle-class Americans joined in the charity movement. By the last decades of the century the list of voluntary agencies in the charity directories of many cities extended 100 pages or more. But private charities were not up to the tasks of dealing with the nation's new urban problems.[28]

America's early failure to cope with the social consequences of industrialization imposed a lasting cleavage between the business culture and the civic culture. In the 1890's many Protestant clergymen scourged the evils of industrialization as their predecessors had criticized slavery. Inevitably industrialization itself became a political issue.

The presidential campaign of 1896, in which William Jennings Bryan confronted William McKinley, was the climax of agrarian populism in America. It was also a contest between two powerful symbols, each seeking to dominate American ideology. One was the vision of a "people's movement" dedicated to democratic ideals and social betterment. The other promised prosperity through patriotism, stability, law, and business. The choice between silver and gold as a standard for currency, although seemingly important to indebted farmers, was almost irrelevant to the economy, with only minor implications for currency volume or interest rates. But the two sets of symbols were potent, and America's emerging business leaders sensed a looming threat. Largely as a result, the 1896 election was the first in which the money of wealthy industrialists played a significant part, under the skillful tutelage of an Ohio industrialist named Mark Hanna. Hanna's money raising set a precedent for modern American politics. Standard Oil contributed $250,000. So did J. P. Morgan. The railroads contributed even more. Receipts and expenditures soared into the millions, enabling the Republicans to finance America's first concentrated mass political advertising campaign and to send hundreds of paid speakers into the field. It was also the first national election in which employers intimidated factory workers into voting against their will. American business literally bought its way into an emblematic battle —a battle from which it has never emerged. The divisive struggle between business culture and civic culture had been joined.[29]

Other industrializing nations, better organized to smooth the social disruptions of large-scale production, avoided this ideological trap. The major cities of Western Europe had strong traditions of municipal government, which aided them in planning and administering programs of public health, housing, transport, and general assistance to soften the transition to industrialization. National governments, having helped mobilize resources for industrialization, possessed the administrative machinery and public legitimacy necessary to provide social services on a large scale. Fearful of a growing Social Democratic movement in the newly founded German Empire, for example, Bismarck established by 1888 a national system to provide his "soldiers of industry" with pensions and insurance against sickness and unemployment—a system so patently linked to the maintenance of social order that an exhibit at the 1904 St. Louis world's fair described the system as "the German Worker Insurance as a Social Instrumentality." In 1911, under the leadership of David Lloyd George, Britain established a comprehensive system of unemployment and health insurance. Between 1880 and 1912 twelve major European nations developed programs of workmen's compensation for injuries; ten established programs of insurance against sickness; eight had national old-age pension schemes; and five developed national unemployment insurance. Japan had a national pension plan by the 1880's and was the first Far Eastern nation to develop a modern social security system. In America, by contrast, social programs like these had to await the New Deal.

Without a tradition of public administration, the United States could not make an effective response to the new social problems of industrialization. The widespread sense of frustration and insecurity that resulted therefore turned against the only target that was available: the process of industrialization itself and the large enterprises that embodied it. The muckraking exposés of industrialists like Harriman, Astor, Carnegie, Swift, Morgan, Vanderbilt, Rockefeller, Armour, and Schwab and of the oil, sugar, railroads, tobacco, and meat-packing industries fed off this frustration. So did the wave of reforms which followed. The readiness of America's new business leaders to resort to ideological battle instead of supporting the evolution of a strong public sector to respond to the new social needs of industrialization confirmed them in the role in which they had been cast.

7.

Between 1900 and 1920 the rate of increase in output per worker (and per person) in the American economy declined by approximately 50 percent from the rate prevailing over the previous decade. This deceleration marked the end of the first era of American productivity. The enormous spurt in productivity of the late 1880's and 1890's had been due to an extraordinarily efficient mobilization of resources into high-volume production: machinery which incorporated new technology; disciplined workers from the farm and from overseas; and advances in transportation and communication that enabled goods and materials to flow continuously through the manufacturing process and into distribution. But the processes underlying the surge of mobilization could not sustain the dynamic they had set in motion.

In sum, the problems that stalled the next stage of industrialization stemmed from failures of organization. When America's new engine of production began to overrun its capacity to distribute, market, and consume, business sought to remedy the problem through mergers and consolidations. But this reorganization did not suffice. Some of the mergers let manufacturers reduce capacity and limit competition without any real gains in the efficiency of production, distribution, or marketing. Even the combinations that did yield new efficiencies were suspect in the eyes of many Americans, who doubted their accountability either to the market or to the political process. And many of the risks of overcapacity remained.

The shop floor itself suffered from organizational inadequacy. Foremen's authority over their subordinates was arbitrary and unchecked, resulting in worsening labor unrest and mounting difficulties in coordinating production within the firm.

A third organizational failure plagued public administration. American government lacked the capacity to respond efficiently and equitably to many of the social ills of industrialization. The result was the beginning of a sharp ideological cleavage between the ideals of social welfare and industrial growth.

The evolving American economy required systems of organization that could give it stability and legitimacy. Large, newly consolidated enterprises needed an institutional structure that could confirm their new role and help shield them against the ravages of the business cycle. Within their own enterprises, businessmen required a system of rules and policies to check the arbitrary actions of foremen, legitimize their authority in the eyes of workers, and aid them in coordinating production within the firm. And within society at large, popular acceptance of industrialization depended on a system of public administration to soften its social impact.

In the absence of these organizational systems, the continued growth of high-volume production in America was stymied. Labor unrest, social disruption, and political turmoil in the first decades of the new century constrained productivity and raised fundamental questions about the role of the large corporation in American life. America searched for an answer to what appeared to be an impasse in its politics and economy. The answer came in the form of a new political and economic vision: that of management.

THE ERA
OF
MANAGEMENT
1920–1970

Part Two

III
THE MANAGERIAL
IMAGINATION

1.

From 1920 to 1970 output per worker in the American economy grew at an average rate of 2.3 percent per year—faster than in any other industrialized nation. Some of this increase was simply due to more and better machinery. But a larger part of the expansion was due to changes in the way America organized itself to produce.[1]

The first American era of productivity had been a direct extension of Britain's Industrial Revolution. The United States had merely added huge doses of capital and labor, and a large national market, to Britain's basic inventiveness. The recipe had generated enormous increases in production, for a time. But America could not continue this expansion without an organizational network to coordinate and monitor the use of its resources. Its new business enterprises and its newly mobilized society both needed management.

Management emerged around 1920 as a philosophy, a science, and a pervasive metaphor which would dominate the way Americans viewed themselves and their institutions for the next fifty years. Management was

America's own creation. No other industrialized nation so fully embraced it or experienced its spectacular capacity to generate new wealth.

The paradigm of management deserved to dominate its time. Many of the problems that emerged in America before World War I—within its factories, among its enterprises, and in society at large—had been rooted in bottlenecks, inefficiencies, poor coordination, and inadequate controls. The managerial ideas and institutions that arose after the war solved many of these problems. They bore for America the fruits of high-volume, standardized production. The managed organization replicated itself across the country—in businesses, government agencies, and labor unions —promising stability, order, and prosperity. For fifty years it faithfully delivered.

Business enterprises that standardized and coordinated their work achieved spectacular efficiency. Management hierarchies that employed sophisticated techniques to supervise and monitor subordinates gained a cost advantage over their competitors. Thus, a sort of organizational "natural selection" set in: Firms that invested heavily in machine production bested those that did not, while those that took the next step and developed superior managerial systems outpaced more traditionally managed firms. The ability to innovate and to mobilize resources was still important to competitive success, of course. But throughout this era real advantage lay in the relative efficiency with which these inventions and resources were managed.

Managerial ideas and institutions also emerged in government. High-volume producers needed government's help in creating a stable environment for planning and coordinating their investments. Mergers and consolidations at the turn of the century had helped eliminate distribution and marketing bottlenecks and thereby mitigated the initial problem of overcapacity. But after World War I had triggered an enormous surge in industrial capacity, the problem reappeared. Plant and equipment in the new business enterprises imposed such high fixed costs that production at less than full capacity severely threatened the firms' profitability. Unless each firm within the industry could somehow coordinate its investment decisions with other firms, it ran the risk of investing in too much capacity. As we shall see, the remedy was to be found in a government-managed network of regulatory agencies, advisory boards, and trade associations which enabled companies to coordinate their investment decisions informally but effectively.

Management pervaded government largely because interaction with business engendered a kind of bureaucratic emulation: In mobilizing businesses for war and coordinating businesses to avoid excess capacity, government inevitably came to draw upon the business organization as a model of effective administration. The problems of mobilizing and coordinating business firms were, after all, just one level removed from those of mobilizing and coordinating productive units within a single firm. Management techniques applicable to the firm level naturally seemed appropriate to the economy as a whole.

These relationships were, of course, less direct than they might appear in hindsight. Causes and effects were often indistinguishable. Managerialism offered America a set of organizing principles at precisely the time when many Americans sensed a need for greater organization, and these principles soon shaped every dominant American institution precisely as they helped those institutions become dominant. The logic of routine, large-scale manufacturing first shaped its original business environment and then permeated the larger social environment. And American society embraced and duplicated it because it was the very engine of prosperity.

2.

Managed organizations achieved an extraordinary stability during this period. Notwithstanding two world wars, several regional conflicts around the globe, a major depression, and several deep recessions, the institutions that dominated America in 1920 continued to dominate it for the next fifty years.

America's major companies changed very little over the era. Of the 278 largest industrial companies at the start, only 14 had been liquidated, dissolved, or discontinued by the end. Companies that were household words in 1920—Quaker Oats, American Tobacco, Eastman Kodak, Procter & Gamble, Libby, Borden, Carnation, Campbell Soup, Heinz, Ford, U.S. Steel, Pillsbury Flour, International Harvester, B. F. Goodrich, Singer, Diamond Match—were still household words half a century later.

If anything, stability increased during the era: Half of America's 50 largest manufacturing companies in 1947 were still within the top 50 twenty-five years later. The other half were still in the top 200. Viewed from the perspective of the 1970's, the stability is equally remarkable: All but 5 of America's 50 largest manufacturing companies in 1972 were among the top 200 in 1947. Nor was the era's stability restricted to manufacturing. The banking and insurance industries followed a similar pattern, with the major companies enjoying relatively constant market shares over the entire period.[2]

Just as the same firms dominated industries, so the same industries dominated America's economy as a whole throughout the period: In 1920 and in 1970, 22 of the 200 largest companies were in petroleum; 5 of the 200 largest, at both ends of the era, were in rubber; 18, in machinery; 20, in food products; and 20, in transportation equipment. Chemicals, primary metals, and tobacco also started as, and stayed, key industries.[3]

The same set of industries (with the addition of electronics and aircraft, which were just emerging in 1920) led the economy in technological advances, the production of capital goods, overall growth, and wages.[4] A businessman of 1920, suddenly transported to America in 1970, would have felt more or less at home.

Government institutions also achieved a stability and continuity little perturbed by changes in administration. Of 175 federal government units identified in a 1923 survey, 148 (or nearly 85 percent) were still in operation fifty years later, and most of them retained the same responsibilities.[5] Some units changed their names, but not their character. The War Industries Board and its related industry committees, for example, were transmogrified during the 1920's into the various associations and boards that Herbert Hoover coordinated as secretary of commerce. This apparatus formed the organizational foundation for Franklin Delano Roosevelt's National Recovery Administration and in World War II was once more transformed into the War Production Board and Office of Price Administration. These institutions lived on in the 1950's and early 1960's as industry committees within the departments of Commerce, Interior, and Defense. Indeed, many of the same staff members served throughout: General Hugh Johnson, liaison officer between the War Industries Board and the Army in World War I, became the first director of the NRA; Hoover himself had been director of the Food Commission in World War I; Donald Nelson, an NRA official, subsequently headed the War Production Board in World War II, while Leon Henderson, another NRA official, headed the Office of Price Administration.

Meanwhile, government agencies that had been established at the start of the era to promote and to regulate transportation, communications, energy, and agriculture became permanent fixtures. Hoover's Federal Radio Commission of 1927 had become the Federal Communications Commission a decade later, with responsibility for allocating frequencies, setting rates for long-distance telephones, and promoting the infant television industry. Hoover's Aeronautics Branch at the Commerce Department, established in 1926, became the Civil Aeronautics Administration in 1938, then the Civil Aeronautics Board in 1940. A Federal Power Commission, established in 1920 to supervise hydroelectric development, gained control over natural gas pipelines in 1938 and lived on in various guises until the early 1970's. The Interstate Commerce Commission had by 1920 been given responsibility for managing railroad terminals, abandonments, mergers, construction, and securities; it preserved that bailiwick for the next half century. So, too, with the Farm Bureau in the Department of Agriculture, the various commissions and boards established to oversee the production of coal, the Federal Reserve Board, and the Shipping Board, which became the Federal Maritime Commission. All these agencies, which had been designed primarily to stabilize the economic environment for specific industries, proved remarkably enduring.

The managerial era also witnessed the labor movement's metamorphosis into a formal network of large, permanent, managed institutions. Labor militancy was forcefully subdued. In the "open shop" campaign of the 1920's, for example, city-wide associations of businessmen, backed by the National Association of Manufacturers, provided individual employers with legal advice and financial assistance in warding off union militants. They sent spies into the union to get information on their plans.[6] And by promoting the reorganization of municipal governments through zoning, housing, and parks projects, they gradually gained control over the use of public space. Requirements for park permits, ordinances against disturbing the peace, and restrictions on trespassing and soliciting made it more difficult for union militants to "take to the streets." The annual ledger of the police barracks in one steelmaking town

(Ellsworth, Pennsylvania, 1927) records the pervasiveness of control: Exactly 2,088 visitors were excluded from the town; twenty-eight labor assemblies were patrolled and dispersed; and there were 175 arrests for disorderly conduct.[7] Labor Day in Muncie, Indiana, was devoid of ceremony in 1924; by contrast, a quarter century earlier, celebrations had begun at 4:00 A.M. with a forty-four-round artillery salute and had featured oratory, pie-eating contests, dancing, parades, and evening fireworks.[8] Although these efforts, combined with the post World War I recession, discouraged unionization in many industries, overall membership during the latter 1920's remained constant at about 2 million. Membership increased to 4 million in the organizing drives of 1933 and 1934. With the founding of the Committee for Industrial Organization in 1936, the growth of unions in America's heavy industries accelerated. During World War II the ranks of organized labor swelled to 14 million. By the mid-1950's the number had reached 17 million, and by the late 1960's, 20 million.

More important than numbers alone was labor's new institutional character. Beginning in the 1930's, American labor unions began to resemble the business organizations they confronted—hierarchical, departmental, and structured along industry lines. Indeed, both in the style of its organization and in the nature of its agenda, unionism absorbed management values. Industrial concentration was perceived to be inevitable. Labor came to concede management's authority to make policy for the workplace, an authority resting on technical expertise. Union leaders limited their concerns to hours, wages, job classifications, and work rules. By the late 1930's, after this agenda had been codified into law, the institutional relationships which it implied had become well established in most major industries.

Despite the periodic threat of strikes and walkouts, organized labor fitted nicely into the emerging structure of American production. Both business management and government management could deal more efficiently with a formal structure of labor management. The three management spheres coordinated their activities to mobilize the nation for war and to guard against excessive industrial capacity. There were tensions in these relationships and occasional confrontations over specific issues, but the three nevertheless learned to communicate and bargain smoothly, orchestrating decisions through their hierarchical control over vast reservoirs of complementary resources. By the late 1920's, after four decades of stormy conflict, the relationship between capital and labor in America had been rendered relatively stable.

This stability was no more a "success" for labor than it was for business. It represented, rather, an efficient accommodation. Both sides had discovered their roles in a nexus of mutual control. As the forces of labor militancy were progressively blocked, more managerial forms of unionism became the only possible routes to large-scale organization. In many respects, the emergence of the Committee for Industrial Organization was a logical outcome of this increase in institutional control. By 1937, with General Motors' recognition of the United Auto Workers and U.S. Steel's recognition of the Steelworkers' Organizing Committee, the transformation to industrial unionism was complete. Collective bargaining had become an efficient managerial method of maintaining a stable work force and minimizing unexpected disruptions.

Business, government, and labor all became efficient managerial organizations, controlling large numbers of people. Sophisticated monitoring and reporting systems let centralized staffs maintain order. And because this new form of bureaucratic control rested on standardized "rules," it constrained the discretion of lower-level supervisors. Arbitrary authority —whether exercised by factory foremen, municipal bosses, or maverick labor leaders—was sharply checked. Managerialism installed authority at the top of the hierarchy, where decisions could be made in an efficient and impartial way.

The capacity to control rested on the capacity to exclude. The Federal Exclusion Acts of 1921 and 1924 drastically limited immigration. The total annual quota from Eastern and Southern Europe was set at only 20,000. Immigrants did not stop coming, of course. But the U.S. government now had the organizational capacity to find and expel them if they came illegally or if their activities offended local authorities. The number of people evicted from America rose steadily, reaching 26,674 in 1927 and 30,212 in 1933.[9]

Institutional stability and predictability enabled managers at all levels of American society to coordinate and plan their activities better than before, nurturing the emerging system of high-volume, standardized production. Advances in productivity were matched by increases in real earnings throughout the period (with the exception of the Depression decade of the 1930's). And apart from the late 1920's, the distribution of income remained relatively stable as well. But the price of such stability was occasionally high, particularly when it expressed itself in outbursts of racism, religious intolerance, xenophobia, and a fear of Communist insurrection.

3.

In 1913 a scientist named John B. Watson asserted that there were purely objective causes of human behavior. He and his followers claimed that people were born as passive, pliant beings that could be trained, through structured regimes of stimulus and response, to do almost anything. The managerial imagination drew upon this new science of behaviorism, based on the notion that human action could be manipulated through selective conditioning.

If human nature was so malleable, it seemed only sensible that the institutions which controlled and directed human behavior should be designed in such a way as to bring out the "best" in people: Social institutions should promote civic virtue; business institutions should promote productivity. The institutional settings in which people lived and worked took on new instrumental importance. One logical behaviorist inference was that legal institutions, for example, should no longer be mired in precedent. Oliver Wendell Holmes, Jr., suggested that judges should replace fixed legal principles with a new organic view of the law as a social instrument. He argued that law should refer less to abstract norms and more to the particulars of social reality: Criminals should be diagnosed and treated to overcome the warping environments that had led them astray; separate courts, emphasizing counseling and mediation, should be established to deal with the special problems of juveniles and of families. Louis Brandeis peppered his legal arguments with social data. His view of the law's proper role was encapsulated in the famous Brandeis briefs, which advanced an instrumental view of the Constitution as a document open to reinterpretation to address new social needs that the Founders could not have anticipated.

If law could be managed, so could every other human institution. The problems of urban squalor could be ameliorated through reshaping the family and urban environments. Productivity could be increased by modifying the factory environment and providing workers with more effective incentives. Sales could be expanded through more scientific techniques of marketing and advertising. In short, human nature could be shaped through social engineering, a project of psychological retrofitting requiring the same fundamental approach—if somewhat more complex specifications—as designing a machine production process.

Social engineers needed appropriate training, of course. And the channels for providing such training were themselves becoming institutionalized. *Ad hoc,* amateur responses to the problems of a particular neighborhood or factory were giving way to professional solutions, generalized to suit all cities and workplaces. The original settlement workers of the turn of the century, for example, had been ordinary citizens concerned with particular groups of poor people in specific urban settings. By the 1920's settlement workers like Jane Addams and Lillian Wald were joining reformers from other cities to study and to recommend changes in urban life benefiting poor people in general. The settlement houses became centers in which experts developed ideas for efficient city management. People devoted to helping the poor increasingly came to view themselves as professional social workers and sought specialized training and formal accreditation. As private philanthropy became the domain primarily of large charitable foundations, professionals assumed responsibility for allocating funds according to objective criteria.

Professional social engineers also came to dominate the workplace. Industrial psychiatrists, who began to appear in the 1920's, sought to improve "human relations" at work through group and individual counseling. Professionally trained personnel managers set out to select, train, place, and promote people efficiently, according to the workers' measured aptitudes. Specialists in labor relations advised managers about how to deal with labor unions. Industrial physiologists concerned themselves with factory lighting, noise, the speed of tools and machines, and the overall design of the workplace. And professional advertisers and marketers increasingly came to control company decisions about how products were distributed and sold.

Social engineers left an indelible mark on American education. The comprehensive high school, tracking, educational testing, home economics, student council, daily flag pledge, high school athletics, school assembly, vocational education, vocational guidance, clubs, and school newspapers together transformed the American school from a place for teaching basic skills into a laboratory for shaping basic attitudes and habits. Inculcating a sense of good citizenship became the schools' central mission. But they served an important sorting function as well, separating children into different categories according to their "aptitudes" and their "potential." By the end of the 1920's objective educational testing was used extensively at all levels. The College Entrance Examination Board and Cooperative Testing Service were conducting national examinations. Many occupational groups were establishing programs of "accreditation" at state universities. Increasingly a child's future station in society was determined by his or her performance on a series of formal tests and programs extending over a dozen or more years.[10] In the era of management, direct personal authority gave way to indirect control exercised by the architects of institutional settings.

There was nothing sinister about all this. Social engineers and the people who hired them rarely, if ever, questioned the legitimacy of their undertaking because their goals seemed beyond reproach. Civic virtues, efficiency, productivity, and health were demonstrably aspects of social well-being. Just as obviously, they seemed open to objective definition. If the goals of high-volume machine production could be clearly defined as more production at lower unit costs, so presumably could society's other goals be made explicit and operational so that professionals might get to work pursuing them most efficiently. People might disagree about how the new national wealth was to be distributed among managers, workers, and investors, but few would dispute the fundamental goals— to produce more at less cost, to grow bigger, and to replicate clean, healthful, and prosperous communities across the land. All this seemed within the competence of the new social engineer.

4.

The twin dangers haunting the era—war and industrial overcapacity —gave special urgency to engineering solutions and further focused institutional attention on means rather than on ends. National defense and national prosperity had vivid meaning to most Americans and summoned unambiguous support. The nation had yet to experience either a foreign war which many felt to be unjust or a prosperity for some citizens knowingly bought at the price of massive unemployment for others. The two world wars, the Depression, and the Korean War had touched Americans of whatever social or economic status in essentially the same way. Thus, the dominant public issues concerned technique and strategy. And the professional experts, the social engineers who designed institutions, stood ready with techniques and strategies designed to serve these goals.

Explicit centralized planning had been restricted to the two world wars and the worst years of the Depression. But the habits and attitudes of planning permeated the management era and shaped its institutions. As subsequent chapters make clear, market competition ceased to be the main force behind the evolution of American industry; nor were there many businessmen who could contemplate an unmanaged economy with anything but anxiety. While the ideal of the "free market" excluded planning, the series of economic crises and wars that marked the era had made planning organizations—the superstructures of management—central to the success of the American economy. As we shall see, the real debate centered not on the choice between a free market and planning, but on whether business leaders or government administrators would take the lead in planning.

America's basic goals were so clearly defined that the era of management was marked by a peculiar kind of empirical politics. The success of political rhetoric increasingly grew to depend on the quantity and quality of data the speaker commanded. "Good" policies were defined as those that would most efficiently serve the unquestioned end; "bad" policies were simply less efficient. Quantified costs and benefits were tallied with growing enthusiasm over the course of the era, reducing almost all public issues to questions of empirical fact.

Empirical politics, however, was an exclusive affair. Admission to the political forum came to be limited to experts with special knowledge about a given field or training in the measurement of social costs and benefits. Sociologists who proclaimed the "end of ideology" during this time were, in fact, noting the absence of a politics of values open to every citizen by virtue of his or her capacity for moral judgment. Empirical politics had been a natural outgrowth of a political culture in which the goals of national defense and full-capacity production were obvious and widely shared. Moral judgment had little to do with it. The American penchant for empirical politics would become inappropriate only when the issues of the day ceased to be the sort that were open to factual resolution.

The social planning and empirical politics that dominated national discourse in this era were reflected in government agencies and business corporations. Both sorts of institutions were managed by professionals whose primary concerns were strategic and technical. Indeed, large government agencies and large corporations were almost indistinguishable, both to the people who worked within them and to outsiders who dealt with them. Both institutions were similarly programmed to dispose of the various demands that might be made of them. Standard operating procedures let them routinely process large amounts of data and deliver large quantities of goods and services with remarkable efficiency.

Thus, regardless of who "owned" these institutions or to whom they were accountable, they functioned in predictable ways. Ownership and accountability had little operational significance when tasks were so obvious and goals so unambiguous. Shareholders and citizens alike sought managerial efficiency, and inefficiency was the only legitimate grounds for protest. The moral force of law was substantially replaced by managerial rules emanating from government agencies; the moral force of enterprise, by managerial rules emanating from corporate headquarters.

5.

The managerial imagination conjured stable institutions, carefully designed to encourage certain types of behavior and dedicated to the efficient accomplishment of clear, given ends. These three aspects of management were closely related. Institutional stability was largely a function of successful social engineering, by which the energies of vast numbers of people were directed and coordinated, and of the clarity and durability of institutional goals. Social engineering in turn depended on a sturdy consensus about the purposes that the society should be engineered to promote and about the legitimacy of the institutions that did the engineering. And management's singular attention to efficient production likewise had as its premises stable demand for industrial products and steady supplies of resources. This stability in its turn depended on social engineering to manage consumer demand, labor productivity, and the social consensus that supported the system.

At its base, management entailed a new awareness about how institutions could be organized. The model that inspired this organization was the machine—streamlined, precisely engineered, devoid of superfluous parts. America paid homage to the machine in the gleaming chrome, rounded glass, and stainless steel of its Art Deco buildings and furnishings. And America patterned itself after the machine in the formal bureaucracies that emerged in the 1920's and dominated its business and government for the next half century.

But the managerial imagination reflected more than an aesthetic fashion. The managerial form of organization was the most efficient structure for organizing the performance of an integrated set of simple, repetitive tasks. Managers concerned themselves exclusively with the efficient pursuit of productivity, as they were expected to do and rewarded for doing. Managers' professional code was built upon the ideal of efficiency, and the enterprises they worked in, along with the people they controlled, were cast as agents for achieving that ideal.

The science of management, incorporated into a canon of principles applied by professional managers, determined the shape of America's organizations for half a century.

IV
THE PROFESSION
OF MANAGEMENT

1.

The science of management offered a set of principles for controlling large organizations—principles seemingly as universal and immutable as the laws of physics. Indeed, their progenitors styled themselves as scientists dedicated to discovering —through empirical observation and logical inference—the underlying rules of efficient administration. The science of management spawned the profession of management.

For a half century the profession of management and the science it sprang from shaped administrators' goals and public expectations, defining an ideal of efficient business and government. While institutional reality often fell short of that ideal, the techniques and standards that the ideal inspired both propelled America's economic growth during the era and granted new legitimacy to its large institutions.

The new phenomenon of high-volume, standardized production— whether manifested in sewing machine assembly or the screening of visa applications—imposed wholly new management problems. Previous industrial traditions had bequeathed few useful principles. Historically the few large and complex enterprises in America had had specialized functions requiring more or less idiosyncratic styles of organization. To prevent accidents and control burgeoning costs, American railroads, for example, had established intricate maintenance and operations systems, manned by full-time salaried managers in centralized headquarters. Monitoring thousands of employees and millions of dollars' worth of equipment spread over many hundreds of miles required daily reports, statistical and accounting controls, and regional administrators. Similarly, its sheer size and its widely dispersed services had led the United States Post Office to establish a cadre of professional middle-level and top managers who supervised distribution centers and developed systematic procedures for speeding the flow of mail.

Certain aspects of these two types of organization were, of course, applicable to the needs of the new twentieth-century enterprises, and in the first decades of the century there was a great deal of trial-and-error borrowing from these models. The managers of Andrew Carnegie's steelworks in Pittsburgh, for example, used cost sheets modeled on railroad practices to maintain control over their growing operation. But America needed a generic science of management applicable to the whole set of new problems and opportunities that high-volume, standardized production ushered in.

The earliest intimations of a management science appeared in 1887, in an article entitled "The Study of Administration." The author was Woodrow Wilson, then a young professor at Princeton.[1] Wilson was concerned about the corrupting effects of political patronage on public administration, particularly in light of the "enormous burdens of administration" that government was taking on in America's new industrial society. He proposed the creation of a bureaucracy, to be strictly insulated from politics, in which a "competent body" of administrators could pursue a "detailed and systematic execution of public law." Broad political issues would be left entirely to legislators. "Administrative questions are not political questions," he wrote. "Although politics sets the tasks for administration, it should not be suffered to manipulate its office." For Wilson, good administration was efficient administration, and there was a single most efficient way of accomplishing any administrative task. Public administrators should subscribe to the "one rule of good administration for all governments alike." Wilson called for a new science of administration to discover these neutral and efficient rules.[2]

By a single stroke Wilson divorced much of government from politics. His ideas, developed and expounded in a series of studies by Professor Frank J. Goodnow of Johns Hopkins University, were to have far-reaching effects. No one before had so clearly distinguished policy from administration or argued so persuasively the case for neutral principles of management as Wilson.

The second inspiration for a science of management came from Frederick Winslow Taylor, the engineer who had invented carbon-steel machine tools. Taylor asserted that there was a single "best method" for organizing work. This best method was discoverable through careful study of the time and motion entailed in doing each job. Efficiency could be improved by simplifying tasks, standardizing tools and equipment, testing workers to place them in the jobs for which they were best suited, and offering bonuses for improved efficiency. Taylor predicted that these principles would transform business enterprises into "smoothly running machines."[3]

Taylor's ideas were considered liberal and progressive because they promised for the factory precisely what Woodrow Wilson's ideas promised for the government: an end to arbitrary, corrupt, and inefficient rule. Taylor declared that his "whole object was to remove the cause for antagonism between the boss and the men who were under him." Under scientific management, workers and bosses would be bound to the same set of rules. Taylor wrote:

> The man at the head of the business under scientific management is governed by rules and laws which have been developed through hundreds of experiments just as much as the workman is. Questions which are under other systems subject to arbitrary judgment and are therefore open to disagreement have under scientific management become the subject of the most minute and careful study in which both the workman and management have taken part.[4]

2.

To Taylor and his followers, scientific management promised more production and thus less conflict over its distribution. Under scientific management, workers and employers would "together turn their attention toward increasing the size of the surplus, until the surplus becomes so large . . . [that] there is ample room for a large increase in wages for the workman and an equally large increase in profits for the manager."[5]

Both Wilson and Taylor were confident that efficient management would drive politics out of the workplace and out of government administration, as the benefits of efficiency spread through society. The idea that conflict could be eliminated by improved management had enormous appeal, particularly to business leaders. Sam Lewisohn, president of the American Management Association in 1926, urged Americans to forget past hostilities and wrongs and to concentrate on training effective managers for the future. "The problem of distribution which has so often been regarded as a drama, with labor and capital as conflicting characters, turns out to be largely the prosaic task of using . . . policies to increase national productivity."[6]

Taylor's ideas seemed applicable to the organization of society as a whole. "The same principles [of management] can be applied with equal force to all social activities," he noted, "to the management of our homes, the management of our farms, the management of the business of our tradesmen large and small; of our churches, our philanthropic institutions, our universities, and our government departments."[7]

The very name of the new discipline suggested benign progressiveness. *Management* implied the guidance and restraint necessary for social harmony. *Science* bespoke disinterestedness and rigor. Together, the words "scientific management" provided the perfect banner for a new wave of reformers who sought to control and regulate society rather than to uproot it. Louis Brandeis, for example, saw in Taylor's ideas an ideal vehicle for social reform. Careful planning, along the lines that Taylor recommended, could improve the functioning of the economy as a whole, leading to a higher standard of living for all citizens. Working conditions could be improved, wages increased, hours reduced. Brandeis was the first to use the term "scientific management" to apply to Taylor's ideas, and he became one of its chief proponents. For Brandeis, scientific management presented an opportunity to rationalize society. "Under scientific management," he wrote, "nothing is left to chance."[8]

Brandeis elevated the principles of scientific management to the front pages of America's newspapers in the celebrated Eastern Rate Case of

1910–11, which arose out of the railroads' demands for an increase in freight rates in northeastern states. Representing the eastern shippers before the Interstate Commerce Commission, Brandeis argued that the railroads had not demonstrated their need for additional revenue. Then he shifted to the offensive: Even if they had proved their case, the remedy did not lie in higher rates. Instead, the solution was to introduce the new science of management. Through it, he declared, the railroads could save $1 million every day. Brandeis led a parade of engineers and businessmen before the commission to proclaim the virtues of scientific management.[9]

After the Eastern Rate Case, America embraced scientific management with unabashed enthusiasm. In 1914, 69,000 people attended an efficiency exposition held at the Grand Central Palace in New York City, with Taylor as the main speaker. Its success prompted similar expositions in other cities. Lectures and demonstrations were held all across the country.[10]

3.

Scientific management rested upon three basic principles: specialization of work through the simplification of individual tasks; predetermined rules to coordinate the tasks; and detailed monitoring of performance. In the half century following World War I, these principles were applied to almost every large enterprise in America. A survey of industrial engineers from seven manufacturing firms undertaken in the mid-1950's revealed these principles' durability. When asked how work should be structured, the engineers offered the scientific management litany: Jobs should be broken down into the smallest possible specialties, coordinated according to predetermined rules, and monitored with various data-gathering techniques.[11]

Specialization by Simplification. Specialization was not a new idea, of course. Medieval producers of textiles had divided their work into spinning, weaving, dyeing, and printing. The Gilyak Eskimos had parceled out responsibilities on their seal hunts to harpooners, oarsmen, and helmsmen. What was new was the deliberate, painstaking effort to break jobs down to their basic elements, so that each task would be both precise and extremely simple. "Time and motion" specialists sought to reduce all work to a finite number of elementary steps, each of which could be parceled out as a distinct task. One of Taylor's disciples, an industrial engineer named Frank B. Gilbreth, contended that all manual work consisted of seventeen basic movements; in any given job certain of these movements could be eliminated or combined for greater efficiency.

Specialization by simplification had several distinct advantages. First, it allowed an enterprise to employ inexperienced and unskilled workers —a boon during times of labor scarcity, as in World War I, and a means of keeping wages relatively low when labor was more abundant. Secondly, it enabled workers to become highly efficient through mastery of simple, repetitive steps. (This efficiency gain was assumed to offset any careless indifference brought on by boredom). Thirdly, the system allowed more efficient supervision: Tasks were so simple that foremen could easily recognize when a worker was not doing his or her job. This meant that the foreman's role also was simpler and more easily monitored by middle-level managers. Finally, through specialization by simplification, individual tasks could be better synchronized with one another and with machines, permitting steadier and more intensive use of people and equipment.

Predetermined Rules. The principle of specialization by simplification led naturally to the second principle: explicit and comprehensive work rules fixed in advance. A worker whose job entailed only a small, discrete step in the production process inevitably lacked an overall perspective on the operation. No single worker within a system of specialization by simplification could know exactly how his task meshed with the tasks of other workers or how a slight alteration in his task (caused by a change in raw materials, a breakdown in a machine, or a mistake) might alter the rest of the production process. Thus, increased specialization demanded intricate coordination and control by higher-level supervisors. And to ensure against overly narrow decisions at the supervisory level, supervisors in turn needed to be coordinated and controlled by a still higher level of management with an even broader perspective. Specialization by simplification forced the development of management hierarchies, arranged like a pyramid. Each level up the hierarchy was responsible for a progressively larger part of the operation.

These supervisory jobs could themselves be rendered more efficient by division into simplified steps. The steps would be codified in detailed rules, planned in advance, in anticipation of every contingency. Foremen and middle-level managers would need only to determine which rule to apply to a given situation. Their discretion would be circumscribed, and their overall efficiency enhanced, since they would not need to spend their time devising new solutions to recurring problems. In effect, everyone in the organization would be guided by predetermined rules. "It is absolutely necessary," wrote Taylor, "for every man in an organization to become one of a train of gear wheels."[12]

Rules multiplied within every large organization. Corporations announced "company policy" through written directives and guidelines. Government agencies issued elaborate rules of procedure. Broad "strategic plans" guided decisions at the top of the organization. "Operating rules" governed middle-level decisions about such things as production design, hiring, training, and assignment of personnel. "Standard operating procedures" at the lower levels stipulated how accounting, performance appraisals, and output measurements should be undertaken. Job descriptions at all levels were specified precisely. Explicit criteria determined promotion up established job "ladders." Conditions under which employees could be dismissed were codified. Rules for dealing with other units within the enterprise and in other enterprises were carefully delineated. Exhaustive lists of "what to do if" rules were issued to deal with possible aberrations in the flow of production.

As the management era progressed, the formulation of rules became more sophisticated, particularly at higher levels of planning. The years following World War II marked a great advance in the technology of planning, involving operations research, linear programming, probability statistics, and game theory. All these devices aided professional managers in allocating capital and designing the production process. Rules for day-to-day operations also benefited from theoretical refinements in production scheduling, machine loading, goods distribution, and inventory control.

Management Information. The third principle followed from the first two. In order to know which rule to apply to a specific situation, managers at all levels needed reliable information on the current status of each stage in the production process. Scientific management offered an array of information-gathering tools: cost accounting, inventory controls, budget controls, financial reporting systems, and task reports. It also required a staff of specialized clerks and timekeepers to monitor the results.

These tools, too, grew more sophisticated as the era progressed. Alfred P. Sloan, Jr., when president of General Motors in the 1930's, refined the process of gathering task information. He broke down into very small units the costs of each automobile that GM produced and developed reporting systems to monitor these costs and, over time, to reduce them. After World War II American managers instituted elaborate financial controls tied to program objectives and management information systems based upon electronic data collection and analysis.

These three principles—specialization by simplification, predetermined rules, and detailed management information—allowed the entire system of production to be systematically programmed. The organization was structured like the machines at its core, engineered to follow the sequence of steps specified by the settings on their controls. Scientific management made the large enterprise, and everyone who contributed to it, an extension of the high-volume machine. In so doing, it transformed American production and, with it, American life.

It is important to remember that these principles were embraced by organized labor as well as by management. Labor unions saw in them a means for preventing petty despotism in the shop and for controlling their own members. The clear definition of work rules, the explicit delineation of jobs, detailed rules governing wages and working conditions for each job, and a grievance process based on a highly specialized division of labor —all offered union members a modicum of security against arbitrary actions by the company, and at the same time they provided the union with a way to monitor the behavior of employers and workers alike. By the late 1920's organized labor was advocating scientific management as enthusiastically as were business leaders.

Within a few short years America's factories were governed by rigid job classifications and work rules. Toolmakers did not clean their own tools. Light-machine operators and miscellaneous-machine operators worked on different machines. Millwrights, not electricians, unscrewed the covers of electrical contacts. Specialization by simplification, detailed rules, and accounting systems were to underlie all future union strategies to protect their members.

Who was to set the controls for the machine enterprise? Who was to develop the rules by which it would function? Scientific management had an answer. Every large enterprise would have an elite group of planners trained to exercise this responsibility. Taylor envisioned a planning staff that would schedule operations, establish standard work rules, and allocate resources. These specialized thinkers were to be sharply distinguished from the rest of the work force.

This separation of thinkers from doers was the apogee of specialization: Planning was to be distinct from execution, brain distinct from brawn, head from hand, white collar from blue collar. One cannot overstate the importance of this split to the way America organized itself thereafter. This was not simply a separation between laborers and supervisors; managers with direct responsibility for supervising production were almost as narrowly constrained as manual workers by decisions emanating from the "thinkers." The separation ran between employees responsible for day-to-day production and those responsible for planning the production process; between nonprofessionals, whose training and frames of reference were bounded by the enterprise in which they worked, and professionals, whose competence and allegiance transcended the organization; between "line" and "staff."

The split was accepted by all participants as an inevitable aspect of efficient production. By the 1930's labor unions that had been organized along craft lines, such as the International Association of Machinists and the International Ladies Garment Workers Union, were organizing blue-collar workers by industry, without regard to craft distinctions. Industry-wide unions, like the United Auto Workers and the United Steelworkers, appeared. Each company came to be composed of two groups—professional managers and unionized workers—who had more in common with their counterparts in other companies than they had with each other. Employees at all levels began to function rather like replaceable units of machinery.

The professional manager and his professional staff worked outside the daily process of production, segregated from the middle-level managers, foremen, and workers who were engaged in purely routine tasks. They dealt with the realm outside the routine, with overall strategy. Their competence to engage the nonroutine derived from their professional training. Through that training they had internalized management principles and developed the habits of mind necessary to select, interpret, and apply them. The professional manager and his professional staff therefore were programmed like everyone else in the organization, but at a higher level of generality, with rules meant to apply to any organization in which they might find themselves.

4.

At the turn of the century the disciplines most closely associated with professional management had been mechanical and civil engineering. The heads of almost all of America's railroads at the turn of the century— George Whistler of the Western, Benjamin Latrobe of the Boston & Ohio, Daniel McCallum of the Erie, George McClellan of the Illinois Central, J. Edgar Thompson of the Pennsylvania—had been trained as civil engineers, responsible for railroad construction and bridge building before they became managers. Frederick Taylor and many of his disciples, like Morris Cooke, were also engineers.

The connection between engineering and management seemed obvious. First of all, training as an engineer prepared one to design and construct machines, an activity central to high-volume industry. But more generally, scientific management conceived of work as an extension of the machine. Thus, designing work logically seemed to fall within the engineer's expertise. The analytic techniques developed within the emerging engineering profession also seemed applicable to the new problems of organization. Finally, because of their formal training, engineers— unlike most others associated with industry at the time—carried certified professional status. As authority within the organization passed from craftsmen to foremen and salaried managers, the sources of authority changed from knowledge-specific skills to status within the enterprise. Professional training as an engineer, while perhaps not concerned with skills directly relevant to the job at hand, at least conferred status appropriate to a position of authority.

Between 1890 and 1930 the number of trained engineers in the United States increased by more than 400 percent, from 7,000 to 226,000. Out of 284 top businessmen in 1900, 12.5 percent were originally trained as engineers, the largest proportion of any professional group. Engineering was the fastest-growing profession in America before World War I.[13]

But management was rapidly becoming a profession on its own.

Schools of business were appearing. Both the University of Chicago and the University of California established undergraduate schools of "commerce" in 1899. New York University's School of Business Administration and Dartmouth's Amos Tuck School of Administration and Finance were founded in 1900; then, in 1908, came Harvard's Graduate School of Business Administration. Their curricula centered on accounting and commercial law, suggesting that they were more interested in training commodity traders and arbitragers than managers. But by the 1920's courses were introduced which pertained directly to the management of the large enterprise—marketing, delegation of responsibility, motivation of employees, financial controls, and cost accounting.

Professional journals soon appeared; they included the *Management Review,* founded in 1918, and *Management in Administration,* founded in 1921. Professional societies, like the Administrative Management Association, founded in 1919, and the American Management Association, in 1925, were established. Management consultants also arrived on the scene. By the end of World War I Arthur D. Little, Inc., originally an engineering firm, was including management advice in its services. In 1921 another firm, Day & Zimmerman, was advising General Motors about how it should reorganize itself, and the management consulting firm of Frazer & Torbet was peddling its services to both business and government. In 1925 one of Frazer & Torbet's erstwhile partners, James O. McKinsey, set up his own successful firm.

These specialized schools, journals, societies, and management consulting firms, all of which were flourishing by the mid-1920's, buttressed the idea of management as a distinct profession with its own standards, ideals, and frames of reference, transcending any particular business enterprise. They also reinforced the notions that the professional manager could anticipate a career path passing through many different enterprises and managerial situations; that his training and credentials made his expertise as marketable as any other professional service; and that, for these reasons, his primary loyalty was to the management profession and to his standing in that profession, rather than to any particular organization in which he might temporarily find himself. The professional manager could conceive of a lifetime in management, moving up a managerial career ladder from middle-level to top positions, from smaller to larger firms. This personal agenda inevitably shaped his ambition and his view of each particular job he held along the way.

Professional management did not come to all large firms at the same time, of course. Even by the 1930's, for every Alfred Sloan, Jr., of General Motors (who detached himself from the hurly-burly of production and made key decisions on the basis of statistical data), there was a Henry Ford (who refused to yield control over any facet of the firm's operations, arbitrarily discharged workers and managers alike, and kept the company in a perpetual state of near chaos). But as professionally managed companies like General Motors gradually outcompeted idiosyncratically managed companies like Ford, professional management came to dominate American business. (Ford's near bankruptcy was averted by the succession of Henry Ford II, who promptly instituted professional management practices.[14])

The decline of family ownership accelerated this evolutionary process. Through merger and new stock issues, the voting stock in many large firms became more and more diluted. As inventor-promoters lost control in firms like Du Pont, General Electric, U.S. Rubber, and Standard Oil, professional managers met a growing demand for reliable business leaders who could act in the best interests of all shareholders. The federal securities laws of 1933 and 1934 formalized this emerging relationship between the new professional manager and the growing number of public investors to whom he was responsible. The manager was to be an agent of the shareholders; his control was to be exercised on their behalf. The law thereby legitimized the growing separation of corporate ownership from corporate control and gave its imprimatur to the professional manager's new role.

The ascendancy of professional management in America's large companies was nearly complete by the early 1950's. The professionally managed firm had become the standard form of modern business enterprise. By 1962 in none of America's 200 largest nonfinancial companies did an individual, family, or group hold more than 80 percent of the stock. In only 5 did a family or group have majority control. Professional managers were clearly in control of 169 out of the 200 companies.[15]

Even where inventor-promoters and their families lingered on, professional managers often occupied key staff positions that let them impose professional values on the company. They hired and supervised teams of accountants, budget analysts, industrial engineers, quality-control engineers, manufacturing engineers, lawyers, market analysts. They presided over more specialized professionals—product managers; sales managers; advertising managers; personnel managers. And they contracted with other professionals outside the enterprise for special tasks—management consultants; investment bankers; counsel. Regardless of the formal allocation of authority within the enterprise, therefore, professional managers came to have de facto authority.

The separation of planning from execution, of thinking from doing, became the organizational norm during the era. Professional managers and their planning staffs took on more and more of the responsibility for formulating rules, as they continued to simplify the routine tasks of production. Production workers and the firm's formal owners—the sources of labor and capital—came to have progressively less influence on corporate strategy or operations.

Not surprisingly, professional staffs burgeoned. Between 1910 and 1940 America's employed population increased by 49 percent. But a substantial part of that increase was in the ranks of professional managers and their staffs. The number of individual proprietors in American business increased by only 17 percent, while the number of salaried employees increased by 127 percent. The change was most dramatic within individual companies. In 1923, for example, Swift & Company, the large meatpacking concern, employed 50,000 workers and 500 executives. In 1950 the firm employed 75,000 workers and 2,150 executives. Over 27 years the ratio between the two groups had changed from 1 executive for every 100 workers to 1 for every 35.[16]

The character of leadership also changed. The previous generation of business leaders had stressed strength of character—the Protestant virtues of prudence, punctuality, and perseverance. For them, success in business had been the hallmark of superior personal performance, tangible evidence of the energy and ambition required to mobilize America's resources. Increasingly, however, the business enterprise was too large, and its profitability and growth were dependent on too many factors over too many years, for the business manager to be judged solely by demonstrable results. Personal success came to be weighed by different criteria: the forcefulness of the manager's personality, as evidenced by his ability to shape the organization, to put his "stamp" upon it; his cleverness at analysis, in manipulating numbers, juggling organizational units, and diagnosing problems; his professional detachment, which enabled him to make difficult decisions—like laying off employees or firing subordinates—quickly and dispassionately. These qualities owed more to the right professional education than they did to strength of character. As the *Management Review* noted in 1928, all the attributes the successful manager required "can be developed by training."[17]

The professional manager in America came to exercise his craft above the industrial din, away from the dirt, noise, and irrationality of people and products. He dressed well. His secretary was alert and helpful. His office was as clean, quiet, and subdued as that of any other professional. He organized and controlled large enterprises in a cool, logical, and decisive manner. He surveyed data, calculated profits and losses, and imposed systems for monitoring production, applying a general body of rules to each special circumstance. His professional training was his cachet.

5.

Ironically, as personal character became less germane to the success of the professional manager, the character traits of the production workers took on new importance. Specialization by simplification meant that the production worker need not be particularly bright or skilled. But his reliability, dependability, and attentiveness became progressively more crucial to the overall operation. Carelessness at any small point in the production process could now jeopardize an entire run. Indeed, as the entire company grew to be integrated within a single flow of production, and each step along the way became more tightly synchronized with every other, the enterprise became highly dependent on the precision with which each task was undertaken. And because each task was inherently simple, precision became more a function of attitude than of skill.

Management professionals tackled the issue of shop-floor attitudes the same way they tackled every other issue: by installing a carefully crafted system based on science. Production workers' attitudes were to be managed through systematic recruitment and screening, well-designed programs to educate and motivate new workers, and subtle controls to weed out the poorest performers.

All this testing, motivating, and evaluating were rooted in the new sciences of "human relations" and industrial psychology, pioneered by Harvard psychologist Elton Mayo during the 1930's and 1940's. In his most famous experiment, Mayo had observed six production workers assembling telephones at Western Electric's Hawthorne, New York, plant. He noted that their attentiveness increased consistently, regardless of what experimental changes he introduced into the setting. He concluded that the employees performed better simply because they "felt themselves to be participating, freely and without aforethought"[18] in the experiment. Mayo did not draw the inference that production workers should actually be given more responsibility. The large increases in productive efficiency that high-volume enterprises were now enjoying flowed, after all, from innovations of precisely the opposite sort—specialization by simplification and predetermined rules devised by management professionals. Instead, Mayo (and other industrial psychologists of the era such as F. J. Roethlisberger and W. J. Dickson) urged that professional managers and their staffs be trained in "human–social" skills.[19]

"Human–social" skills soon became another aspect of professional management, another unit of professional training. Production workers needed to be made to feel as if they were involved in the enterprise and were respected as individuals. Actual participation and personal respect were, of course, impractical. But professional managers could at least manufacture the appearance of involvement and respect. Every dimension of management started from systematic planning, and it seemed obvious that managing the social context of the workplace should as well. The irony of standard operating procedures for making employees feel spontaneously involved and individually respected was lost on managers and employees alike because the large enterprise was so pervasively a product of social engineering.

The newly discovered importance of human-social skills in the workplace did, however, provide business reviews, books, and associations a wonderful chance for sounding a hortatory theme the echoes of which can be heard even today. Sounding more like a missionary gazette than a professional journal, the *Management Review* of 1937 urged managers to give their employees "what every human being asks for in life: respect for his personality, his human dignity, an environment that he comprehends, and an assurance that he is progressing." The *Review* revealed that workers wanted to be treated "not as servants, but as cooperators, which is indeed their true status." The popular author Dale Carnegie found his calling teaching managers how to win friends and influence people. Even the National Association of Manufacturers was urging American managers to give "full consideration to the human personality [of their employees] and the need for individual recognition, opportunity, and development."[20]

By the last years of the era human-social management was being exercised in more subtle ways. Specialists in organization development swarmed over the workplace, conducting encounter groups and "sensitivity-training" sessions. Industrial psychologists provided group counseling and programs of "job enrichment." Some companies instituted collaborative teams and "quality circles" within which workers could offer ideas for improving productivity—so long as they refrained from challenging the structure of authority in the enterprise. Management consultants espoused "Theory Y" or, better still, "Theory Z." But these factory-tested techniques for making workers feel better simply constructed a façade of workplace collaboration. The distinction between thinkers and doers remained intact. Ever more sophisticated strategies for improving the "quality of working life" shied away from actually altering the organization of production.

6.

Scientific management spawned professionalism in government in much the same way as in business—by separating thinkers from doers, those who planned from those who executed the plans. The civics-book ideal of popularly elected representatives issuing instructions to appointed administrators came to bear little relation to the realities of large-scale government organization. In practice, Woodrow Wilson's idea of separating legislative policy from administration resulted in two categories of administrator, roughly corresponding to the planners and executors in the large business enterprise: those at senior levels, who transformed vague legislative mandates into concrete policies, and those at lower bureaucratic levels, who were busily engaged in the day-to-day operations of government. Legislative mandates were necessarily cast in general, and often elliptic, terms. Implementation called for nonroutine judgments. Senior administrators thus came to need and use professional discretion in fashioning the rules that guided their agencies.

Just as predetermined rules within business enterprises governed production and the allocation of resources, predetermined rules within government agencies stipulated eligibility guidelines for benefits, criteria for the imposition of fines, how and when taxes and fees could be imposed, and the standards for delivering public services. The vast majority of these rules were routine. Some were internal to the agency, governing the hiring, training, and promotion of personnel or the technical aspects of providing specific services. A very few, at the highest and most general level, concerned broad questions of public policy. Like the rules of the business enterprise, all were grounded in data—reams of reports, inspections, filings.

Administrative rules served much the same functions as business rules. They promoted efficiency by allowing low-level personnel simply to assign the appropriate rule to each situation, rather than constantly to invent new rules. They limited lower-level discretion, making the agency's activities more predictable and permitting people both inside and outside the agency to plan with more certainty. Thus, as in the large business enterprise, predetermined rules within government agencies fostered both evenhandedness and efficiency. Because authority within the enterprise or the agency was explicitly constrained, people who were subject to authority felt it to be more fair. And because they could determine in advance what was expected of them, groups and individuals could better coordinate their activities.

Like their counterparts in business, high-level professional managers in government increasingly took responsibility for fashioning the rules by which their agencies functioned. In both sectors, the managers' license to set rules derived from their professional training and their access to special knowledge. The enactment of civil service reforms, the increasing number of government jobs reserved for specialists, the movement to install city managers, the proliferation of independent regulatory agencies and autonomous "authorities," and the federal government's increasing reliance on empirical analysis—all were manifestations of a trend to insulate the government's professional managers from the hurly-burly of politics as they exercised their professional expertise. Just as professional managers in business came to preempt the authority of inventor-promoters by virtue of their special knowledge, so professional managers in government came to preempt legislators and elected officials by virtue of their technical understanding of the public interest.

At the start of the era professional managers in government shared with their counterparts in business a background in engineering. Many of Frederick Taylor's disciples, all of them engineers, found their way into state and local government. Herbert Hoover, perhaps the most outstanding public administrator of the era, was trained as an engineer and had been president of the Federated American Engineering Societies before coming to government.

But professional management in government, unlike business, never quite achieved the status of a separate discipline. A few schools were established expressly to train government managers—the Training School for Public Service, established in 1911 by the New York Bureau of Municipal Research "to help make the public service a professional of equal standing with law and medicine"; Syracuse University's Maxwell School of Public Affairs (1924); and, later, graduate programs at Princeton, Harvard, and the University of Michigan.[21] But most professional managers in government were trained as lawyers or as experts in some specific field of policy, like agriculture or health. Often a lawyer and an expert would team up, one heading the government agency and the other providing professional advice; they would devise policy in tandem, together functioning as a hybrid between the professional manager and the political official—a hybrid that might be termed the policy professional. They usually stayed in government only temporarily, moving back into their specialties with changes in administrations.

City managers were the first true policy professionals. Their appearance on the national scene was inconspicuous. In September 1900 Galveston, Texas, was demolished by a tidal wave and hurricane. The city's bankers and businessmen, faced with the awesome job of rebuilding, planned a new administration that would be efficient and powerful enough to get the job done. They created a five-man committee, three of whose members were appointed by the governor and two elected by the city. Each member headed a separate municipal department charged with rebuilding a part of the city. Their efforts were coordinated by a professional engineer of their choosing. By 1904 Galveston had been rebuilt.

Business leaders in other cities took note. In 1910 Richard S. Childs, general manager of the Bon Ami Company and an ardent reformer in the tradition of Wilson and Taylor, advocated a modified version of the Galveston plan for all cities: An elected commission would make broad policy, but an official appointed by the commission, a professional manager, would execute it. Childs likened the plan to a large business corporation with a board of directors and a chief executive. City management, he felt, should resemble "the private business corporation, with its well-demonstrated capacity for efficiency." The idea caught on. Following a campaign mounted by its Chamber of Commerce, Dayton, Ohio adopted the city manager system in 1914. By 1920 more than 500 cities were using it.[22]

The concept of professional city management appealed to progressive reformers, businessmen, Protestant ministers, and patricians alike because it promised to undermine the ethnic urban machines. Politics could no longer be trusted to produce good government; the immigrants who crowded the cities seemed willing to sell their votes for spoils. Mindful that the new managers would be drawn from its ranks, America's middle class united behind "good government" movements that called for professional management, insulated from politics.

Civic reformers saw in city management an end to corruption and favoritism. Business leaders saw the possibility of cleaner, safer, more beautiful, and more orderly cities, which would promote economic growth. The two visions of justice and of efficiency were eminently compatible, since both sprang from scientific management's faith in experts and predetermined rules. Indeed, by 1920 the main themes of America's urban reform movement had shifted from moral renewal to far more complex proposals for neutral, professional administration.

It was but a small step from these ideas to those of the city planners of the 1940's and 1950's: to Robert Moses in New York and Edward Logue in Boston, to the vast public works—the bridges, highways, tunnels, and parks—which they created, and to the innumerable "authorities" from which they developed and executed their plans, undisturbed by politics. It was another small step to the "urban renewal" schemes of the 1950's and 1960's, through which vast tracts of single-family houses and smaller apartment buildings were demolished, and "housing projects" built in their places. And, finally, came New York's

Municipal Assistance Corporation, run by financiers, with total authority to close down or reallocate city services and rearrange city financing. These developments all issued from the same basic premise: Politics in American cities was simply too messy and too unpredictable to allow efficient, businesslike reform. Reform would come only if the task of running cities could be entrusted to a profession insulated from politics. In the views of many people of the era, professional management was the only answer.

Another manifestation of the shift from politics to professionalism in government was the advent of the independent regulatory commission. Headed not by an individual but by a group—whose members served set and staggered terms, represented both major political parties, and were protected against removal except for specific cause—the independent commission was a bulwark against political interference. The commission rode the same trend that brought the city manager. At the turn of the century electric power companies, water companies, and other municipal utilities feared that the city machines would seek to control them, if not purchase them outright. The utilities therefore joined in coalition with civic reformers, who feared that if the cities were to own the utilities, even more jobs would be filled through patronage. Progressive governors, like Charles Evans Hughes in New York and Robert M. LaFollette in Wisconsin, responded by establishing independent regulatory commissions to oversee the utilities and keep them safe from the clutches of the urban bosses. By the end of World War I twenty-six states had followed their lead.

The independent commission movement gathered momentum. New York State established a health commission to supervise quarantines, vaccinations, and other matters of public health. Wisconsin set up an industrial commission to develop standards for factory working conditions. Many states established insurance commissions, banking commissions, tax commissions, boards of regents, and independent boards to license doctors, lawyers, accountants, and the scores of other groups that were claiming professional status. At the federal level, Wilson established the Federal Trade Commission in 1914, to exercise expert judgment about how American industry should be organized. The Interstate Commerce Commission was strengthened, and its jurisdiction broadened. And over the next half century more than a dozen other independent commissions were created at the federal level, charged with overseeing industries as diverse as coal and airlines.

To the liberal reformers of the 1920's and 1930's the independent commission was an important vehicle for extending the benefits of scientific management to the economy as a whole. Journalists Herbert Croly and Walter Lippmann and jurists Louis Brandeis and James Landis argued that the regulatory tasks of government could be performed better if removed from politics and entrusted to the expertise of nonpartisan professionals. They assumed that regulatory commissioners, free from political control, would discover and serve an unambiguous and apolitical public interest.

This dispassionate search for regulatory truth was closely analogous to the professional business manager's dispassionate search for efficiency. It entailed complex fact-finding, careful weighing of expert opinion, and judicious decision making. And largely because their legitimacy depended on public confidence in the commissioners' neutral expertise, which alone often failed to yield clear answers, major regulatory decisions came to be clothed in judicial garb. Small wonder that the first chairman of the first federal regulatory agency was a judge and that as the era wore on, regulatory proceedings began to take on more and more of the adversarial character of courts.

Policy professionals also pervaded the executive branch. Franklin Delano Roosevelt placed expert academics in sub-Cabinet posts—Rexford Tugwell in Agriculture, Raymond Moley in the State Department, Felix Frankfurter's "hot dog" lawyers were seemingly everywhere. World War II brought the likes of chemist James Bryant Conant and mathematician Vanhevar Bush to the Office of Scientific Research and Development and inspired sophisticated management decision systems based on statistical inference, probability theory, and game theory. Indeed, in subsequent years the Department of Defense came to embody "the greatest single management system in history," in the words of Robert S. McNamara (then secretary of defense and a fierce proponent of rational program planning).

John F. Kennedy's Camelot further enhanced the professional expert's role in government. In his 1962 commencement address at Yale University, the young President sounded the theme of government management. "What is at stake," he declared, "is not some grand warfare of rival ideologies . . . but the practical management of a modern economy. What we need is not labels and clichés but more basic discussion of the sophisticated and technical questions involved in keeping a great economic machinery moving ahead. . . . [T]echnical answers, not political answers, must be provided."[23] In short, effective policy making—for the economy, for national defense, for the welfare of the nation—depended on policy professionals who were above politics.

The growth of professional policy staffs in the executive branch paralleled the growth of professional staffs in business. In 1923 fully 64 percent of federal government units exercised direct "line" responsibility for processing applications or delivering services, while only 28 percent of the units were "staff," providing expert advice to professional managers. By 1973, however, line units had fallen to 58 percent of the sample; staff units had increased to 38 percent. If units that existed prior to 1923 are eliminated from the sample, the results are even more dramatic. Of 246 new government units created in the half century between 1923 and 1973, fully 42 percent were staff.[24]

7.

During the management era the search for efficiency in business and for the "public interest" in government were closely similar quests. Both business enterprises and government agencies were engaged in high-volume, standardized production, entailing a large number of repetitive tasks with clearly defined goals, in which almost all contingencies could be identified and covered. Under these circumstances, the unit costs of making goods, delivering services, or processing applications were reduced substantially through specialization by simplification, predetermined rules, and detailed task information—the management science prescription for rendering work routine. The expertise of professional managers in business and government lay precisely in their ability to create such systems. If they were to use their expertise effectively, professional managers had to be separated from the distractions of routine production or routine politics.

Its occasional excesses notwithstanding, the profession of management was enormously successful in its own terms. It designed and maintained an organizational structure that supported American prosperity and enabled it to wage war effectively. The managerial ideal of professional impartiality meant that Americans (with the marked exception of black citizens) were treated evenhandedly by their public and private institutions. It was only later, when goals became less straightforward and external factors less predictable—when the key tasks of business and government became less routine and the preeminence of high-volume production began to decay—that the profession of management began to threaten the next advance in American prosperity.

V
THE
SUPERSTRUCTURES
OF MANAGEMENT

1.

The management era saw America's economy come to depend on the strength of large industrial enterprises producing long runs of standard goods. Capital-intensive industries, like steel, automobiles, chemicals, textiles, rubber, and electrical equipment, combined large-scale machine production with scientific management to achieve extraordinary efficiency. Specialized machines meshed with simplified jobs as the whole production process was guided, coordinated, and monitored by professional managers and their professional staffs. Productivity continued to increase. High volume and new techniques pushed down unit costs, and firms enjoyed economies of scale that would have been inconceivable in earlier eras. The benefits of these new efficiencies spread through the economy both in the form of higher salaries and dividends and as lower-priced products. We may take issue with how equitably these benefits were distributed. But there is little doubt that steadily, except for the Depression decade of the 1930's, almost all Americans saw their standards of living increase. America became the envy of the world.

These remarkable efficiencies depended on huge investments in plant, equipment, and professional talent. These were firms' fixed costs of production. When plants operated at full capacity, the fixed costs could be spread over a large volume, so that the average cost of producing each unit was low. But even when a firm operated at less than full capacity, it still had to maintain its machinery and buildings and retain a core of professional managers or leave the industry altogether. Thus, the large industrial firm faced a dilemma: The combination of machine production and scientific management was a boon when the firm was functioning near capacity, but because fixed costs were so high, idle capacity often meant disaster. Large capital-intensive firms, therefore, energetically sought ways to reduce this risk.

2.

The end of World War I first demonstrated the large-scale risks of large-scale production. The war had stimulated unprecedented new investments in capital-intensive process industries. The Du Pont Company had become an enormously efficient and profitable producer of munitions. Firms such as General Electric and Westinghouse had prospered by supplying the war effort with heavy equipment like electrical generators, motors, and switch gears. But much of this demand evaporated with the Armistice, and by 1920 America had entered a severe recession. Companies that had invested in new capacity were caught with huge fixed costs and dwindling sales.

Scientific management said nothing about over capacity. It focused exclusively on the individual firm's efforts to increase volume and reduce costs. America's growing mastery over production imposed an urgent new problem: managing consumption. How could professional managers ensure that demand for their products would be sufficient to clear their inventories?

One approach was to find new products and markets to compensate for the declining ones. If chosen correctly, the new products could employ facilities and professionals that were not fully occupied with the old products. For this strategy to work, the new products had to be sufficiently similar to the old in the resources they required, but different enough in use or appearance to appeal to a separate market.

Beginning in the mid-1920's, large American firms began to search out

The Superstructures of Management

such new product opportunities. Du Pont enlarged its product line—previously based on explosives—to include paints, dyes, film, fibers, and synthetic chemicals. General Electric expanded into various household appliances as well as radio and X-ray equipment. General Motors offered a wide range of styles of automobile. Under the leadership of Alfred Sloan, Jr. (who described himself as being in the business of making money, not cars), GM also began to manufacture diesel locomotives, tractors, and airplanes. The Aluminum Company of America moved into kitchenware and household fittings. U.S. Rubber expanded into rubber chemistry.

The strategy of grafting on new product lines had built-in limits. If extended too far, the firm would need to add so much additional plant, equipment, and professional talent that any savings gained by using existing assets more efficiently would be vitiated. And diversification carried the risk of making the firm unwieldy. Scientific management was premised on a single-line firm, with a single core of production workers each engaged in a simple operation, and on a professional staff responsible for personnel, engineering, procurement, marketing, finance, sales, and research. As the single-line firm grew, scientific management assumed that the productive core would simply expand, while the professional staff would divide into departments, each with its own set of routines to be handled by clerical employees. The addition of another product line complicated this picture enormously. How were resources to be allocated among products? How could the goal of unified control be met? How were separate operations to be monitored, controlled, and coordinated?

The organizational problems posed by multiple product lines were solved by creating separate divisions for each product. Each division would have its own productive core and its own specialized staffs for personnel, finance, marketing, and so on. Professional managers in central headquarters would mobilize and monitor the firm as a whole, shifting resources among divisions according to market demand for each product and the cost of producing it, setting overall firm strategy to guide professional staffs in each division, and directly attending to a few firm-wide functions like legal services and product research.

This divisional structure seemed ideal. It enabled the firm to achieve large economies of scale both in each product line and in the performance of firm-wide functions. Even more important, a divisional structure gave the firm substantial flexibility to shift resources as demand dictated, thereby employing its facilities to the fullest. Alfred P. Sloan, Jr., reorganized General Motors into divisions in the 1920's. Allied Chemical, Du Pont, Union Carbide, and General Electric soon followed. U.S. Steel adopted the form in the 1930's, along with U.S. Rubber and Armour, Inc. By World War II the multidivision structure had become the dominant form of American business enterprise, including nearly all of America's leading firms in chemicals, rubber, electric machinery, and transportation vehicles. By 1969 fully 76 percent of the nation's 500 largest nonfinancial firms were multidivisional.[1]

Yet diversification imposed the problem of allocating resources among product lines without clear market signals on relative product costs and profitability. Because many of its internal operations were now insulated from market forces, and its overhead costs were spread over several separate product lines, the diversified firm did not automatically know where its profits lay. Thus, to discover where resources could most profitably be applied, it had to rely on complex systems of accounting and techniques for predicting the results of shifting resources from one product line to another. Strategic planning of this sort implied a radical extension of traditional scientific management. Professional managers at headquarters were now less concerned with the efficiency of a particular production line than with how profitably the firm's pool of resources could be allocated among production lines.

The problem of allocating corporate resources did not increase in proportion to the number of divisions. The central apparatus for monitoring divisional performance and shifting resources among divisions could manage many divisions almost as easily as a few, and new ones could be added readily. Mindful of the advantages of diversification, professional managers in corporate headquarters set about accumulating new product lines. But this planning apparatus further increased the bureaucratic distance between senior managers who allocated resources and the divisional managers and workers who dealt with the routine tasks of actual production.[2]

3.

The growing importance of strategic planning for diversified firms meant that for the first time in the American economy a central core of professional managers had authority to shift resources among product lines and to determine the direction of new investment according to analytical criteria. Detailed economic planning had come unannounced to American industry.

This planning apparatus, developed to guide the firm's internal operations, could also be directed outward—toward other companies in the same industry. The tools used to plan and coordinate various lines of production within a single firm could in principle be extended to encompass an entire industry. Instead of each firm's responding in isolation to economic upturns or downturns by expanding or contracting its capacity —resulting in cycles of overcapacity or undercapacity—industry-wide coordination could enable each to accommodate its investment and production plans to the plans of every other firm.

In practice, of course, industry-wide coordination often was complicated by the presence of too many firms in the industry, disparate accounting practices, dissimilarities among products, antitrust rules against agreements to restrain competition, and the understandable reluctance of some firms within the industry—particularly those with the brightest prospects —to cooperate in any effort that might constrain their future profits. But as America's capital-intensive industries grew and consolidated their operations during the 1920's, and as the capacities of the government also grew in response to progressive reforms, war mobilizations, and economic crises, these complications were gradually overcome. Industry-wide coordination became the rule.

Strategic planners in major firms and within the government strove to "rationalize" each industry. The task was made easier by the fact that they all shared a professional culture and a set of analytic approaches. They were already applying principles of scientific management to their firms and government agencies; it was relatively easy to devise similar rules and standards to govern the industry as a whole. Antitrust laws continued to prohibit price-fixing, of course, but not strategic coordination of investment and production among firms, particularly if undertaken by government or at least with the government's blessing.

Industry-wide management took many forms. Trade associations were often actively involved. Federal regulatory agencies played an important role in coordinating certain industries, like commercial aviation, shipbuilding, communications equipment, transportation equipment, coal, and oil. A few regulatory agencies, like the Federal Trade Commission, functioned as broad forums in which business and government professionals together could set rules. Woodrow Wilson remarked in 1916 that the FTC "has transformed the Government of the United States from being an antagonist of business into being a friend of business."[3]

Meanwhile, war-related agencies, like the boards which oversaw production during the world wars, and, later, the Department of Defense and the National Aeronautics and Space Administration were central to the coordination of industries like steel, automobiles, rubber, chemicals, electrical equipment, electronics, and aircraft. Other federal agencies powerfully influenced agriculture, housing, and health, particularly after World War II.

The actual form of business-government planning varied by industry. Typically, three or four dominant firms in the industry set the agenda, determining what aspects of production were to be coordinated, and how. By 1947 almost one-quarter of the earnings of American manufacturing originated in industries with four or fewer dominant firms, each of them holding a highly stable market share; by 1963 the percentage had increased to one-third.[4] The government facilitated these agreements indirectly (by standardizing production in the industry), gave them formal legitimacy (by expressly delegating coordinating authority to industry leaders), or directly enforced the agreements (through, for example, regulatory agency rulings). Occasionally it did all three. In some industries, like automobiles and steel, the government authorized and encouraged coordination for many years and then abdicated in favor of a tight oligopoly that could manage well on its own.

The federal government had become both an agent and a silent partner of industry-wide corporate planning. But only twice did it try to introduce an explicit public agenda for industrial management—during the "Second New Deal" of the late 1930's and in response to the burst of public concern about health, safety, and the environment that came in the late 1960's. The business community greeted both forays with furious indignation, denouncing governmental subversion of the free market.

Whatever form it took, industry-wide coordination usually affected individual firms only indirectly. Rationalization schemes and coordinating mechanisms were devised and implemented by corporate planning staffs. The professional managers maintained complete control. Nor did government agencies, trade associations, or other large firms threaten that autonomy. The American system of industrial coordination was thus only loosely analogous to the management of a single multidivisional firm. Nor, usually, did it resemble a well-disciplined cartel. It was, rather, a loose coupling of major firms within an industry, involving all manner of signals, *ad hoc* compromises, and shifting patterns of leadership. It was a pragmatic management superstructure within which firms sought to coordinate their investment and production with each other.

Coordination entailed bargaining among firms. It also required expert knowledge of the needs of the industry and pending changes in supply and demand. Bargaining implied accommodation and consensus; expertise suggested technical fact-finding. In practice, the two processes were often indistinguishable. Major firms in an industry were "represented" in trade associations, government advisory boards, and rule-making agencies, but the representation often took the form of providing specific data or "perspectives" rather than explicit bargaining. The sharing of information and points of view was usually adequate to ensure coordination.

A final characteristic of these superstructures of management was that they were confined to individual industries. They did not span industries. Even in diversified firms, most lines of business were closely allied to a major industry, through which investment and production decisions were coordinated with other firms. Trade associations, regulatory agencies, and government boards and departments tended to be organized by industry. The expertise of most strategic planners in business and government was focused on a specific industry. There was no organization and little professional expertise which pertained to whole sectors of the economy and to relationships among industries.

In heavy industries, like automobiles, rubber, steel, chemicals, and electric equipment, industry-wide coordination reduced the risks of large-scale production. Coordination allowed greater productive capacity and lower unit costs. But it also reduced competitive pressure in the industry, particularly in fundamental technical innovation. Individual firms did not need to worry that their competitors might suddenly introduce a new innovation that would render current technologies obsolete since they already knew what their rivals were planning. Firms, therefore, felt less compelled to invest in the development of radically new products or processes. As a result, while the unit costs of production continued to decline, there were few major breakthroughs, and industries were often slow to apply new technologies.

The automobile and steel industries illustrate these developments. At the turn of the century American auto manufacturers operated under considerable uncertainty about the direction of technical change in the infant industry. Fifty-seven firms were producing about 4,000 cars a year, three-quarters of which were fueled by steam or electricity. (Interestingly, most of the experimentation with gasoline-fueled engines took place in the less developed Midwest; the better established northeastern manufacturers were wedded to the more conservative technologies.) Several British and French firms were already manufacturing faster and more efficient cars than the U.S. varieties. Of the 181 separate American companies that made automobiles between 1903 and 1926, 28 percent remained in business three years or less; 49 percent, six years or less. But when Ford successfully introduced interchangeable parts and continuous assembly lines, the terms of competition in the industry were fundamentally changed. By 1921 Ford had 60 percent of the world automobile market, and every other car on the road was a Model T.

During the 1930's Chrysler boosted its market share from 10 percent to 30 percent, while Ford's share declined to 20 percent. By the end of the 1930's the American auto industry had become relatively stable. Six major automakers informally coordinated their production and investment decisions. Most had become static, production-oriented manufacturers. By the 1950's the market share of the three major manufacturers was constant. General Motors had emerged as the industry leader, informally coordinating its annual model changes with Ford and Chrysler. With the federal government pouring money into highway construction and home mortgages, America's suburbs began to sprawl, and the demand for automobiles skyrocketed. During the 1950's automobile registrations increased 4.7 percent annually—nearly three times the birthrate. The industry experienced enormous economies of scale, but few innovations. Most changes occurred in styling; engines and transmissions remained much the same from year to year. Americans joked about how little the "new" models differed from the old. Of course, had the new models been truly new, they would have been significantly more expensive, since the auto manufacturers could not have realized the substantial cost reductions of high-volume production.[5]

The American steel industry followed a similar course. After a period of intense competition and innovation before World War I U.S. Steel emerged as the industry leader, with five other firms sharing the rest of the market. The first chairman of U.S. Steel, Judge Elbert H. Gary, became de facto manager of the industry. He even hosted dinners for steel company executives to meet for the purpose of coordinating their firms' investment and production. Gary also worked closely with the federal government during and after the war. When the government brought an antitrust action against U.S. Steel, Gary skillfully transformed the issue from whether the company had inordinate market power to whether it was exercising that power responsibly. The answer to the latter question came to depend, of course, on how well Gary maintained his relations with the government.

Gary's understanding with the federal government inaugurated fifty years of stability for the steel industry. Franklin Delano Roosevelt's National Recovery Administration offered a convenient forum for straightforward price-fixing by industry leaders. During World War II the government financed the construction of several steel plants, which were sold at a fraction of cost to the largest steel companies immediately after the war. This cooperative relationship was perturbed only by President Harry Truman's attempt to commandeer the strike-idled steel mills in 1952 and by the face-off over steel prices between U.S. Steel chairman Roger Blough and President Kennedy ten years later.[6]

This relative stability enabled steel manufacturers to develop very large facilities for producing basic carbon steel. But the industry was slow to innovate. By the late 1950's and early 1960's American steelmakers were balking at the chance to shift from open-hearth furnaces, in which they had heavily invested after the war, to newer technologies: basic oxygen furnaces and continuous casting. No single firm needed to innovate because each knew that its competitors would not.[7]

Yet these examples do not prove the case that industrial coordination retarded the American economy. Quite the contrary. Coordination allowed vast economies of scale, and the essence of efficient standardized production in the management era was scale rather than innovation. The agenda for the management era was embodying earlier technical advances into a working system of machine production and scientific management. Over the fifty-year course of the era, America reaped the full benefits of its earlier innovations by systematizing them. The collection of industry-wide management superstructures sacrificed innovation in favor of high-volume production. For most of the era this was a wise trade. Only toward the end of the period did organizations dedicated to static efficiency begin to threaten the nation's economic vitality.

The new capital-intensive industries were not the only ones that sought industry-wide management, of course. The rise of large industrial enterprises was accompanied by the emergence of politically powerful groups that felt themselves threatened by industrial change—in particular, farmers, shippers, railroads, and small manufacturers. These industrial losers sought public mechanisms—like the Federal Reserve Board, the Federal Trade Commission, and the railroad and farm programs of the 1920's and 1930's—to halt, or at least cushion, their relative decline.

The labor movement had its own stake in industry management. With labor increasingly organized along industry lines, a similar structure on the management side facilitated collective bargaining. Industry-wide coordination of investment and production also made firms more generous with wage increases because—if all companies granted them—wage concessions would not harm any one firm's competitive position and could safely be passed on to purchasers in the form of higher prices. Small wonder that by the end of the era workers in the most tightly managed industries, like automobiles, steel, rubber, and chemicals, enjoyed the highest wages of all industrial workers—at least twice the hourly rate of workers in loosely coordinated industries like apparel and footwear.[8]

The federal government itself had a stake. In no meaningful sense was the government "captured" by industry, for there was no clear distinction between what industry sought from government and what government sought from industry. Both were concerned with promoting efficient high-volume production.

Indeed, the federal government was instrumental in building the super-structures of management. In 1912, for example, Charles Nagel, then secretary of commerce and labor under President William Howard Taft, worked with local chambers of commerce to design a national business organization. Nagel eventually invited managers from 2,000 firms to

Washington, D.C., for a conference to draft a charter for the Chamber of Commerce of the United States.[9] From such beginnings the federal role in industrial coordination grew more extensive. After World War I the government was continuously active in organizing industry trade associations and convening various advisory boards and councils consisting of industry representatives.

Such superstructures of industry-wide management enabled the federal government to deal efficiently with business. Professional managers at the heads of the trade associations and government advisory boards could relay government proposals and rules to their members and communicate back to the government information and opinions to guide new initiatives. Sometimes the government simply delegated the task of rule-making to the association or board, informing it of the goal to be achieved—such as rationing certain raw materials for war production—and then leaving it up to the industry to decide how best to pursue it. Industry-wide management enhanced the power both of the federal government and of the large enterprises that dominated each industry association. Together they "rationalized" the economy for large-scale industry and for public missions—like waging war—that depended on efficient, high-volume production.

4.

World War I shaped the superstructures of industrial management. In the war America found a singleness of public purpose perfectly compatible with large-scale industrial efficiency. Ideas and institutions which were born then lived on, in various guises, through World War II and on into the cold war. The war established the legitimacy of the federal government's role in public education, health, research, welfare, and labor reform. It also gave birth to patterns and mechanisms of business-government cooperation that lasted into the peace—ready to be activated whenever business needed government assistance or whenever government needed business support. Perhaps most fundamentally, the experience of war and of the federal government's role in managing the nation for war legitimized in many people's eyes the role of the government (and, in particular, of the President) as general manager of the economy, responsible for the overall health of American business.

The institutional legacy was powerful. Key economic functions of the federal government—which came to be taken for granted by the end of the management era—had their beginnings in World War I. The War Finance Corporation, which underwrote bank loans to war industries, for example, was the precursor to decades of active government involvement in providing low interest loans to specific industries and firms. It was the direct precedent for Hoover's Reconstruction Finance Corporation, designed to bail out banks and railroads, and for the various schemes of government-backed loans and loan guarantees which marked the New Deal. We shall soon examine its more recent incarnations.

Public institutions concerned with education, public health, and research were also created during World War I. In 1917 Stanford psychologist Lewis Terman developed the Army Alpha exam to screen soldiers for officers' training. It was the first widely used aptitude test, and it set a precedent for decades of ever more sophisticated aptitude testing by schools and businesses. The service academies were the first form of federally funded education. War-related research in navigation and engineering involved the government in sponsoring basic research. Marine hospitals, becoming Veterans Administration hospitals after the war, established the government's role in public health and medical research. The U.S. Housing Corporation condemned land and built housing for defense personnel during the war; this inaugurated a trend toward federal responsibility for America's housing stock.

The federal government's role in labor relations was largely a product of the war. The President's Mediation Commission, headed by the secretary of labor, encouraged collective bargaining. The National War Labor Board, established to promote good labor relations during the mobilization, instituted workplace grievance procedures involving elected worker representatives. The board also actively supported the development of labor unions, seeing in them an orderly channel for resolving industrial disputes. Backed by threats of government seizure and warnings of "work or fight," the board moved boldly to put an end to conflict. When the Smith & Wesson plant at Springfield, Massachusetts, rejected a labor board ruling, the plant was commandeered. When machinists at Bridgeport, Connecticut, defied the board, they were drafted. The board's grievance mechanisms became models for the national structure of labor-management relations established almost two decades later. And when a railroad strike threatened the war effort, Congress passed legislation setting an eight-hour day for railroad workers, forming a precedent for labor reform in other industries.

Enduring patterns for business–government relations were established. The War Industries Board, under the able direction of financier Bernard Baruch, functioned as what one participant called a "town meeting of American industry." Its Commodity Division, staffed largely with professional managers on temporary leave from business, represented the "public" side of the operation; the War Service Committee, whose members were chosen by industry trade associations, represented the large industrial enterprises. The Commodity Division determined overall allocations of commodities to particular industries, while the War Service Committee divided them among firms. The result was an efficient delegation of authority to industrial managers, who invariably favored the largest and best-established enterprises. The Food Administration rationed agricultural commodities in much the same way; like the War Industries Board, it delegated primary responsibility to major agricultural producers. And the Fuel Administration allocated coal and petroleum according to the dictates of major industry groups.[10]

This practice of delegating significant public responsibilities to industry-wide management superstructures was retained in the interwar years as Herbert Hoover's elaborate programs to "rationalize" American industry through trade associations, and as Roosevelt's National Recovery Administration. And almost precisely the same model of organization was instituted in World War II, but on a larger scale: Then 7,000 industrial committees were attached to the War Production Board, and 4,000 to the Office of Price Administration.[11]

Finally, World War I established government's responsibility for gathering information on the overall health of the economy. During the war the government set up four major statistical agencies to gather industrial data: the Central Bureau of Planning and Statistics, the Planning and Statistics Division of the Shipping Board, the Planning and Statistics Division of the War Industries Board, and the Research and Tabulation of Statistics Bureau of the War Trade Board. These agencies—the forerunners of more elaborate data-gathering agencies within the Department of Commerce and the Federal Trade Commission—provided government and industry with the information they needed to coordinate invest-ment and production. (Not insignificantly, all four groups were chaired by Edwin F. Gay, then dean of the Harvard Business School.)

Other war programs established the federal role in economic planning. The Fixed Nitrogen Research Laboratory, created to ensure adequate supplies of nitrates for war munitions, put the government in the business of guaranteeing the availability of strategic materials. Government-sup-ported energy projects, such as the dam at Muscle Shoals (a point of origin for the Tennessee Valley Authority twenty years later), became prece-dents for the massive public works programs of the New Deal. And the war experience convinced many people of the need for a central mecha-nism for coordinating government expenditures, leading ultimately to the adoption in 1921 of an executive budget system for the federal govern-ment, directed by a new Bureau of the Budget.

The government institutions, patterns of organization, and economic planning functions that emerged from World War I were, of course, embryonic. The federal government was still small relative to the indus-trial enterprises that were coming to dominate the economy. In 1923 there were only about 70,000 federal employees in Washington. The govern-ment did not yet provide a comprehensive superstructure of management. But in legitimizing the government's responsibilities for underwriting loans to industry; running large training programs, hospitals, and housing programs; establishing mechanisms to mediate labor disputes and regulat-ing hours and working conditions in the factory; setting allocation targets and delegating authority to industry to implement them; and gathering economic data, anticipating the nation's need for strategic materials, planning massive public works projects, and centralizing the govern-ment's budget-making authority, World War I set the stage for joint business and government institutions for each major industry that would mirror the structure of strategic planning evolving within individual firms.

5.

Superstructures of industrial management continued growing in the interwar years. As America's key capital-intensive industries came to be dominated by a few major firms, strategic planning became both more important and considerably easier to arrange. The federal government, its role established during the war, took an active part in industrial management.

For strategic coordination to work, each major company had to be aware of other firms' investment and production plans. In 1912 a lawyer named Arthur Jerome Eddy published *The New Competition,* an influential book which proposed a network of statistical exchange among companies, administered by open price associations.[12] (The book's frontispiece bore the telling inscription "Competition is War, and War is Hell.") Eddy's ideas reached receptive ears. By 1921 at least 150 open price associations were in operation.

Herbert Hoover sought to expand this system. Appointed secretary of commerce in the midst of the postwar depression, Hoover concurred in business managers' diagnosis of industrial overcapacity as a technical problem that would yield to the industry-wide application of the principles of scientific management. Earlier, as president of the Federated American Engineering Societies, he already had initiated a study of waste in industry that had, in his words, sought "to visualize the nation as a single industrial organism and to examine its efficiency toward its only real object—maximum production." The study found inadequate management to be the source of most of the problems and prescribed industry-wide coordination.[13]

The secretary of commerce saw in Eddy's ideas a way to stabilize production by eliminating wasteful competition. Trade associations, collecting and disseminating industrial data, could further increase industrial efficiency by elaborating on the system of voluntary cooperation and collective planning that had guided the wartime economy. The Commerce Department under Hoover's direction soon became a whirlwind of activity—helping trade associations become organized, promoting statistical exchanges and codes of business practice, and protecting these activities from antitrust scrutiny by having the department itself formalize the agreements and run the exchange machinery.[14]

Hoover did not stop there. Industrial coordination could be further improved if all firms used similar product specifications and cost accounting systems. To this end, he created the Division of Simplified Practice within the department's Bureau of Standards. Between 1921 and 1928 the division worked with more than 900 trade associations and 7,000 firms to standardize and simplify specifications for a huge number of products, including cans, bottles, tires, electrical fixtures, nuts, bolts, pipes, and toilet paper. Hoover also convened industry conferences to standardize accounting and data collections systems and brought together firms in the housing and construction industries to standardize construction materials. He transformed the Census Bureau into a repository of business information about production, prices, and inventories, all categorized by industry.

The campaign to "rationalize" American business for high-volume production gave special attention to the key energy, transportation, and communication industries. Hoover established within the Commerce Department a Federal Power Bureau to manage hydroelectric development; regional power committees; regional shipping boards to plan transportation facilities and guard against shortages of railroad cars; a Radio Division to allocate wavelengths for broadcasting; an Aeronautics Branch to develop aviation aids and controls; and an elaborate program to stabilize coal production. Not surprisingly the details of these plans were worked out by professional managers and engineers from the industries involved.

Finally, Hoover set out to promote American exports. He established a Bureau of Foreign and Domestic Commerce, which advised firms on obtaining foreign loans and investments, analyzed overseas markets, searched for foreign sources of raw materials, and maintained an extensive worldwide network of intelligence about foreign competitors. In all these respects Hoover anticipated the kind of government role in industrial development that Japan's Ministry of International Trade and Industry (MITI) would undertake forty years later.

The Department of Commerce was not the only force pushing the government into industrial management, of course. The distinction between large industrial enterprises and the federal government was becoming blurred on many fronts, with industries taking on more and more governmentlike responsibilities. The Federal Reserve System, which had been established in 1914 to control bank reserves and improve the quality of bank management, was by the 1920's becoming an economic planning agency. The evolving Federal Reserve was strongly influenced by the New York banking community. In 1923 Benjamin Strong, the governor of the New York Federal Reserve Bank and a leading banker, established an Open Market Investment Committee, which bought and sold government securities to balance American industry's needs for adequate credit and economic stability. In 1935 the committee was absorbed by the newly created Federal Reserve Board. The Securities and Exchange Commission, established in 1934, similarly delegated substantial responsibility for developing and enforcing rules to the stock exchanges and to associations of professional accountants. The Civil Aeronautics Board, formed in 1938 to promote as well as to regulate civil aviation, relied almost entirely on industry experts to shape its decisions. And by 1935 oil transported between states could be pumped only in accordance with quotas established by a chain of authority running from the Interior Department's Bureau of Mines to the Texas Railroad Commission, with the entire chain staffed by professionals from the oil industry.

The movement toward industrial management was not confined to one side of the ideological spectrum. Franklin Roosevelt's election marked a shift in public policy and signaled a far more active government role in the economy. But it did not signal a substantial change in the pattern of business-government organization; the superstructures remained intact. Indeed, New Deal economists like Rexford Tugwell, George Soule, and Stuart Chase envisioned a system of national planning—modeled after the ideas of Frederick Taylor and embellished by economist Thorstein Veblen —in which the principles of scientific management would largely supplant the price system. Their only criticisms of the superstructures already in place were that their goals were too narrow and that they were too exclusively controlled by professional managers in industry. The New Deal planners wanted a system of industrial coordination that would manage profits along with investment and production and would give more authority to professional managers in government and labor.

Roosevelt's National Recovery Administration represented a crude compromise between the superstructures already in place and the vision of the new national planners.[15] The NRA had no more specific mandate than somehow to get the economy moving again by coordinating American industry. Theoretically the federal government was in charge, and labor was duly represented. In fact, the NRA's deputy administrators were drawn from industry, and its code-writing committees were dominated by the largest firms in each industry.

By the summer of 1933 codes had been drafted to guide America's major industries: electrical manufacturing, shipbuilding, steel, petroleum, lumber, automobiles, and bituminous coal. The codes substantially extended the principles of Hoover's old industry associations. They set minimum prices, prohibited sales below cost, established uniform cost accounting formulas, formalized statistical exchanges, limited machine or plant hours, constrained additions to capacity, and set up elaborate administrative and enforcement machinery.

In short, the NRA created cartels. Because these rigid and formal cartels made highly visible the pattern of coordination that had come to dominate many industries, they aroused public concern over price-fixing. They also left little room for compromise and accommodation among firms within an industry. Thus the NRA was doomed even before the Supreme Court declared it unconstitutional. While short-lived, the NRA nonetheless left a legacy of new industrial superstructures incorporating the interests of previously excluded economic groups: new trade associations of smaller manufacturers; state "fair trade" laws which protected small retailers from price discounting by larger ones; "trade practice" conferences for smaller industries, hosted by the Federal Trade Commission (which inherited most of the NRA staff); and laws establishing workers' rights to bargain collectively.

The concept of industrial management continued to take on institutional form throughout the New Deal, transcending the disputes that still raged over the relative power of business, labor, and government within the superstructures of management. There was a strong consensus that America's economic system, based as it was on long runs of standardized products, required industry-wide schemes to rationalize investment and production. But there was no consensus about how the superstructures were to be organized. It would take another world war and the consequent transformation of the government into the economy's main customer to temporarily settle the issue.

6.

World War II plunged the federal government far more deeply into industrial management than it had ever been before. At the height of the war 40 percent of everything manufactured or grown in the nation went to the war effort. Planning on the scale the war required had never been attempted. But all the institutional precedents were there—the superstructures of industrial management, in the form of trade associations, industry commissions, boards, regulatory agencies, and labor unions.

They needed only modification and enlargement to meet the industrial challenge of war mobilization.

Unlike the First World War, however, the Second failed to end with the last shots. Instead, it became a permanent mobilization, punctuated by Korea and Vietnam. Many of the superstructures of industrial management were incorporated into a permanent defense production system. Others migrated to the departments of Commerce and Interior. Anticipating the war's end the Commerce Department's Business Advisory Council, for example, estimated postwar production levels industry by industry, devised programs to cushion companies and workers against the decline in the defense market, and encouraged large firms to integrate their plans with suppliers and customers.

Soon after the Korean War the Commerce Department established a Business and Defense Services Administration. Its role, in the words of Sinclair Weeks, secretary of commerce under Dwight D. Eisenhower, was "to see to it that, while private business, of course, cannot dictate government policy and plans, it be placed in a position where it can effectively approve or disapprove of the implementation of such policy and plans from the standpoint of their practical workability in everyday industrial operation."[16] In practice, the agency allocated materials required in military and atomic energy programs and advised the President on accelerated tax depreciation schemes, loan assistance, stockpiling, and other forms of federal support for industry.

By organizing the Business and Defense Services Administration along industrial lines, the Commerce Department sought to give each industry "its own special division for receiving government information and service." Each division was, naturally enough, dominated by the industry's major firms. The staff of the Aluminum and Magnesium Division, for example, came from the three largest integrated producers—Alcoa, Kaiser, and Reynolds. The Forest Products Division was staffed by the vice-president of the Weyerhaeuser Company.[17]

Other government departments had their own business committees. The Department of the Interior, for example, inherited the Petroleum Industry War Council, which had served as part of the War Production Board. During peacetime its membership—including every major American oil company—supervised voluntary industry agreements on the allocation of oil transportation facilities and equipment. Every other raw materials industry had a similar committee within the Interior Department. A 1956 survey found more than 5,000 business advisory committees spread throughout the federal government, many of them carrying out delegated responsibilities for managing their industries.[18]

The Pentagon's role in industrial management was perhaps the most important of all. Unlike the other superstructures of management—which delegated to industries the authority to coordinate production—the Pentagon spawned superstructures that contracted directly with the government. It was American industry's largest single purchaser. In 1952, 11.6 percent of the nation's gross national product was purchased for defense. In the next two decades the percentage never fell below 6 percent.

The government provided a substantial market for several industries. In 1977, for example, government purchases accounted for 56 percent of all U.S. aircraft shipments, 56 percent of the sales of radio and communications equipment, 12 percent of engineering and scientific instruments, and 12 percent of transmitting electron tubes.[19] By the end of the era the Pentagon was funding approximately 30 percent of all U.S. research and development and more than 80 percent of all government-financed research. For basic research with few immediate commercial applications, federal funding exceeded two-thirds of the total. In some industries, government research support reached particularly high levels. In 1977, for example, the government funded 70 percent of research and development in the aircraft industry and 48 percent in the communications equipment industry.[20]

Significantly, government purchases not only underpinned old industries but also shaped the development of new ones. Large-scale defense and aerospace contracts provided emerging industries in the United States with a ready market that let them quickly expand production and thus gain scale economies and valuable experience. The Pentagon's willingness to pay a high premium for quality and reliability, moreover, helped emerging industries bear the cost of refining and "debugging" their products. Largely as a result of government contracts, for example, the U.S. semiconductor industry was able to reduce its unit costs quickly during the 1960's and emerge as a commercial leader in the world market. Because the arms race and the moon race both demanded smaller, faster, and more reliable memory units, the Defense Department and the National Aeronautics and Space Administration became the largest purchasers of semiconductors, together accounting for almost one-third of the market by 1967. While in 1962 an integrated circuit cost $50, by 1968 its cost had dropped to $2.33, making it commercially attractive for use in many consumer products. Over the same period the semiconductor market grew from $4 million to $31 million.[21]

Many other emerging industries followed the same pattern. In 1950 government purchases accounted for 92 percent of aerospace sales. Advanced aircraft originally developed for the military were adapted to civilian uses, the Boeing B–47 and B–52 bombers evolving into the Boeing 707; the Douglas A–3D, A–4D, and B–66 military aircraft becoming the DC–8. The nascent computer industry also relied on federal support. In 1954 the government was the only major purchaser of computers; by 1962 the government market still represented almost one-half of total computer sales. Defense purchases and research support spurred other industries as well: hard plastics, synthetic rubber, lasers, fiber optics, nuclear power, radio and television communications equipment, and optical and scientific instruments.

In many industries, military contracts reinforced the dominance of the largest producers. Although defense contracts often required that firms cooperate on research projects or subcontract the work to smaller manufacturers, the Pentagon tended to rely on the largest firms by awarding them contracts without competitive bidding. Even when firms had to submit bids, they were often rendered meaningless by routine cost overruns. And major defense contractors developed the specifications on which future contracts were to be based, thus guaranteeing their continued favored status.[22]

In his farewell address President Eisenhower warned the nation of a growing military-industrial complex which was gaining enormous power. Yet the superstructures of industrial management spawned by the Pentagon's permanent war mobilization were in fact little more than larger versions of the superstructures that had already dominated the American economy for decades. There was nothing inherently mischievous about these superstructures. On the contrary, they were necessary for efficient high-volume production. The Pentagon's purchases and research subsidies enabled new industries, like electronics and jet aircraft, to gain high-volume scale quickly. Innovation may have been slowed in some instances, but so long as America's economic growth was based not on industrial change but on ever greater production of standardized goods, these superstructures were central to the nation's economic health.

7.

In sum, the profession of management fitted hand in glove with the superstructure of management. The profession and the organizational network that gave it force perfected the American system of high-volume production. Long runs of standardized products brought America to world leadership in the manufacture of automobiles, steel, home appliances, transportation equipment, farm machinery, rubber, and chemicals. From its roots in these industries, high-volume production extended into the rest of the economy.

America's prosperity was a product of the alliance between high-volume machinery and large-scale organization, which was forged by scientific management. Specialization by simplification, predetermined rules, and feedback information separated the professional managers who undertook industrial planning from actual production. Employees and their organizations embraced the same principles and sought to protect their economic status through clearly defined jobs and explicit work rules.

To let firms cover the high fixed costs of specialized machinery and professional staffs, the large-scale enterprise required mechanisms for coordinating its investment and production with other firms in the industry. Trade associations, public boards and regulatory agencies, and other planning authorities provided each major industry with a management superstructure that let data be pooled, products be standardized, and firm strategies be made compatible. Professional managers in government, insulated from politics and dedicated to neutral efficiency, facilitated this strategic coordination. Organized labor concurred in this agenda since strategic coordination smoothed industry-wide bargaining and encouraged larger wage concessions.

The style of business organization that evolved over America's management era was ideally suited to high-volume production. That evolution followed a clear path: The goal of industrial efficiency, valued both for the wealth it generated and for its incalculable importance in wartime, led to the development of supportive superstructures of industrial management. The new wealth created by this organization of high-volume production fueled its further success as rising real wages and the development of a comfortable, consumption-oriented middle class spawned a mass market for standardized goods. The federal government, its abilities built and tested in war mobilization, took an ever larger role in coordinating and developing the huge domestic market. So successful was this organizational structure that, as we shall see, it was retained long after the economic conditions that had shaped its evolution had fundamentally changed.

VI
THE NOVELTY
OF MANAGEMENT

1.

The profession of management and its industrial superstructures presided over America's rise to a prosperity and national power unparalleled in history. The economic logic of this American style of production was so compelling, and its success so spectacular, that one might assume that high-volume, standardized production is simply "modern" production—that essentially the same system of specialized, simplified industrial work, with a separate group of professional managers controlling firms and coordinating industries, has evolved in every other nation as it emerged from underdevelopment or the ravages of war.

Any such assumption would be wrong. This evolution was uniquely American. The industrializing nations of continental Europe and Japan followed other paths. Each developed its own structure of industry, but these countries shared important characteristics which distinguished them sharply from the United States. (Great Britain, as will be seen, was a separate case.) First, their mass markets developed far later than did America's. This was because class and regional tastes were more differentiated, the distribution of incomes was more skewed, and unskilled labor was in relatively greater supply, resulting in lower real wages. Thus, high-volume production in continental Europe and Japan tended to be confined to primary metals, shipbuilding, chemicals, and other heavy industries. And even in these industries production was never as standardized as it was in America but was typically involved in a range of products, tailored more closely to the specific needs of different industrial purchasers. Secondly, craft guilds retained substantial political power, making it difficult for industry to replace skilled craftsmen with salaried managers schooled in scientific management.

For both these reasons, high-volume, standardized production came later to continental Europe and Japan than to America, and it was never central to the organization of business and government. To be sure, scientific management was widely discussed in all these nations. Just before World War I Louis Renault, André Citroen, and other European inventor-promoters visited the United States and brought back to the Continent the concepts of assembly lines and specialized departments. French Premier Georges Clemenceau ordered that scientific management be applied in military plants. Later Japanese firms undertook time and motion studies modeled on Taylor's teachings, in an effort to simplify manufacturing tasks.[1]

But the principles of management which took hold on the Continent and in Japan were addressed more to effective supervision than to the simplification of production. The most influential management theorist in Europe was Henri Fayol, whose *Administration industrielle et générale,* published in 1916, emphasized patterns of formal authority in the organization. Fayol recommended that no subordinate in the hierarchy should report to more than one superior (he called this unity of command) and that no superior should supervise more than a few subordinates ("span of control"). Thus, Japanese and European business enterprises tended to worry about the "vertical" flow of information and commands, instead of about the American preoccupation with simplifying rules and tasks to accelerate the "horizontal" flow of production. This concern with rationalizing the vertical chain of command was consistent with smaller-scale production and with the lingering authority of skilled craftsmen.

In continental European and Japanese enterprises those who planned the work were not so strictly separated from those who executed it.

Professional managers simply did not exist. Even today no single word in French, German, Swedish, or Japanese corresponds very closely to our term "management." Professional management societies, journals, and consulting firms did not appear in these countries until the late 1950's, under American influence, and they never achieved the status they did in the United States.[2]

Long after the norm for business leaders in America came to be specialized training in business administration, business leaders on the Continent and in Japan continued to be trained in engineering or applied economics. Of 20,000 West German managers surveyed in 1967, 44 percent had university degrees in engineering or economics; only 3 percent, in business administration. In a corresponding survey 60 percent of French managers were found to have been trained as engineers. The percentages were similar in Sweden and Japan.[3] In all these nations, in fact, government experience rather than business school was the most common source of training in administration. Many top-level salaried managers were former civil servants, who brought to their industrial careers a familiarity with government organization and public concerns. By the 1960's there were institutes of management training in Western Europe and Japan, but they were peripheral to the traditional education systems and served mainly mid-career executives seeking specific training in particular aspects of management. They did not give degrees, nor did they confer professional status. In continental Europe and Japan business administration was more a job than a profession.

Because scientific management never took firm root, labor unions in continental Europe and Japan came to rely less upon rigid job classifications and rules to guarantee their members' job security than upon schemes of labor participation in company decisions. In these nations, organized labor is rarely present in the shop; instead, unions typically negotiate general standards for the industry as a whole, leaving managers free to change the details of work. And because the distinction between planners and actual producers has been less sharply drawn than in American firms, schemes of employee participation can more easily be meshed with the productive process. Workers in Germany are represented in works councils and on company supervisory boards. Since World War II managers and workers in Japanese firms have developed elaborate methods of consultation. Workers in France and Sweden participate in company decisions through workers' councils. In all these countries labor unions have grown to claim a much larger proportion of the work force than in America. By 1980, 83 percent of Swedish workers, 56 percent of Austrian workers, 42 percent of West Germans, and 33 percent of Japanese were organized, opposed to 21 percent of the workers in the United States.[4] Japanese and European unions also included many white-collar workers. And because of their size and their influence on industrial decisions, these unions came to be a force in the development of national economic policy.

2.

As relatively late industrializers dependent on international trade, continental Europe and Japan relied to a far greater extent than did America or Britain on national economic strategies, spearheaded by their governments. In sharp contrast to the American pattern, these governments were the driving forces behind economic development—the vehicles through which middle-class business interests overcame the inertia of an older economic order based upon landed wealth. The governments and central banks of these countries designed, financed, and operated the railroads and telegraph systems. They supplied capital for steel mills. They disseminated new technologies. During the 1920's and 1930's they directly supervised industrial cartels in raw materials and semifinished goods, in order to maintain earnings during periods of declining demand. After the nearly total devastation of World War II, governments and central banks orchestrated economic reconstruction.

They also pursued deliberate and detailed strategies to promote economic development. Because international trade loomed so large in their economies, these strategies necessarily emphasized international competitiveness. By the 1960's European and Japanese governments and banks were carefully monitoring changes in world markets, helping their firms line up sources of supply, and arranging export financing. They were, in short, directly and openly intervening to propel their economies toward growth. In several of these countries—especially Japan, West Germany, and France—these public efforts have successfully accelerated economic adjustment. This governmental economic management did not usurp decision making by individual firms. Rather, it shaped firms' decisions through carefully chosen tax, credit, and tariff policies.

The organizational mechanism for economic management varied substantially from nation to nation, but a few features were broadly shared: First, instead of the *ad hoc* scatter of separate industrial superstructures that developed in the United States, the tendency in continental Europe and Japan was to unify and coordinate economic policy making across industries. Business and labor organized themselves nationally to participate in these deliberations. Secondly, because ministries and central banks were able to undertake specific strategic interventions, they were spared the comparable American agencies' nearly impossible task of devising programs and regulations appropriate to all firms at all times. Instead, their programs were tailored to meet the needs of particular firms and markets at particular times. Their decisions, therefore, were more flexible, and less bound up with precedent, than were those of American agencies. Thirdly, because of their pivotal roles in the economy, these bureaucracies attracted to their ranks some of the most talented university graduates in each nation. They were places of high prestige, and their decisions, though seldom legally binding, were generally accepted by business and labor because of the respect and confidence—and, often, the financial clout—they commanded. America, by contrast, never developed a permanent and prestigious cadre of senior public officials. For all these reasons the superstructures of industrial management in continental Europe and Japan came to be dominated by governments and by government-connected banks—in contrast with American industrial superstructures, in which the largest firms in each industry typically took the lead.

The different structure of industrial management in Europe and Japan shaped a different pattern of business organization. Business enterprises relied less than did American firms on diversification into unrelated fields as a hedge against economic change, for example. Their fixed costs were often lower than those of American firms, and their governments and central banks undertook to spread the risk of new investment. Through most of the era mergers and acquisitions were rare.[5]

In many respects, Britain's industrial organization during the management era was more closely akin to the American model than to that of the rest of Europe and Japan. Professional management came to Britain —although later than it did to the United States—after the spectacular performance of American industry during World War II had drawn British attention to American management techniques. Sir Stafford

Cripps, chancellor of the exchequer in the postwar Labour government, sent teams of businessmen to America to bring home the secrets of professional management, which soon permeated British institutions, perhaps because the ideal of a select corps of trained managers harmonized well with Britain's tradition of training its elite, through public schools and Oxbridge, to manage its far-flung colonial possessions.

By the 1970's Britain shared with the United States some of the world's largest manufacturing enterprises. In 1972 thirty of them employed more than 40,000 people apiece. (The five other European Economic Community nations, with three times Britain's population, shared among them about this same number of giant enterprises.) Many of Britain's large companies were highly diversified.[6] Mergers and acquisitions were common. British labor unions, like their American counterparts, had come to depend on scientific management's system of job classification and work rules as the primary means of protecting their members.

Britain's superstructure of industrial management also resembled America's. Because Britain had industrialized early, its government and central banks had taken no formal role in its economic development. Nor had war so ravaged the British economy that reconstruction demanded detailed government planning. Shaping national economic strategy had therefore never become a central function of British government. Instead, the superstructures of management developed much as they had in America—*ad hoc,* largely hidden from public view, organized by industry, and dominated by the largest firms.

3.

In continental Europe and Japan social welfare was intimately bound up with economic organization. For these relatively recently feudal nations industrialization was as much a matter of social transformation as of technical progress. Social change and economic development went hand in hand. Bismarck's Germany had led the way in the nineteenth century with schemes of health insurance and old-age pensions, followed shortly by other European nations. Japan's Meiji government had instituted comprehensive old-age pensions and pioneered a system of universal primary education, which produced close to 100 percent literacy by the 1920's.[7] By the time America enacted Social Security legislation in 1935 twenty other nations had had such schemes for almost a generation. Even by the end of the era social welfare, unemployment insurance, and publicly financed health care were still more generous in continental Europe and Japan than in the United States.

The integration of social welfare and economic development was critical to these nations' futures. To catch up economically, they had to transform their societies quickly. Peasant farmers had to become urban workers. Rapid industrialization was soon seen to depend on the health and economic security of the work force. Thus, the government bureaucracies that ushered in new industry also—often almost simultaneously—established national insurance schemes which spread the cost of ill health, unemployment, and old age over the population as a whole.

These governments also well understood that failure to adapt could threaten social stability. In many of these nations the interwar years were marked by large-scale syndicalist, socialist, Communist, Fascist, and anarchist movements. After World War II bureaucracies in these nations oversaw programs of economic and social reconstruction, which integrated public welfare with the imperatives of growth. In Japan this responsibility came to be shared by major firms that provided their workers with a broad array of social services. The postwar "welfare states" of Europe emphasized public services and comprehensive income maintenance as a means of rebuilding community and reestablishing solidarity among their citizens.

In America, by contrast, the process of industrialization had been led by business enterprises rather than by government. At least until World War I the country had had no national bureaucratic apparatus to administer broadly based social insurance schemes and no tradition of collective spending for public welfare. Americans, spared the need to transcend a harsh tradition of feudal class distinctions, found it difficult to appreciate the strength of the link between social welfare and economic growth.

Even after World War II the relationship remained elusive to most Americans. The nation had not suffered the dislocations and deprivations that war had wrought in Europe and Japan. America did not need to concern itself with social and economic reconstruction. Nor—so long as the nation held unrivaled economic strength—was active adjustment required; there was little competition to adjust to. High-volume, standardized production required social stability rather than social change. America occupied itself with the task of shifting the direction of its high-volume production from war mobilization to mass consumption.

The closest America came to broad-based programs of social reconstruction were the GI Bill, Veterans Administration housing loans, and the Eisenhower highway construction program, which together spawned the postwar boom in housing, home furnishings, home appliances, and automobiles. America's programs of public assistance, meanwhile, were far less comprehensive than those in Europe and Japan. Instead of providing a system of common social services, its welfare programs were narrowly targeted to specific categories of unfortunates who were conspicuously distinct from everyone else—the aged; the blind; single mothers; the medically indigent; the handicapped. Rather than emphasize the different needs that any citizen might experience over a lifetime, America's welfare programs emphasized the differentness of the needy. Designed solely to save the unfortunate from destitution, the programs were not geared to helping the poor change their economic status. Indeed, public housing, urban renewal, public hospitals, Medicaid, and food stamps tended to perpetuate poverty by defining a separate welfare economy segregated from the system of production.

Britain's organization of social welfare, like its organization of industry, lay halfway between that of America and those of other industrialized nations. Although Britain had pioneered a national scheme of health insurance in the early decades of the century and had extended its comprehensive welfare programs after World War II, the programs remained similarly segregated from the British economy and involved no efforts to link social welfare with industrial growth. Indeed, the programs' maintenance rested on a precarious political consensus. British management never fully embraced them as aspects of industrial strategy. Instead, the programs became isolated symbols of contention between the British right and left. By the late 1970's a Conservative government in Whitehall was actively dismantling them.

4.

America had followed Britain's lead into industrialization. Britain in turn followed America into high-volume production. In both nations there developed a sharp division between the planning and the execution of work, which came to be reflected in their social policies. In Great Britain social welfare became the exclusive concern of the Labour party.

In the United States it became the special cause of postwar liberals, whose vision was transmuted into bureaucratic programs which stigmatized many of their recipients. In neither country was social welfare perceived as an integral part of industrial development. On the contrary, high-volume production consigned it to a peripheral role. The model in both countries was an earlier tradition of charity, oriented to delivering succor to the helpless rather than to accelerating social evolution. As we shall see, in marked contrast with the delivery of social services on the Continent, eligibility in Britain and America has depended primarily on one's income. These programs have been viewed as means of tidying up industrialization—responding to its unfortunate side effects, rendering it slightly more humane.

That the process of industrialization in both Britain and America had been led by business enterprises rather than by government, and that both nations had avoided the worst devastations of World War II and the subsequent need for social and economic reconstruction, brought them a continuing ideological and institutional distinction between social welfare and industrial development. Governments in Britain and America had neither the historical precedent nor the formal authority to integrate social policies with industrial policies.

The British and American failure to appreciate the connection between social welfare and economic change began to take its toll only toward the end of the management era, when both nations found themselves locked into a structure of organization that was rapidly becoming obsolete without any means of speeding or easing their adjustment. And the organizational systems built around high-volume, standardized production were so pervasive—permeating business, government, and labor—that economic change would prove to be especially painful to both.

IMPASSE
1970-

Part Three

VII
GLOBAL CHANGE

1.

The management era ended for America around 1970. Its decline began, ironically, just as many Europeans were coming to view the mastery of high-volume production as the "American challenge" which Europe had either to emulate or to succumb to. Gradually the economic cycles began to track a downward trend, and over the next decade America's resources were progressively idled. The proportion of U.S. manufacturing capacity employed in production, which had reached 86 percent in 1965, averaged in the range of 80 percent during the 1970's and fell to less than 70 percent by 1982. Only 3.5 percent of America's labor force was jobless in 1969, but thereafter unemployment climbed persistently, reaching almost 11 percent in 1982.

Measured in constant 1981 dollars, the Dow-Jones industrial average declined from 2,624 in 1965 to around 1,000 in 1982. The profit rate of America's nonfinancial corporations declined steadily from 12.7 percent in the late 1960's to 10 percent by 1975 and has not risen above 10 percent since then. By the 1980's the core industries of the management era—

steel, automobiles, petrochemicals, textiles, consumer electronics, electrical machinery, metal-forming machinery—were in trouble. And many of the giant firms of the past half century—U.S. Steel, General Motors, International Harvester, RCA—were suffering sharply declining profits. Some faced bankruptcy.

Productivity growth slowed from an average yearly increase of 3.2 percent between 1948 and 1965 to an average of 2.4 percent between 1965 and 1973. The rate of growth then plunged to 1.1 percent between 1973 and 1978, and in 1979 American productivity began actually to decline. At the end of 1979 the average worker was only 98 percent as efficient as he was at the beginning of the year. Productivity continued to fall in 1980. (Since then, productivity has edged upward, but largely because fewer workers are employed.)

The average American's standard of living has inevitably begun to suffer. After 1965 real incomes slowed their long climb. Between 1968 and 1981 the average American worker's real wages declined by one-fifth. The engine of prosperity had stalled.

The decline is particularly startling when compared with the performance of several other industrial countries. From the mid-1960's the economies of Japan, West Germany, France, and even Italy and Britain grew faster than America's economy. From 1976 to 1981, Japan's productivity grew at an annual rate of 7.1 percent, France's productivity at 3.9 percent, and West Germany's productivity at 3.4 percent. By some measurements, the per person national product of several other nations actually exceeded that of the United States.[1]

When all industrialized countries were gripped by a worldwide recession in 1981 and 1982, America was among the hardest hit, suffering slower economic growth and higher unemployment than France, Japan, or West Germany and higher inflation than Japan or West Germany. America's standard of living has stayed high in absolute terms, in large part because its stock of wealth is still immense. But that lead is eroding quickly. The relative decline in the American standard of living manifests itself in a variety of ways. Life expectancy at birth is lower in the United States than in fourteen other nations. Seventeen countries have infant mortality rates lower than America's. And levels of air pollution in this country are worse than in many other industrial nations.[2]

2.

With the close of the management era America has abruptly faced a stark challenge of economic transformation, but the old organization of business, labor, and government has resisted change. High-volume, standardized production was the engine of prosperity for so long that fundamental change threatens the well-being of too many people. So the nation has pretended that the management era has not really ended. America has dismissed its economic troubles as the work of OPEC and the oil shocks of 1973 and 1979. It has blamed regulations, inflation, taxes, government deficits, and subsidized imports.

As the trusted formula of high-volume, standardized production has ceased to deliver prosperity, America has been ready to embrace any explanation but the most obvious: The same factor that previously brought prosperity—the way the nation organizes itself for production—now threatens decline. Everywhere America has looked, it has seen the symptoms of its economic impasse, but the nation has been unable to recognize the problem because its roots are deeply embedded in the organization of America's business enterprises, labor unions, and government institutions.

Government regulation served as a convenient rhetorical scapegoat in the 1980 presidential election but offers no real explanation. Environmental laws indeed require firms to invest in new equipment, but those requirements have imposed only modest costs. Safety regulations also add some costs to operations, but the reduction in accidents has meant savings in time and expense that go far to offset these extra costs. Capital expenditures on pollution control and safety combined have never exceeded 6 percent of industrial investment and may be blamed for at most around a tenth of the slowdown in productivity. Significantly, pollution control and mandatory safety laws have been more stringent in many other countries, including Japan, that have still surpassed American rates of productivity growth. As we shall see, during the 1970's Japanese steelmakers spent almost twice as much as their American counterparts on pollution control and worker safety.[3] Finally, many critics of regulation underscore the obvious when they claim that safety and a clean environment cost something. The issue is whether they are worth it. Considering the relatively modest cost of the regulations and the importance Americans place on these aspects of their well-being, the claim that measures to maintain the environment and protect workers are responsible for a declining American standard of living is simply not plausible.

Nor do government deficits explain any major part of America's problem. There is no evidence that deficits have been nearly large enough to discourage private investment and economic growth substantially. What matters is not the total dollar debt but its relationship to the economy's size. In the period from 1956 to 1973, when the U.S. public sector mushroomed, the rest of the economy also grew in proportion. After 1973, as overall growth slowed dramatically, the government's share of the economy stabilized.[4] Today's debt is less than 30 percent of the nation's gross national product, about the same proportion as it was in the late eighteenth century. By comparison with other industrial countries that have outpaced America, the U.S. government sector has stayed quite small as a proportion of the economy. Indeed, throughout the 1970's the governments in West Germany, Japan, and France maintained a larger public debt in proportion to their national economies than did the American government. And tax revenues as a percent of national product increased substantially more in every other major industrialized country than in the United States.[5]

Inadequate capital formation has not been the problem either. Between 1965 and 1980, even in the face of inflation, America continued to invest about 10 percent of its gross national product in plant and equipment; since 1977 the rate has exceeded 11 percent, and in the first quarter of 1982 it reached 11.7 percent—its highest level since 1928. Indeed, investment in *manufacturing* as a percent of the total output of goods in manufacturing increased substantially—from 10.8 percent between 1960 and 1964 to 14.8 percent between 1973 and 1978. This level of manufacturing investment was not significantly below that of America's foreign competitors.[6]

Nor can other proposed explanations really explain America's decline. Investment in research and development declined from 3 percent of the gross national product at the start of the 1970's to 2 percent at the start of the 1980's. But this decline stemmed mostly from the slowdown in publicly financed defense and space programs which affected American industry only indirectly. And U.S. expenditures for research and development were still higher than those of its competitors. In any event, the decline in America's productive growth actually began in the late 1960's, well before any cutback in research expenditures. Nor can responsibility be placed on escalating energy prices. The oil shock affected all nations, many of which were much more dependent on imported energy resources than was the United States. Even more to the point, America's economic decline predated the oil embargo.

Nor was it the inevitable drop in output from the nation's mines; or the slowdown in the movement of American labor out of agriculture; or the entrance of women and young people into the labor force; or unfair competition by foreign manufacturers. Even taken together, these explain only a small part of America's gradual, steady economic decline relative to other leading industrial nations. They fail to take into account the worldwide reorganization of production and America's failure to adapt to it.

3.

America's relative decline has been rooted in changes in the world market. Prior to 1965, foreign trade did not figure significantly in the U.S. economy. Only a small proportion of American-made goods were traded internationally; an equally small amount of foreign production entered the United States. This situation has changed dramatically.

In 1980, 19 percent of the goods Americans made were exported (up from 9 percent in 1970), and more than 22 percent of the goods Americans used were imported (up from 9 percent in 1970). But those figures understate the new importance of foreign competition. They show only where American producers had already been bested on their own ground, and they mask the vastly widened scope of world competition. The most telling statistic is this: By 1980 more than 70 percent of all the goods produced in the United States were actively competing with foreign-made goods.[7] America has become part of the world market.

American producers have not fared well in this new contest. Beginning in the mid-1960's, foreign imports have claimed an increasing share of the American market. By 1981 America was importing almost 26 percent of its cars, 25 percent of its steel, 60 percent of its televisions, radios, tape recorders, and phonographs, 43 percent of its calculators, 27 percent of its metal-forming machine tools, 35 percent of its textile machinery, and 53 percent of its numerically controlled machine tools. Twenty years before, imports had accounted for less than 10 percent of the U.S. market for each of these products. Between 1970 and 1980 imports from developing nations increased almost tenfold, from $3.6 billion to $30 billion (in constant dollars).[8]

During the 1970's the share of American manufactured goods in total world sales declined by 23 percent while every other industrialized nation, except Britain, maintained or expanded its share. Japan's share rose from 6 percent to 10.5 percent. The developing nations as a group expanded their share to 10 percent of world trade in manufactured products by the mid-1970's, up from just 4 percent a few years before. By 1980 their share had increased to 13 percent.[9]

America's diminishing presence in the international market has been particularly marked in capital-intensive, high-volume industries. Since 1963 the U.S. proportion of world automobile sales has declined by almost one-third. United States' sales of industrial machinery also declined by one-third; sales of agricultural machinery, by 40 percent; telecommunications machinery, by 50 percent; metalworking machinery, by 55 percent.

The growth of the developing countries' world market share has several related causes. Beginning with the General Agreement on Tariffs and Trade in 1947, industrialized nations gradually reduced their tariff levels, often granting special preference to developing countries. Simultaneously with trade liberalization, developing countries have gained relatively easy access to international capital through the World Bank and eager lending by European, American, and Japanese banks. By the 1970's even the private Eurodollar markets were prepared to finance new ventures.

Technology has also moved more fluidly across the globe. Developing countries can now purchase (from international engineering and capital equipment firms) the world's most modern steel-rolling mills, paper machines, computer controlled machine tools, or fertilizer plants. They can also get training and technical supervision to accompany the new production facilities. And they send growing numbers of their citizens to industrialized countries for training. By the early 1970's more than 20 percent of the doctoral degrees in science and engineering conferred by American universities were going to foreign students, and in Europe nearly 50 percent of the university students in science and engineering were foreign-born.[10]

Global channels of sales and marketing have opened up. The growth of large-scale retail outlets in industrialized nations has given developing countries an efficient way to distribute their wares. Korean television manufacturers, for example, have gained a sizable share of the U.S. television market simply by supplying a dozen large American department store chains.

All these changes have been accelerated by new transportation and communications technologies. Beginning in the 1960's, containerized shipping, specialized tankers, and jet air-cargo carriers substantially reduced international shipping costs. Even in the 1970's, when fuel prices multiplied, these new technologies held down the costs of moving goods around the world.[11] Many developing nations have also improved their internal rail and road systems and invested in central ports and airports. At the same time data processing machines, microprocessors, and satellite communications facilities have enabled businesses efficiently to divide the production process into separate operations that can be performed across the globe at different production sites and then integrated into a single product. Developing countries have been ideally suited to the standardized parts of this fragmented production process.

These dramatic changes in the world economy, starting in the 1960's, have enabled developing countries to move quickly into global industries. By the mid-1960's Korea, Hong Kong, Taiwan, Singapore, Brazil, and Spain had begun specializing in such simple products as clothing, footwear, toys, and basic electronic assemblies, which required substantial amounts of unskilled labor but little capital investment or technology. Between 1970 and 1975 South Korea's exports of textiles increased by 436 percent; Taiwan, by 347 percent; Hong Kong's, by 191 percent.[12]

As newly industrialized countries expanded production of labor-intensive goods, Japan's export mix was shifting out of these simple products and into processing industries, like steel and synthetic fibers, which, while requiring substantial capital investment and raw materials, used mostly unskilled and semiskilled labor and incorporated relatively mature technologies that were not subject to major innovations. Between 1966 and

1972 the Japanese steel industry increased its assets by over 23 percent a year—expanding capacity, investing in highly efficient basic oxygen furnaces and continuous casting facilities, and building cargo ships that could carry large quantities of high-quality ore from Australia and Brazil and coal from Australia and Canada. As its own steel needs began to level off in the early 1970's, Japan increased its exports of raw steel. It invested in more than fifty finishing facilities in developing countries in order to expand its market share.[13]

By the mid-1970's Korea, Hong Kong, Taiwan, Singapore, Brazil, Spain, and Mexico had followed Japan by shifting their export mix toward the basic capital-intensive processing industries. By 1977 Brazil, with probably the largest iron ore reserves in the world outside the Soviet Union, had become the world's eighth largest steel producer; Mexico, the tenth largest. Korea and Taiwan were adding steelmaking capacity that would produce 20 million tons of raw steel by the mid-1980's. All told, these developing countries increased their share of world steelmaking capacity from 9 percent in 1974 to 15 percent by 1980.[14]

As less developed countries moved into steel production, Japan was *reducing* its domestic steelmaking capacity and becoming a major exporter of steel technology, engineering services, and equipment. In 1978 Korea's steel exports to America rose 24 percent while Japan's fell 17 percent. Japan moved its industrial base into more complex products, like automobiles, color television sets, small appliances, consumer electronics, and ships—industries requiring considerable investment in plant and equipment as well as sophisticated new technologies.[15]

At the same time Malaysia, Thailand, the Philippines, Sri Lanka, India, and other poorer countries were taking over the production of clothing, footwear, toys, and simple electronic assemblies. Workers in these countries earned, on average, no more than $25 per month. In the Dominican Republic's La Romana free zone, workers were paid thirty-four cents an hour. Before the overthrow of the Somoza government Banco Central de Nicaragua was advertising that its country's workers would assemble electronic components for twenty-five cents an hour. In Mauritius unskilled female workers were paid seventy cents a day.[16]

By 1980 Korea, Hong Kong, Singapore, Brazil, Spain, and Mexico had increased their production of complex products like automobiles, color television sets, tape recorders, CB transceivers, microwave ovens, small computers, and ships. These developing countries now supply 16 percent of the world shipbuilding tonnage. Korea already has the largest single shipyard in the world, and with its salary rates averaging only one-third those of major Japanese shipyards, Korea may surpass Japanese tonnage in five years.[17] Brazil is becoming a net exporter of automobiles, commuter aircraft, and hydroturbine generators. Mexico is developing into a center for world automobile engine production.

Almost all of the world's production of small appliances (whether labeled Panasonic, Philips, GE, Sony, Zenith, or unrecognizable brands) is now centered in Hong Kong, Korea, and Singapore. Components and product designs are purchased from major companies; financing is arranged through Japanese, U.S., and European banks; and distribution is handled through large retailers like Sears or through the established distribution channels of large Japanese or American consumer electronics companies.

Certain oil-rich nations—Mexico, Saudi Arabia, Indonesia, and Nigeria—are building huge petrochemical complexes. They seek to take advantage of their relatively cheap feedstocks in order to provide large-volume commodity chemicals like ethylene, methanol, and basic fertilizers.

Poorer nations are expanding their electronics assembly operations. Malaysia now has 240 electronics assembly plants, and the electronics industry is the nation's second largest employer, accounting for 100,000 jobs. Even the People's Republic of China has announced that it is creating six "special economic zones"—four in Guangdong Province and two in Fujian Province—which will specialize in electronics assembly.[18]

In short, the globe is fast becoming a single marketplace. Goods are being made wherever they can be made the cheapest, regardless of national boundaries. And the most efficient places for much mass production of standardized commodities are coming to be third world countries. Over a period of only fifteen years many of the world's developing countries have begun to specialize in high-volume production, featuring long runs of standardized products. Their production costs are lower than America's both because their workers are content with lower real wages and because some of them have favored access to cheap materials.

One important trend is often overlooked: The hourly output of workers in these newly industrialized nations is catching up to that of American workers because of the simple fact that they are beginning to use many of the same machines. Meanwhile, other, poorer nations themselves are rapidly moving toward capital-intensive, high-volume production. The International Labor Office estimates that every year between 1980 and 2000, 36 million people will enter the world labor force, and 85 percent of them will be from developing nations.[19] The newly integrated international market will put many of them to work at America's old specialty of high-volume, standardized production.

This type of production is also moving to developing countries because many of them constitute the world's fastest-growing markets for standard products. Sales of automobiles, home appliances, and basic steel are growing much faster in Southeast Asia and South America, for example, than in North America and Europe, where markets for standard durable goods are relatively saturated. Consumers in industrialized countries want specialized products.

The trend is becoming clear. First, America's basic steel, textile, automobile, consumer electronics, rubber, and petrochemical industries (and the other high-volume industries that depend on them) are becoming uncompetitive in the world. Secondly, now that production can be fragmented into separate, globally scattered operations, whole segments of other American industries are becoming uncompetitive. Whatever the final product, those parts of U.S. production requiring high-volume machinery and unsophisticated workers can be accomplished more cheaply in developing nations.

Automation, far from halting this trend, has accelerated it. Sophisticated machinery is readily moved to low-wage countries. Robots and numerically controlled machines further reduce the need for semiskilled workers in high-volume production (except for workers with easily learned maintenance and programming skills). For example, robots in the automobile industry are replacing more semiskilled jobs, like arc welding and spot welding, than unskilled jobs. In the ball bearing industry, fully automated plants require only 30 percent fewer workers than standard plants of the same size. Most of this saving is in semiskilled workers. Meanwhile, automated inspection machines are reducing the cost of screening out poor-quality components, thereby encouraging firms in industrialized nations to farm out the production of standardized parts to developing nations.[20]

Thus, automation has made developing nations still better suited to high-volume, standardized production. Not surprisingly, ball bearing plants and automobile-manufacturing facilities are being established in several third world nations. Some of the most automated clothing plants in the world are now found in Hong Kong; some of the most advanced steelworks, in South Korea.

What began in the 1960's as a gradual shift became by the late 1970's a major structural change in the world economy. Assembly operations are being established in developing countries at a rapid clip, and America's manufacturing base is eroding precipitously.

4.

Other industrialized nations of course confront the same competitive threat. Since the mid-1960's European industries have faced an ever greater challenge from low-wage production in developing countries. Since the late 1970's Japan has been challenged as well. Japan is no longer a low-wage nation—the real earnings of Japanese workers are approaching those of their European and American counterparts.

Japan, West Germany, France, and other industrialized countries have sought to meet this challenge by shifting their industrial bases toward products and processes that require skilled labor. Skilled labor has become a key barrier against low-wage competition for the simple reason that it is the only dimension of production in which these countries retain an advantage. Technological innovations may be bought or imitated by anyone. High-volume, standardized production facilities may be established anywhere. But production processes that depend on skilled labor must stay where that labor is. The competitive fate of British industry over the last twenty-five years illustrates this pattern. Great Britain has consistently led the world in major technological breakthroughs, like continuous casting for steel, monoclonal antibodies, and CAT-scanning devices.[21] But because its businesses lacked the organization and its workers lacked the skills necessary to incorporate these inventions into production processes quickly enough, they have reaped no real competitive advantage from them.

Industrialized countries are therefore moving into products like precision castings, specialty steel, special chemicals, process control devices, sensor devices, and luxury automobiles as well as into the design and manufacture of fiber-optic cable, fine ceramics, lasers, integrated circuits, and aircraft engines.

Some of these products or processes require precision engineering, complex testing, and sophisticated maintenance. Others are custom-tailored to the special needs of particular customers. The remainder involve technologies that are changing rapidly. These three product groups are relatively secure against low-wage competition because they depend on high-level skills rather than on standardized production.

Precision Products. Products that require precision engineering, testing, and maintenance cannot easily be made in most developing countries. In the precision casting industry, for example, highly skilled labor is required first for making the dyes and tools and then for forming, finishing, and correcting the resulting products. Because these highly skilled jobs must be performed in the same place as the rest of the production process and because they involve a significant percentage of the total labor required to produce precision castings, the whole process is protected against low-wage competition. The assembly of process control devices similarly demands exacting mechanical adjustments, which can be undertaken only by skilled technicians.

Custom Products. Products custom-tailored to buyers' specific needs are also immune to rapid competitive decline. Turned out in relatively small batches and in close coordination with their customers, these products inevitably depend more on the skill and knowledge of their designers, fabricators, and marketers than on unskilled labor. Examples include numerically controlled machine tools and multipurpose robots; auto body sheet steel that is resistant to corrosion on the inside and smooth and paintable on the outside, made in a small-batch process that coats galvanized sheet on one side; steel rods and bars, which are produced from scrap metal in minimills; telecommunications switching equipment, each installation requiring a separate, customized software system; computer hardware and software systems designed to solve specific problems, like inventory control; made-to-order semiconductor chips designed to fit into particular machinery; special chemicals prepared for particular industrial uses; and custom-designed office equipment.

Computers can add to the efficiency of small-batch, custom-tailored production by controlling the pace and performance of various machines.

This innovation permits skilled workers to make rapid changes in product design after short runs and avoids expensive retooling. The inherent analytical strength of computers complements uniquely human advantages in recognizing patterns, assessing complex problems, and making intuitive leaps to new situations. For example, computerized machinery has been installed in a new Canadian chemical plant that custom-blends a wide range of alcohol products for use in carpets, soaps, and containers. Rather than have all possible blends programmed into the machinery in advance, the computers provide teams of workers with technical and economic data for refining their own decisions about which blends are needed and how they should be produced. The production process is thus constantly changed and upgraded.

When computers are used in predetermined ways, however, the production process does not need skilled workers. Computer-aided manufacturing processes that do not rely on skilled workers are migrating to developing countries in which low-wage labor or cheap raw materials can reduce the cost of production still further.

Technology-Driven Products. The third group of products that are relatively protected against foreign competition is that that depends on rapidly changing technologies. When major innovations occur so frequently that new product generations appear every few years, high-volume, standardized production confers little competitive advantage. By the time high volume is reached the product has already been outdated. Mass production can still yield economies of scale (Japanese production of semiconductor chips is a prime example), but real competitive advantage derives from technological advances. Under these circumstances, production facilities must be in close contact with research and development efforts, so that the latest innovations can be incorporated quickly and efficiently. Examples of products or processes that depend on rapidly changing technologies are computers, integrated circuits, biotechnologies, fiber optics, lasers, and ceramics.

These three product categories—precision-manufactured, custom-tailored, and technology-driven—have a great deal in common. They all depend on the skills of their employees, which often are developed within teams. And they all require that traditionally separate business functions (research, design, engineering, purchasing, manufacturing, distribution, marketing, sales) be merged into a highly integrated system that can respond quickly to new opportunities. A useful shorthand term for this general type of production is "flexible system."

Flexible-system production has an advantage over high-volume standardized production in any enterprise in which production costs can be reduced more sharply by solving new problems than by making routine the solution of old ones. The unit costs of producing simple, standardized products like cotton textiles, basic steel, or rubber tires generally decline more with long production runs than with improvements in the production process. Manufacturers of these products therefore do well to emphasize large capacity, cheap labor, and cheap raw materials rather than flexible systems.

This does not mean that industrialized countries must abandon their older industries, like steel, chemicals, textiles, and automobiles. These industries are the gateways through which new products and processes emerge. It is far easier to move into flexible-system production by upgrading manufacturing skills and know-how and by elaborating networks of suppliers, distributors, and customers already in existence than by leaping into a totally uncharted sea of products and processes unrelated to an industrial base of the past. Rather than abandoning these older industries, America's industrialized competitors are seeking to restructure them toward higher valued and technologically more sophisticated businesses—like specialty steel, special chemicals, synthetic fibers, and precision-engineered automobiles and auto components.

Specialty steels—comprising new additives and different levels of purification and cast into customized shapes—can be adapted to diverse industrial needs; such products now account for almost half of Japan's and West Germany's steel output. Meanwhile, European and Japanese chemical manufacturers are moving swiftly into special, complex chemicals like high-performance plastics, ceramics, and insecticides and herbicides that are custom-tailored to the ecologies of particular regions. West German shipbuilders have shifted to producing more technically advanced ships and other customized engineering projects. Swedish aircraft manufacturers are concentrating on specialized airplanes capable of taking off and landing on very short runways, and Swedish electric machinery manufacturers are focusing on high-voltage transmission. European automakers are developing specialized trucks, vans, and touring vehicles.

Of all industrialized countries, Japan's shift from capital-intensive, high-volume production to flexible-system production has been the most rapid. But Japan has not abandoned its older industries; it has accelerated their evolution. Its automakers are experimenting with a variety of fuel-saving materials—graphite fibers, dual-phased steel, and advanced plastics. They are designing highly efficient microcars. They are developing complex manufacturing systems to reduce production costs further. In this way, the automakers have reduced to fifteen hours the amount of labor required to assemble a small car (in contrast with thirty hours per car in America). By the same token, Japan's production of high-quality polyester filament fabrics, requiring complex technologies and skilled labor, now accounts for 40 percent of its textile exports. Japan has substantially reduced its capacity to produce basic steel, basic petrochemicals, small appliances, ships, and simple fibers, while dramatically expanding its capacity in the higher valued, more specialized segments of these industries. To accomplish this transformation, it has applied such innovations as process control devices, fiber optic cable, complex polymer materials, and very-large-scale integrated circuits. Japanese companies are also packaging their more standard products within technologically complex product systems, such as office communications and computer-aided manufacturing, which require custom design and servicing. In Japan's flexible-system enterprises the distinction between goods and services is becoming blurred.

Japan has reduced its capacity in the capital-intensive, high-volume segments of its basic industries by scrapping plants and equipment, by simultaneously investing in new high-volume capacity within Korea, Taiwan, Singapore, and Brazil, and by retraining its workers for higher skilled production.

West Germany and France are having more difficulty shifting their economies, but each country is making progress. Although the current recession has taken its toll in both nations, Germany nevertheless has reduced its basic steel, chemical, and automobile making capacity somewhat and shifted more of its production into specialty steel, pharmaceuticals, and precision machinery. France has reduced its capacity in heavy industries and is seeking larger positions in the design and fabrication of computers, aircraft, nuclear power generators, satellite technology, and electronic switching equipment.

Other industrialized countries are at various stages of this industrial evolution. Even Taiwan and Korea are seeking to shift into flexible-system industries. Korea is now establishing a semiconductor research and development association, jointly funded by government and industry. Taiwan is building a science-based industrial park at Hsinchu.

America's evolution has so far been sluggish. America has been far less successful than other leading industrialized nations in increasing its manufacturing exports to cover its import bill. The nations of Western Europe and Japan have been selling America more manufactured goods than it has been selling back to them.[22]

Sales of grain, coal, and revenues from services have of course helped ease America's trade imbalance. (Of the $22 billion of goods the United States shipped to Japan in 1981, by far the largest category—$6 billion—comprised agricultural products.) But these enterprises cannot alone guarantee the nation's economic future. The most accessible coal will have been mined within the next few years; additional coal will be more costly to retrieve, not only in terms of machinery and equipment but also in damage to the environment and injuries to workers. Nor can grain exports fill the gap indefinitely; improvements in agricultural production are spreading to other areas of the globe with favorable climate and soil conditions, and America's soil will gradually become depleted.[23]

Moreover, the nation cannot rely on services. America's sales of services depend on the vigor of its future manufacturing base. Approximately 90 percent of America's income from services consists of the investment income of its manufacturing firms and, to a lesser extent, of individuals. This income has declined significantly since the mid-1960's. In 1965 the United States received 3.6 times as much investment income as it paid out to foreign firms and individuals in dividends and royalties, but by 1978 the ratio of investment income to payments was down to 1.8 to 1. As foreign firms continue to gain strength relative to their American counterparts in merchandise businesses, this trend will continue.[24]

Other sources of service income face similar declines. Fees and royalties paid from subsidiaries abroad now account for 8.5 percent of America's service income. This income has also declined rapidly as American merchandise firms have lost their competitive strength. Banking, insurance, and consulting services constitute the remaining 1.5 percent. These services are also directly linked to the manufacturing base of the country and surely will diminish as merchandise trade declines. German, Japanese, and Middle Eastern banks, for example, have largely supplanted U.S. banks as their economies have become relatively stronger. By the same token, engineering services depend upon ongoing experience in building up-to-date plants; indigenous engineering firms are already being established in South Korea, Taiwan, and Brazil. And other nations are moving to substitute their own legal and insurance services for those supplied by Britain and America.

5.

These trends pose a troubling question. If it is true that the economic future of the industrialized countries lies in technically advanced, skill-intensive industries, why have American firms failed to respond by adopting the new products and processes?

The answer has several aspects that are dealt with in more depth in other chapters. First, some U.S. firms *are* adopting flexible-system production, but they are very much in the minority, far short of the proportion required for any kind of truly national adjustment. Secondly, few of America's business leaders have been trained and selected for the role of guiding product and process innovation, nor—when the legal and financial manipulations of paper entrepreneurialism offer so lucrative a short-run substitute—do many of them have much taste for it. Thirdly, flexible-system production is so fundamentally different from standardized production that the transition requires a basic restructuring of business, labor, and government; any reorganization of this magnitude threatens vested economic interests and challenges established values and is thus bound to be resisted. Finally, as we shall see, the transition also requires a massive change in the skills of American labor, requiring investments in human capital beyond the capacity of any individual firm.

As America has forfeited world industrial leadership to Japan, its businessmen have become obsessed with Japanese management. The business press daily praises practices such as "quality circles," said to encourage worker commitment, soften workplace conflict, and improve product quality. U.S. management consultants recommend the sorts of investments in new products and processes that are hailed as the key to Japan's success. American business schools are returning to the "basics" of production management and engineering, the managerial orientation thought to underlie the speed of Japanese firms in responding to new business opportunities. American businessmen aspire to new Japanese-style "understandings" between labor and management. New secrets of Japanese success are regularly revealed—profit-sharing schemes, joint research ventures, divestment programs, "Theory Z," and so on.

But American business leaders are responding only to the superficial novelty of Japanese management without acknowledging the underlying differences in the organization of production. They hope simply to upgrade their management techniques, while retaining intact the old structure of high-volume, standardized production. Yet the answer lies not in new techniques but in a new productive organization requiring a different, less rigidly delineated relationship between management and labor and a new relationship with government.

6.

Flexible-system processes cannot be simply grafted onto business organizations that are highly specialized for producing long runs of standardized goods. The premises of high-volume, standardized production—the once-potent formula of scientific management—are simply inapplicable to flexible-system production. First, the tasks involved are necessarily complex since any work that can be rendered simple and routine is more efficiently done by low-wage labor overseas.

Secondly, skill-intensive processes cannot be programmed according to a fixed set of rules covering all contingencies. The work requires high-level skills precisely because the problems and opportunities cannot be anticipated. The organization must be able to respond quickly to emerging and potential markets. Delicate machines break down in complex ways. Technologies change in directions that cannot be foreseen. The more frequently products and processes are altered or adapted, the harder it is to translate them into reliable routines. Again, if the problems and opportunities could be anticipated and covered by preset rules and instructions, the production process could be moved abroad.

Finally, workers' performance cannot be monitored and evaluated through simple accounting systems. In flexible-system production the quality of work is often more important than quantity. As machines and low-wage labor overseas take over these tasks that demand only speed and accuracy, workers' skill, judgment, and initiative become the determinants of the flexible-system enterprise's competitive success. Moreover, tasks are often so interrelated that it becomes impossible to measure them separately; since each worker needs the help and cooperation of many others, success can be measured only in reference to the final collective result.

For these reasons, the radical distinction heretofore drawn between those who plan work and those who execute it is inappropriate to flexible-system production. Not only is advanced planning often impossible, but problem solving also requires close working relationships among people at all stages in the production process. If customers' special needs are to be recognized and met, designers must be familiar with fabrication, production, marketing, and sales. Salespeople must have an intimate understanding of the enterprise's capability to design and deliver new or customized products. Flexible systems can adapt quickly only if information is widely shared and diffused within them. There is no hierarchy to problem solving: Solutions may come from anyone, anywhere. In flexible-system enterprises nearly everyone in the production process is responsible for recognizing problems and finding solutions.

In high-volume, standardized production, professional managers, staff specialists, and even low-level production workers typically get much of their training before joining the organization and seldom venture far from a fairly narrow specialty. They conduct their careers between organizations, but within that single specialty.

By contrast, in flexible-system production much of the training of necessity occurs on the job, both because the precise skills to be learned cannot be anticipated and communicated in advance and because individuals' skills are typically integrated into a group whose collective capacity becomes something more than the simple sum of its members' skills. As the group members learn how to solve various problems, they also learn about each other's capabilities. They become familiar with complementarities between their own talents and the capabilities of others in the group, of other groups, and of the organization as a whole. As is true of a baseball team, practice together increases their collective prowess. Flexible-system workers see their individual skills enhanced and their efforts amplified through work in an ongoing group, and thus, their identification with the enterprise is generally stronger than their allegiance to their profession or occupational group. Flexible-system workers often pursue their careers between specialties, but within a single organization.

In contrast with the high-volume, standardized enterprise—which is organized into a series of hierarchical tiers arranged like a pyramid—the flexible-system firm has a relatively "flat" structure: In most firms that stake their success on specialized or technology-based products, there are few middle-level managers and only modest differences in the status and income of senior managers and junior employees. The enterprise is typically organized as a set of relatively stable project teams that informally compete with one another for resources, recognition, and projects.

Finally, because flexible-system production is conditioned on ever-changing markets and conditions, it is less vulnerable than high-volume production to shifts in demand. Its machines and workers are not locked in to producing long runs of any single standardized good. For this reason, flexible-system enterprises have less need to diversify into several lines of business as insurance against declining demand in any one. Nor do they require the same types of superstructures of industry-wide management to coordinate their firms' investment and production decisions and to stabilize the industry. Flexible-system producers thrive on instability. Too much stability, and they would gradually lose their markets to high-volume, standardized producers around the globe.

In all these respects the organization of high-volume production is so fundamentally different from that of flexible-system production that the transformation from one to the other is exceedingly difficult. Because the roles, experiences, training, and expectations of professional managers and workers in high-volume production differ so sharply from those flexible-system production calls for, neither group is prepared to adapt smoothly to such a transformation. In fact, they are likely to resist it. Professional managers are apt to be uncomfortable in work structures in which authority is informal and *ad hoc,* deriving more from technical knowledge than from hierarchical rank. By the same token, employees are prone to feel threatened by the lack of the explicit work rules and well-defined job descriptions which in the past have provided some security against arbitrary authority. Workers at all levels are likely to resist any change that might reduce their economic security in the short term, even if the change promises greater prosperity.

Part of workers' and managers' resistance stems from their accurate recognition that their training and hard-won experience are often simply inappropriate to flexible-system production. The expertise of professional managers lies in devising rules and scrutinizing numbers rather than in collaborating to solve novel production problems. By the same token, specialists may know a great deal about engineering, marketing, or some other facet of producing and distributing goods but have no experience in integrating these approaches to respond to new product opportunities. Unskilled or semiskilled workers know how to follow simple rules; but they are seldom accustomed to exercising discretion or accepting responsibility as members of a team, and they may not have developed the basic verbal and mathematical skills that are prerequisites to team learning. And no one in the typical high-volume enterprise is accustomed to intense, ongoing collaboration.

The very techniques by which decisions are made within high-volume enterprises inhibit change toward flexible-system production. Because profits in high-volume enterprises derive from very long runs of standardized units, managers balk at making changes that might reduce capacity and jeopardize volume, and investors are similarly reluctant to underwrite this sort of risk. American industry has a tradition of marginal, incremental change—like the annual alterations in automobile styling—that maintains high-volume production of essentially the same goods. American managers and investors have generally found wholly new products or processes simply too risky.

Indeed, change toward flexible-system production cannot even be evaluated according to traditional investment criteria, by which the anticipated direct returns on new investments are toted up against their direct costs to calculate the all-important rate of return. High-volume enterprises have no simple way to estimate the return on investments in flexible systems. How can the benefits of greater adaptability be precisely forecast before problems and opportunities become apparent? How can such contingent advantages be measured against the more certain benefits of greater volume? Managers' analytical tools, designed for an era of stability, are inadequate to process the subtler, less certain factors that govern the success of flexible-system enterprises.

7.

The profound difference of flexible-system production helps explain America's nostalgia for the management era. Long runs of standardized products brought America unparalleled prosperity. True, that prosperity was interrupted by a great depression and by periodic recessions. But these were interruptions, nothing more. High-volume, standardized production always restored prosperity. Indeed, it steadily surpassed its previous levels, achieving more efficiency, longer production runs, and greater volume than before.

America has been unwilling to give up this vision. The present economic decline, after all, superficially resembles earlier ones. Many people cling to the hope that it is also temporary, caused by passing phenomena which have little to do with the underlying organization of American production—"instabilities" in Middle Eastern oil fields; momentary industrial overcapacity; government regulations inspired by episodic environmental and consumer movements; inflation caused by excessive government spending. Once these scourges are behind us, so this reasoning goes, America's prosperity will be restored, on the same basis as before. We have had unemployed workers and idle factories in the past, but our engine of prosperity has always come through. The enduring faith is that it will do so again.

Too many of us have too much of a stake in the old patterns of organization to acknowledge comfortably the magnitude of the shift that must be undertaken. This institutional inertia can be overcome only when the pain grows almost unbearable, when the standard of living falls even more precipitously than it is now falling, when the reality of what must be done becomes irrefutable. But economic decline also hardens the resistance to change because many people are made more vulnerable to the risks attendant on change. They feel they are on the verge of poverty or at least deprived in relation to the standard of living they once knew. Such feelings engender a widespread conservatism. Let us at least preserve what we have, retreat to the ways we used to do things, and return to "basics." Everyone involved in the creation of wealth—investors, professional managers, production workers—grows less willing to take risks. The cycle of decline is set in motion.

America's industrial base must change radically. If American prosperity is to be truly restored, a substantial fraction of capital and labor must shift toward flexible-system production. But the organization of high-volume, standardized production permits change in only one dimension: toward greater scale and a larger volume of the same standardized products. As shall be discussed, because America's professional managers are ill-equipped to undertake the necessary shift, they have resorted to various ploys designed to maintain or increase their firms' earnings without new productive investment. Paper entrepreneurialism of this kind merely rearranges industrial assets while wasting the time and abilities of some of America's most talented people.

Organized labor, meanwhile, also resists industrial change, ready to sacrifice growth and even to roll back wages as the price of preserving America's old industrial base. The superstructures of industry-wide management, dominated by the largest and most entrenched firms within each industry, have joined in coalition with organized labor to lobby—successfully—for protection against imports (see Chapter IX).

And America's social welfare and employment policies continue to seek stability rather than social change, thereby relegating the poor to permanent poverty and making the prospect of economic change particularly threatening to everyone whose economic well-being depends on older industries. Failing to adapt to skill-intensive labor implies, by default, an adaptation to dead-end labor (see Chapter X).

The shift has been slow and painful because America is simply not organized for economic change. Its organizations are based on stability rather than on adaptability. The extraordinary success of high-volume, standardized production during the half century of the management era has left America a legacy of economic inflexibility. The institutional heritage of our past success now imperils our future.

VIII
PAPER
ENTREPRENEURIALISM

1.

During America's management era industrial firms prospered by producing ever longer runs of standard goods, at ever lower unit costs. Managers were judged and rewarded by their skill in applying professional principles to plan and monitor this process. But as competitive advantage in high-volume, standardized production progressively shifts toward the newly developed and developing countries, and as competition among advanced countries has come to turn less on scale or the static efficiency of machine production than on skilled workers and organizational adaptability, America's professional managers have found themselves in a difficult bind. Unable to accommodate the institutional changes required for flexible-system production, they have sought ways to maintain or increase their firms' profits while avoiding the cost and risk of investing in fundamentally new products or processes.

Managers have indeed adapted by innovating. But the innovations have not been technological or institutional. Rather, they have been based on accounting, tax avoidance, financial management, mergers, acquisitions, and litigation. They have been innovations on paper. Gradually, over the past fifteen years, America's professional managers have become paper entrepreneurs.

Paper entrepreneurialism is the bastard child of scientific management. It employs the mechanisms and symbols developed to direct and monitor high-volume production, but it involves an even more radical separation between planning and production. It is a version of scientific management grown so extreme that it has lost all connection with the actual workplace. Its strategies involve the manipulation of rules and numbers that in principle represent real assets and products but that in fact generate profits primarily by the cleverness with which they are employed.

At its most pernicious, paper entrepreneurialism involves little more than imposing losses on others for the sake of short-term profits for the firm. The "others" are often taxpayers who end up subsidizing firms that creatively reduce their tax liability. The "others" are sometimes certain of the firms' shareholders, who end up indirectly subsidizing other shareholders. Occasionally the "others" are unlucky investors, consumers, or the shareholders of other firms. Because paper gains are always at someone else's expense, paper entrepreneurialism can be a ruthless game. It can also be fascinating and lucrative for those who play it well. It therefore attracts some of our best minds and most talented citizens. But it does not create new wealth. It merely rearranges industrial assets. And it has hastened our collective decline.

2.

When the management era began to collapse in the mid-1960's, professional managers, seeking to limit the damage, turned to the tools at hand. The ideology of management control was so deeply ingrained that the instinctive reaction of professional managers was typically to define, even more precisely than before, the rules and working relationships within their firms, seeking thereby to solidify their control. But because the environment was changing so rapidly—with the entrance of new foreign competitors, new products, new manufacturing processes, and the opening of new global markets—the rules and controls had to be extraordinarily elaborate. They became yet more intricate as the pace of change accelerated.

To coordinate the increasingly complex tasks of production specialists with the tasks of specialists concerned with individual product lines and with those in particular marketing territories, managers introduced the complex organization and techniques of matrix management, through which employees reported to several different managers for different dimensions of their work. (An employee engaged in, say, the marketing of refrigerators in South America would report to three managers—in charge of marketing, refrigerators, and South American sales, respectively.) When the matrices became too complicated, resulting in endless conflicts and confusion, organizational development consultants were called in to design and coordinate project teams. When this team structure had so muddled personal accountability that employees began to engage in buck-passing and bureaucratic gamesmanship, managers added still more controls: budget reviews, computer-based management information systems, narrative reports on operations, monthly "flash" reports, formal goal-setting systems, and detailed performance evaluation and incentive compensation systems.

These ever more elaborate systems of managerial control brought with them additional layers of staff to devise the new rules and procedures, to design and monitor systems of performance appraisal, to referee the inevitable confusion over responsibility, and to mediate conflicts. Between 1965 and 1975 the ratio of staff positions to production workers in American manufacturing companies increased from 35 per 100 to 41 per 100. In certain industries the jump has been even more dramatic. In electrical machinery the ratio increased from 46 staff jobs for each 100 production jobs to 56 per 100; in nonelectrical machinery, from 43 to 59; in chemicals, from 66 to 78. Companies with 2,500 or more employees have had a higher proportion of staff positions relative to production workers (44 per 100 in 1972) than firms with under 500 employees (32 per 100). The largest companies have the highest ratio of staff to production workers. At AT&T, for example, the ratio went from 72 per 100 in 1958 to 99 per 100 in 1976.[1] By 1979 half the employees of Intel—the microprocessor manufacturer—were engaged in administration. When an engineer wanted a mechanical pencil, processing the order required twelve pieces of paper and 95 administrative steps. It took 364 steps to hire a new employee.[2]

This sudden proliferation of staff positions within U.S. firms is particularly striking by comparison to other nations. In the typical Japanese factory, for example, foremen report directly to plant managers. The foreman in the typical American factory must report through three additional layers of management. Until very recently the Ford Motor Company had four more levels of managers between the factory worker and the company chairman than did Toyota.

Bureaucratic layering of this sort is costly, and not only because of the extra salaries and benefits that must be paid. Layers of staff also make the firm more rigid, less able to make quick decisions and adjust rapidly to new opportunities and problems. In the traditional scientifically managed, high-volume enterprise, novel situations are regarded as exceptions, requiring new rules and procedures and the judgments of senior managers. But because there are now so many layers of staff specialists and managers, the enterprise cannot accommodate novelty.

The typical sequence now runs something like this: A salesman hears from a customer that the firm's latest bench drill cannot accommodate bits for drilling a recently developed hard plastic. The customer suggests a modified coupling adapter and an additional speed setting. The salesman thinks the suggestion makes sense but has no authority to pursue it directly. Following procedures, the salesman passes the idea on to the sales manager, who finds it promising and drafts a memo to the marketing vice-president. The marketing vice-president also likes the idea, so he raises it in an executive meeting of all the vice-presidents. The executive committee agrees to modify the drill. The senior product manager then asks the head of the research department to form a task force to evaluate the product opportunity and to design a new coupling and variable-speed mechanism.

The task force consists of representatives from sales, marketing, accounting, and engineering. The engineers are interested in the elegance of the design. The manufacturing department insists on modifications requiring only minor retooling. The salespeople want a drill that will do what customers need it to do. The finance people worry about the costs of producing it. The marketing people want a design that can be advertised and distributed efficiently and sold at a competitive price. The meetings are difficult since each task force member wants to claim credit for future success but avoid blame for any possible failure. After months of meetings the research manager presents the group's findings to the executive committee. It approves the new design. Each department then works out a detailed plan for its role in bringing out the new product, and the modified drill goes into production.

If there are no production problems, the customer receives word that he can order a drill for working hard plastics two years after he first discussed it with the salesman. In the meantime, a Japanese, West German, or South Korean firm has already designed, produced, and delivered a hard-plastics drill.

As the bureaucratic gap between corporate officials and production workers continues to widen, the enterprise becomes more dependent on quantifiable data and less sensitive to qualitative information. Professional managers concentrate on month-to-month profit figures, data on growth in sales, and return on investment. Less quantifiable information—product quality, worker morale, and customer satisfaction—may be at least as important to the firm's long-term success but cannot be conveyed upward efficiently through the layers of staff. Even if such qualitative information occasionally works its way to senior executives without becoming too distorted in the process, it is often still ignored. Information like this does not invite quick decisions and crisp directives. It is frequently too "soft" to allow decisive action; it may be vague and impressionistic or anecdotal; it may hint at much deeper problems.

Even quantifiable information becomes distorted as it moves up the corporate hierarchy because it must be summarized and interpreted. Distortions arise whenever information must be relayed through a long sequence of people. (The practice of relaying messages along the trenches in World War I once resulted, so the story goes, in the message "Send reinforcements—we are going to advance" reaching headquarters as "Send three and four pence—we are going to a dance."[3]) Distortions also occur intentionally. Lower-level managers, dependent on senior managers for rewards and promotions, naturally want to highlight good news and suppress bad news. In reporting their costs, for example, they may seek to outmaneuver the accounting department (which determines how overhead costs are distributed among units) by shifting some overhead to another unit. Since lower-level managers are competing with other managers for scarce investment resources, they are likely to present overly optimistic estimates for the projects they seek to fund. Their forecasts may underestimate costs, overestimate market demand, and leave out certain expenses altogether. The planning systems that process these estimates become arenas for organizational gamesmanship.

For all these reasons, professional managers at the tops of American firms have come to preside over a symbolic economy. The systems of management control which they initiated in the mid-1960's in efforts to maintain profitability have become more intricate and elaborate as the global market has grown less predictable, requiring additional layers of managers and staff specialists. While the bureaucratic distance between senior managers and production workers has increased, the rules and numbers in which senior managers deal have become more and more disconnected from the everyday processes of production and distorted by excessive reliance on "hard" data, by communication failures, and by gamesmanship. Lacking the familiarity with operations that would give them more concrete tools than these disembodied symbols, professional managers at the tops of our large business enterprises have turned—by necessity—toward the manipulation of rules and numbers as the primary means of maintaining the profitability of their firms.

Paper entrepreneurialism relies on financial and legal virtuosity. Through shrewd maneuvering, accounting and tax rules can be finessed, and the numbers on balance sheets and tax returns manipulated, giving the appearance of greater or lesser earnings. Assets can be rearranged on paper to improve cash flow or to defer payments. And threatened lawsuits or takeovers can be used to extract concessions from other players. Huge profits are generated by these ploys. They are the most imaginative and daring ventures in the American economy. But they do not enlarge the economic pie; they merely reassign the slices.

3.

The conglomerate enterprise is one manifestation of paper entrepreneurialism. Before the mid-1960's American business enterprises generally expanded only into lines of business related to their original products. They entered markets appropriate to their managerial, technical, and marketing capabilities, where they could achieve real competitive advantage.

The conglomerate enterprises that were born after the mid-1960's—multibusiness giants, like Gulf & Western, LTV, Textron, Litton, United Technologies, Northwest Industries, and ITT—are entirely different.

They have grown by acquiring existing enterprises, often in wholly unrelated fields. Gulf & Western, for example, owns Paramount Pictures, Consolidated Cigar (America's largest cigarmaker), Kayser-Roth (one of America's largest apparel makers), APS (an auto parts supplier), one of America's largest zinc mines, Madison Square Garden, Simon & Schuster (publishers), Simmons (mattresses), the Miss Universe and Miss U.S.A. pageants, a large sugarcane plantation, four insurance companies, and Oscar de la Renta fashions. ITT (the world's eighth largest corporation) owns Wonder Bread, Sheraton Hotels, Hartford Insurance, Bobbs-Merrill Publishing, and Burpee Lawn and Garden Products.

Conglomerate enterprises rarely, if ever, bring any relevant managerial, technical, or marketing skills to the enterprises they acquire, for the simple reason that they have no direct knowledge of these unrelated businesses. Their expertise is in law and finance. Their relationship to their far-flung subsidiaries is that of an investor. Indeed, many conglomerates function almost exactly like mutual funds, except that the staff at conglomerate headquarters presumably has somewhat more complete information about their subsidiaries than mutual fund advisers have about the companies in their portfolios. Some conglomerates have come a step closer to mutual funds by becoming minority owners of a variety of other companies. Gulf & Western actually maintains a $536 million portfolio of stocks in sixteen companies; both the Reliance Group and Sharon Steel maintain minority positions in twenty or so companies at any time. Financial advisers within conglomerates like these decide which stocks to purchase or sell according to precisely the same criteria that advisers to mutual funds employ. The conglomerate spreads the risk of investment over its entire stock portfolio, just as the mutual fund does. And like the mutual fund, the conglomerate does not create new wealth or render production more efficient. It merely allocates capital.

The paper advantages of conglomeration extend beyond speculation and risk spreading, however. Whenever a firm's stock market price falls below its book value (the assumed market value of the firm's total assets, if they were sold bit by bit), another company can post significant gains on its balance sheet simply by acquiring the undervalued firm and consolidating the two sets of books. Thus, the acquiring firm's earnings increase, as if by magic. As the American economy has declined, the stock of many companies has fallen to less than book value in this way. The stock market is not being irrational; companies like these are probably worth more disassembled than they are as continuing operations. But conglomeration does not redeploy these assets; it merely displays them more attractively on a new, consolidated balance sheet.

If the acquired firm has lost money in recent years, so much the better. The conglomerate that acquires it can use the losses to reduce its tax liability. Even if the assets of the acquired firm are purchased for more than their stated value in its books, the game is still on—the acquiring company has a higher basis for depreciating its new assets for tax purposes. (The 1982 tax law has made this route somewhat more treacherous.) U.S. Steel's purchase of the Marathon Oil Company, for example, saved the steelmaker about $500 million in taxes in the first year and will save at least $1 billion more over the productive life of Marathon's Yates oil field since tax laws let the oil field be valued for tax purposes at a higher cost than the property represented in Marathon's books. Because U.S. Steel can take new depletion deductions against this high-valued property, the Yates reserves are worth far more to it than they were to Marathon, which had already extracted what it could of the oil field's tax-deduction potential. The field's tax benefits were renewable through transfer, even if the oil was not.

Conglomeration has been proceeding at a breakneck pace. In 1972, 33 percent of the employees of America's manufacturing companies were involved in lines of business totally unrelated to their companies' primary businesses. In 1977 American companies spent $22 billion acquiring one another. By 1979 they were spending $43.5 billion. That year sixteen firms, each worth more than $500 million, were gobbled up, including CIT Financial ($1.35 billion, purchased by RCA), and Reliance Electric ($1.16 billion, by Exxon). All records were shattered in 1981, when $82 billion were spent on acquisitions. Du Pont paid a staggering $7.5 billion for Conoco; Fluor, $2.7 billion for St. Joe Minerals; Gulf Oil, $325 million for Kemmerer Coal; and U.S. Steel, $5.9 billion for a controlling interest in Marathon. The pace continued in 1982.[4]

Despite widely advertised concern over a capital shortage and calls for corporate tax breaks to spur new investment, firms bent on aquisition have seldom been deterred by price. Corporations have been paying premiums of 50 to 100 percent over market value for the stock of the companies they seek to acquire. Even during the "go-go-years" of the late 1960's, when "funny money" fueled a short-lived merger explosion, premiums rarely exceeded 25 percent.

All this has been accompanied by some of the heaviest bank borrowings in history. Du Pont borrowed $3.9 billion to purchase Conoco, at an interest rate close to 20 percent. Texaco negotiated a loan of $5.5 billion from an international consortium of banks, led by Chase Manhattan. Fluor Corporation, having borrowed $1 billion to buy St. Joe Minerals, poured virtually its entire cash flow for the first half of 1981 into interest payments.

Before 1965 "unfriendly" takeovers were almost unheard of. Since then they have become an important aspect of paper entrepreneurialism. Fear of a takeover bid haunts America's corporate boardrooms. In a 1981 survey of chief financial officers in America's 480 largest industrial firms, 49 percent thought that their companies were vulnerable to takeovers; even of the remaining group, 38 percent said that they had developed formal plans aimed at thwarting takeover bids. The fear is well founded. Of the 249 firms that have faced unfriendly takeover attempts within the last three years, only 52 have successfully withstood the assault and remained independent.[5]

The fear of takeover has generated an array of paper entrepreneurial strategies. Many targets of takeover bids, fleeing acquisition by companies unfriendly to their present managers, are running into the arms of other, more congenial firms. When WUI, an international telecommunications firm, learned that the Continental Telephone Corporation was on its trail, it sought to be acquired instead by Xerox. Some target companies seek immunity by themselves buying companies in the would-be acquirers' own industries, so that antitrust laws block the acquisition attempt. Daylin, Inc., defending itself against W. R. Grace's recent tender offer, sought to purchase Narco Scientific, Inc.—a maker of equipment in a product line so similar to Grace's that the latter would be barred from taking over Daylin. One of the more bizarre—and expensive—defense strategies is for a target company simply to reduce its cash reserves and thus become less attractive to potential predators. This may explain the J. Ray McDermott Company's recent $758 million acquisition of Babcock & Wilcox, and the Kennecott Copper Corporation's $567 million purchase of Carborundum.

Increasingly, target companies are paying would-be acquirers high premiums to buy back blocks of stock that the acquirers have amassed. The acquirer says, in effect, "I now have eight or nine percent of your stock. I am not going after your company. But unless you buy the block from me at a premium, I know five or six other companies that are interested and could take you over." This is the corporate equivalent of a demand for ransom. Paper entrepreneurs are generating large earnings from such threats. Even if the target company refuses to pay the ransom, its stock typically shoots up when Wall Street learns that a takeover may be afoot. Thus, the paper entrepreneur can generate earnings simply by selling the block of stock in the open market. Bendix recently made $75 million after taxes by buying and then selling back 20 percent of the outstanding stock of Asarco. Gulf & Western announced in September 1981 that it had made open-market purchases of large blocks of stock in two companies: a 7.4 percent interest in Oxford Industries, Inc., and a 10.4 percent interest in the Robertshaw Controls Company. Two months later both Oxford and Robertshaw bought back their shares, for a total of $2.1 million more than Gulf & Western had paid for them.[6]

The wheeling and dealing are sometimes Byzantine. The Kennecott Copper Corporation recently bought back (for $168 million in cash) shares that Curtiss-Wright had amassed in Kennecott, giving Curtiss-Wright a premium of $10 a share over market value. Six weeks later Kennecott fell into the arms of Standard Oil of Ohio, which, in a $1.7 billion deal, acquired it at $62 per share, up $27 from what Kennecott had just paid Curtiss-Wright. In another recent battle the Bendix Corporation made a surprise $1.7 billion takeover bid for Martin-Marietta, only to have Martin-Marietta retaliate with a $1.5 billion offer to purchase a controlling interest in Bendix. When Bendix appeared to be winning the fray, Martin-Marietta enlisted the help of Harry Gray, the master conglomerator who heads the United Technologies Corporation. United Technologies promptly put in its own $1.5 billion bid for Bendix, agreeing to divide the spoils with Martin-Marietta. Faced with a stalemate in which each of the companies would own controlling shares in the other, Bendix finally turned to the Allied Corporation to bail Bendix out by merging with it.

The largest gains for conglomerates, however, lie in their potential for opening access to ready cash at low or no cost, while simultaneously avoiding or deferring income taxes. Financial conglomerates offer particularly rewarding possibilities along these lines. Consider, for example, Baldwin-United, a company that until 1968 was known for the Baldwin piano, which it had been making since 1891. But piano sales were growing slowly, and the pressure from foreign competition was increasing. So Baldwin purchased a bank, twelve insurance companies, a savings and loan company, some mortgage banking companies, America's largest mortgage insurance company, and its two largest trading stamp companies. Many of these acquisitions have been cheap sources of cash. The insurance companies have provided low-cost funds in the form of premiums; the savings and loan company has brought in deposits at low passbook rates; the mortgage banking and servicing companies have transferred billions of dollars in mortgage and real estate tax payments from borrowers to lenders while holding the funds for up to several weeks in the process; and the trading stamp companies sell stamps to merchants, who give them to customers, who are unlikely to redeem them for months or years, if ever. Baldwin has further enlarged its earnings by avoiding or deferring taxes on these cash flows. Its mortgage banking acquisition had unrealized losses in its loan portfolio, which the company then used against its overall earnings; it also deducts the commissions it pays to its brokers in the year paid, occasionally generating large tax losses. With these ample deductions, Baldwin has been able to redeem the bonds that its mortgage insurance company purchased, with tax impunity. As a result of all these financial and tax ploys, the firm's return on equity increased from 13 percent to 31 percent between 1968 and 1980.[7] In 1982, however, the bubble burst, and Baldwin faced imminent bankruptcy.

Other companies have followed suit. The Xerox Corporation, suffering from intense Japanese competition in its copier business, recently paid $1.6 billion in cash and stock for Crum and Forster, a property and casualty insurance company. Crum and Forster's main attraction was the tax write-offs of underwriting losses, which gave it an annual average tax rate of 12 to 14 percent; Xerox had paid a 38 percent tax rate in 1981. The new acquisition thereby lets Xerox accept its weakened position in the copier business with less anxiety, as tax losses shield its balance sheet. Following a similar strategy, the American Can Company has been moving out of packaging and into financial services, culminating with the purchases last year of three major insurance companies.

Conglomerates serve no useful financial purpose. Investors who wanted to buy into a particular bundle of industries could simply have bought stocks separately. American investors gain nothing from having the bundle prepackaged in the form of a diversified conglomerate. Indeed, conglomerates undermine the efficiency of America's capital market by eliminating investors' options to buy into Bobbs-Merrill alone, for example, without taking stock in all the rest of ITT's hodgepodge of businesses.

Nor do conglomerates serve any useful industrial purpose. Unlike earlier multidivisional firms, which featured some complementarity among operations, modern conglomerates are generally little concerned with the actual economic functions of the various subsidiaries, beyond the interest a landlord might take in a sharecropper's labors.

Nor do they benefit employees. When one of a conglomerate's businesses begins to falter, only capital assets are salvaged and redeployed. Workers typically are left to fend for themselves.

Paper entrepreneurialism does not rely solely on acquisitions, of course. Every month or so another innovative paper ploy is unveiled. For example, many companies are now engaging in an expensive and financially empty exchange of new stock for old bonds. It works like this: A company that sold long-term bonds when interest rates were lower— thus, so was the yield, or "coupon," the bond had to offer—still carries the debt on its books at the original face value, even though the outstanding bonds are in fact being traded on the market at a discount since they yield less per dollar of face value than newer financial assets. This debt bothers the firm's managers, who want the balance sheet to seem as unencumbered by indebtedness as possible.

As a result, investment brokers have gone into the business of buying up old bonds at their (low) market value and offering to return them to the issuing firm in exchange for new shares of common stock. By buying back its old bonds, the company can claim to have "retired" a chunk of debt based on the financially irrelevant face value of the bonds. Thus, managers are willing to pay the broker handsomely for engineering the swap.

The company makes a precisely offsetting trade—a certain market value of stock for an equal market value of bonds. The cost: millions in brokers' fees and premiums. The only result: Some gullible investors may be led to believe that the company has suddenly become less burdened by debt and therefore more valuable. The ruse is tax-free, with the exchange of stock for bonds treated as a nontaxable corporate reorganization so long as the broker handles the mechanics. Since August 1981 more than 100 such exchanges have swept some $1.8 billion in debt from corporate balance sheets. Even U.S. Steel managed to use the ploy to report a profit for the depressed second quarter of 1982, despite sizable losses in its steel business. Like other gimmicks, this one will go out of fashion in a year or two, when investors and the Internal Revenue Service catch on, and another innovation will replace it.

A similar maneuver called defeasance lets companies cheaply erase old debts without paying off a single bondholder. A company buys old, discounted government securities, puts them into a trust account, and pledges the income to meet obligations on its own old, discounted bonds. The old debt is proudly declared paid off. Here again, the firm exploits the ambiguity of "value"—face value versus market value—to try to fool investors. Like the stock swap, equal value is traded for equal value, and the lower debt levels or increased profits that firms announce are purely illusory. Morgan Guaranty Trust has engineered defeasance deals for fifteen companies since 1977. Exxon "increased" its earnings by $130 million in the second quarter of 1982, while Kellogg declared paper profits of eight cents a share on defeasance transactions. (In mid-1982 the Financial Accounting Standards Board declared a moratorium on defeasance deals while it considered whether to ban them.)

Paper entrepreneurs also display their virtuosity in "creative" accounting. Many firms increase profits by adopting more liberal bookkeeping methods for depreciation, investment tax credits, and interest costs incurred during construction. They also redistribute income and expenses from good years to bad or recognize profits in advance of sales. Through such techniques of earnings management, firms manipulate their financial statements to create the impression of greater earnings than they have actually achieved.

During the late 1960's and early 1970's, as corporate balance sheets began to show the damage of lagging sales and mounting inventories, companies developed an array of practices to inflate their earnings, including rainy-day reserves and off-the-books financing. After tighter accounting rules curbed these highly publicized abuses in the mid-1970's, the sleight of hand had to become more sophisticated. In 1978, for example, when slumping car sales began to push the Chrysler Corporation into the red, forcing the automaker to halt production at many plants and slash its dividends by 60 percent, the company still managed to project a fourth-quarter profit. Thanks to a little-noticed actuarial adjustment, Chrysler merely changed the assumed rate of return on its employee pension portfolio to 7 percent from 6 percent, reducing pension costs and adding about $50 million to its profits. The alteration was likely to escape the eyes of analysts and auditors, who are seldom trained in pension matters. Chrysler did nothing illegal. Indeed, it disclosed in a footnote to its annual report that it had made the actuarial change, although it did not state any figures.[8]

Other methods of "earnings management" abound: showing certain transactions as collateral borrowings rather than as sales; overstating or understating inventories; failing to account fully for the effect of inflation on the value of inventories or profits; overstating the value of goodwill gained from a merger or acquisition; and understating the price paid for an acquisition (GE paid about $2 billion worth of stock to acquire Utah International in 1976, but pooling of interest accounting rules let GE show a price of only $548 million on its balance sheet; Utah International's $196 million profit in 1977, of course, looked much better on $548 million than it would have on $2 billion[9]).

None of these ploys is illegal. Nor—with the possible exception of defeasance—do they violate generally accepted accounting principles, which give firms wide latitude in reporting their earnings. Given the complexity of modern business practices and the uniqueness of each firm, more rigid accounting rules might actually lead to greater distortions. And that is the point: The set of symbols developed to represent real assets has lost the link with any actual productive activity. Finance has progressively evolved into a sector all its own, only loosely connected to industry. This disconnectedness turns business executives into paper entrepreneurs—forced to outsmart other participants or to be themselves outsmarted.

The manipulation of symbols takes many forms. At its most crass, it has become an exercise in public relations. During the past fifteen years corporations have invested increasing sums in image advertising, and researchers have found such advertising campaigns to have had a significant positive effect on stock prices. W. R. Grace's 1980 television campaign, for example, extolled the company's business and financial attributes. After the commercial had run in test markets for thirteen weeks, studies showed that the public had a greater familiarity with the company and gave it a higher approval rating than before; Grace's stock price rose impressively.[10] Some image advertising campaigns have been extraordinarily expensive. In 1979 Gulf & Western took out the most elaborate print advertisement in history—sixty-four pages in *Time* magazine covering the company's entire annual report. The cost: $3.3 million. The Mobil Oil Company's annual "public affairs" budget is $21 million.

Indeed, over the last fifteen years corporate public relations has become one of America's growth industries. Company annual reports have grown more lavish. E. F. Hutton Group's seventy-six-page report for 1981 offers full-page photos of executives posing in libraries and drawing rooms. The embossed cover portrays the investment company's chairman and president standing in an ornate entrance hall with marble floor and chandeliers. The production costs of annual reports for America's largest companies now average $3 apiece.[11]

As elaborate paper transactions crowd America's financial markets, their proper role—allocating capital—has become at least in part a matter of public relations. When Rory F. McFarland, founder and president of Advanced Energy Technology, sought funding for his new "antifriction" gear, he hired the huge public relations concern of Hill and Knowlton to issue press releases.

International trade has multiplied the opportunities for paper entrepreneurialism. Companies speculate on changes in the values of international currencies. (Two weeks before the peso's big devaluation in the summer of 1982, Coca-Cola increased its Mexican subsidiary's debt by 30 percent; the loan can now be repaid in cheaper pesos.) They set up paper "domestic international sales corporations," through which they indefinitely defer the payment of U.S. taxes on foreign earnings. They allocate profits to foreign subsidiaries in countries like the Netherlands Antilles, where taxes are very low. Du Pont has established in Switzerland a "distribution" subsidiary into which profits from other subsidiaries as far off as Australia and South Africa have been channeled. The drug companies Schering-Plough and Abbott Laboratories both allocated most of their worldwide 1977 profits to tax-free Puerto Rico. (The ruse gave Abbott a 285 percent return on its Puerto Rican assets.) Other U.S. companies have retained an estimated $6 billion in untaxed profits there.[12]

There is also, of course, straightforward speculation. As late as 1970, for example, only 12.4 million commodity futures were traded in the United States, and 90 percent of these were in agricultural commodities. The annual volume has now reached 101 million contracts, an eightfold increase. The single most active contract traded is the Chicago Board of Trade's Treasury Bond contract, and approximately half the industry-wide volume is in contracts for nonagricultural commodities. The volume of financial futures alone is now almost double the finance industry's entire volume in 1970.[13]

Of course, many traders are using the futures market as a legitimate "hedge" against unexpected change in the prices of commodities or financial instruments important to their businesses. But trading in futures also invites a substantial amount of pure finagling, as evidenced by the Hunt brothers' silver-buying spree and the bursting of the silver bubble in March 1980. In February 1982 the Kansas City Board of Trade launched a new trading instrument—the stock index future, pegged to a composite index of stock market prices. The Chicago Mercantile Exchange and the New York Commodity Exchange soon followed with their own stock index futures. The Commodity Futures Trading Commission is now considering applications to trade futures on fifteen additional common stock groupings and even to trade options on stock index futures. These new instruments turn stocks into "commodities" and let speculators play with stocks under the accommodating rules of the commodity markets instead of the more stringent requirements of the stock exchanges. For example, margin requirements are much lower for commodities than for stocks. The Federal Reserve has imposed a 50 percent rule for equity margins; an investor must put up cash to cover one-half the value of the stock he intends to purchase. But the Kansas City Board of Trade is setting an analogous "consumer deposit" of only 10 percent. Options on stock index futures will require even less cash—just a relatively small premium for the right to buy or sell the underlying index future.

Here, too, lurk profitable tax avoidance schemes. A few years ago (before the IRS cracked down) trading in futures often involved a lucrative maneuver known as the tax straddle, in which an investor purchased a futures contract and simultaneously sold an identical contract. Obviously the investor would make money on one of the contracts and lose the same amount on the other. But the loss could be deducted immediately from taxable income, while the profit could be deferred indefinitely. Similar but more sophisticated strategies are now being actively promoted by the "commodities advisory services" that have sprung up in recent years.

All this paper entrepreneurialism is played out against a background of mounting lawsuits, for the obvious reason that losers do not like to lose. Professional managers in companies targeted for takeover are suing their predators. Shareholders are suing managers. Acquiring companies are suing the officers of the companies they acquired. Purchasers of futures contracts are suing sellers who cannot meet the payments. The number of business lawsuits stemming from breach of contract, antitrust, or alleged "wasting" of corporate assets has increased fourfold since 1965.[14] In what is becoming a typical step in the asset rearrangement game, Borden filed suit against the Acton Corporation, charging that Acton had overstated the value of the inventory, receivables, and plants of some of its snack food operations Borden had bought for $11.6 million in 1980. In a recent antitrust action MCI was awarded $1.8 billion in damages from AT&T—an amount that dwarfed MCI's net income that year of $13.3 million and was three times the total revenues it had earned since its incorporation in 1969. The lawsuit was much more important to MCI than were its products. And nearly 25 percent of Bendix's pretax income in 1981 came from a favorable legal judgment.

Paper litigation is becoming as complex as the paper transactions that underlie it. Nearly six months after Exxon bought the Reliance Electric Company for $1.24 billion in 1979, Reliance had to recall faulty commercial and industrial circuit breakers that had been manufactured by its Federal Pacific Electric Company unit. Reliance had itself acquired that unit from UV Industries for $345 million earlier in 1979. Lost production and lost sales attributed to the recall reduced Reliance's 1980 profits by about $80 million. In June 1980 Reliance filed suit against UV Industries Liquidating Trust, Inc. (successor to UV Industries, which had been liquidated three months before) and against the Sharon Steel Corporation, which had purchased all of UV's assets and assumed its liabilities. The suit alleges that UV failed to disclose that its financial results were tainted over a period of years by inadequate inspections of its circuit breakers. Meanwhile, Sharon Steel is embroiled in litigation with two New York banks and twenty institutional investors that are trying to force the redemption of $130 million of low-interest UV bonds. Sharon is suing to be allowed to replace UV as debtor and thereby reap the capital gain. The outcome of all these actions is certain in only two respects: Some money will change hands, and no new wealth will be created.

4.

One must be clear about the problem of paper entrepreneurialism in America. Paper entrepreneurialism does not directly use up economic resources. Assets merely change hands. Nor, of course, are all paper transactions wasteful. Every economy needs some paper entrepreneurs to help allocate capital efficiently among product entrepreneurs.

The problem is that that paper entrepreneurialism is supplanting product entrepreneurialism as the most dynamic and innovative business in the American economy. Paper entrepreneurs provide nothing of tangible use. For an economy to maintain its health, entrepreneurial rewards should flow primarily to products, not to paper.

Ours is becoming a symbolic economy in which resources circulate endlessly among giant corporations, investment bankers, and their lawyers, but little new is produced. Financial resources are kept liquid in order to meet the next margin call, to enter the next position, or to exploit the next takeover opportunity. They are not applied in earnest to any single undertaking, for fear that they will soon be needed for something else. Investments in plant and equipment have been incremental and short-term. There is scant investment in new products or processes, for the simple reason that longer-term endeavors tie up resources for too long. In 1979 the RCA Corporation complained publicly that it lacked the $200 million that would be needed to develop a video cassette recorder, although recorders are the fastest-growing appliance of the decade. But RCA had no qualms about paying $1.2 billion to buy a lackluster finance company that same year. Socal's 1980 bid for Amax included a cash payment that would have entirely consumed the $1 billion surplus with which Socal had begun the year. Only after Amax spurned the offer did Socal decide to spend the surplus on new oil leases instead. In 1979, after the chairmanship of U.S. Steel had gone to David Roderick (whom *The New York Times* described as even "less a creature of the mill than most of the top executives, having been groomed entirely on the financial side of the company"), the company decided to scrap its plan for building a new steel plant. Instead, it began building a cash reserve to acquire some other, more promising company, like Marathon Oil.

While business leaders are otherwise engaged, America's industrial base remains wedded to high-volume, standardized production. Flexible-system production does not fit well into large conglomerate enterprises. The enterprises are too diffuse and fragmented to generate team spirit, too unwieldy and bureaucratic to accommodate novel approaches to new problems. Real product entrepreneurs bridle at the red tape. Employees are discouraged from choosing unorthodox solutions. It is often difficult, from the mire of conglomerate headquarters, to identify unique customer needs. Big companies also tend to wait for markets to develop; they are not equipped to pursue successfully the markets that do not yet exist.[15] Exxon's plunge into the "office of the future" has been an unmitigated disaster. The company is losing money at a rate that would bankrupt almost anyone else—in 1980 alone its office equipment division lost $150 million on sales of $270 million. Industrial giants like Monsanto, Ford, and Sylvania, which tried several years ago to develop their own commercial semiconductor operations, failed miserably and withdrew from this rapidly changing market. Other large companies—RCA, TRW, Westinghouse—have not done much better.

Perhaps the largest cost is in human talent. Today's corporate executives spend an increasing portion of their days fending off takeovers, finding companies to acquire, conferring with their financial and accounting specialists, and responding to discovery in lawsuits, instead of attending to their products. Indeed, approximately 40 percent of the chief executive officers of America's largest firms have backgrounds in law or finance and rose to their present positions from company legal or financial staffs. This is in sharp contrast with the past. As recently as 1950 only 13 percent of America's key chief executive officers had legal or financial backgrounds. Most had come up through the ranks from marketing, engineering, or sales.[16]

The rise of the legal and financial executive officer parallels America's decline. In the late 1960's, for example, two of the nation's three major automakers decided to place their destinies in the hands of financial men. Lynn Townsend was picked to cure Chrysler of its financial ills; at General Motors, Frederick Donner was selected to show the company how to use its huge stash of working capital. The same is true in others of America's central industries. Between 1972 and 1978 private business services in law, finance, and accounting absorbed 9 percent of all the hours of work added to the American economy; if the business services which the firms added internally by expanding their legal and financial staffs are included, the figure is approximately 12 percent.[17]

Paper entrepreneurialism now preoccupies some of America's best minds, attracts many of its most talented graduates, employs some of its most creative and original thinking, and spurs some of its most energetic wheeling and dealing. Increasingly over the last fifteen years the most sought-after jobs among business school graduates have been in finance and consulting, where the specialty is rearranging assets and shuffling corporate boxes—and from which bright young MBAs have their best shot at becoming corporate executives. Only 3 percent of Harvard Business School's 1981 graduates took jobs in production and 18.6 percent in sales and marketing, while 21.6 percent went into finance. Young people seeking quick affluence without much risk have turned to the practice of law, where America's highest-paying entry-level jobs are found. In a recent survey, 24 percent of Harvard freshmen said they were planning a career in law; only 7 percent were going into science. In 1982 New York City's largest law firms were paying their recruits, fresh out of law school, salaries of $48,000 per year. In 1980 the median income for partners in New York's largest law firms was $242,685, up 50 percent from 1975. Law firms can afford to pay these exorbitant salaries because legal fees keep rolling in.[18]

While America's graduate programs in law, finance, and accounting are booming, science and engineering programs are foundering. Since the mid-1960's law has been the nation's growth industry. Between 1940 and 1960 only about 1 American in 600 was a lawyer. But between 1971 and 1981 the number of practicing attorneys increased by 68 percent. The country now has more than 590,000 lawyers—1 for every 400 citizens. Over the same decade, however, there was only a 15 percent rise in the number of engineers and a 25 percent rise in the number of laborers. This is in sharp contrast with other industrialized nations. Only about 1 of every 10,000 citizens in Japan is trained in law, while 1 out of 25 Japanese citizens is trained in engineering or science.[19] More than 65 percent of all seats on the boards of Japanese companies are occupied by people trained as engineers; roughly the same percentage of seats on American boards is taken by people trained in law, finance, or accountancy.[20] Thus, in Japan many problems that arise in business are viewed as problems of engineering or science, for which technical solutions can be found. In present-day America the same problems are apt to be viewed as problems of law or finance, to be dodged through clever manipulation of rules or numbers.

Professional education in America is putting progressively more emphasis on the manipulation of symbols to the exclusion of other sorts of skills—how to collaborate with others, to work in teams, to speak foreign languages, to solve concrete problems—which are more relevant to the new competitive environment. And more and more, America's best students have turned to professions that allow them to continue attending to symbols, from quiet offices equipped with a telephone, telex, and a good secretary. The world of truly productive people, engaged in the untidy and difficult struggle with real production problems, is becoming alien to America's best and brightest.

The link between the rise of paper entrepreneurialism and America's economic decline is not a matter of strict cause and effect. Paper entrepreneurialism is a symptom of America's decline, both cause and consequence. It is a consequence in that paper profits are the only ones easily available to professional managers who sit isolated, atop organizations designed for a form of production that is no longer appropriate to America's place in the world economy. It is a cause only in the sense that the relentless drive for paper profits has diverted attention and resources away from the difficult job of transforming that productive base. It has retarded the transition that must occur and made change more difficult. Paper entrepreneurialism thus has a self-perpetuating quality which, if left unchecked, will drive the nation into further decline.

5.

Paper entrepreneurialism has an even more insidious side. The attitudes and frames of reference that have encouraged the rearrangement of industrial assets in the hopes of short-term gains have also encouraged the rearrangement of people, resulting in an increasing velocity of hirings, firings, and layoffs at all levels of American firms.

Insecurity reigns from the bottom rungs to the top offices of America's largest corporations. Companies that enter new lines of business typically are quick to hire new managers and employees but are cautious about investing in new plant and equipment, on the assumption that if the new venture fails, it is far easier to get rid of people than plant and equipment. Companies that are merged or acquired soon put together a new "team" at the top. (A recent survey shows that within one year of a major merger or takeover 32 percent of executives in the acquired firm leave their jobs.[21]) Many companies that have experienced declining earnings for several quarters are quick to "make heads roll" (in another survey, half the managers interviewed attested to personal difficulties with "anxiety" and "restlessness"; one-third complained of "unwarranted fears"[22]). It is hardly surprising, therefore, that each year, over the past six years, 15 to 25 percent of American executives have left their jobs; that the chief executive of the average U.S. firm has now been in office for fewer than five years; and that at any given time almost 30 percent of America's managers and 34 percent of its professional technicians have had résumés making the rounds.[23] One of America's fastest-growing service industries is executive recruitment, now involving 1,300 firms together employing more than 7,000 professional "headhunters."

America's executive suites have become centers of intrigue. The list of executives dismissed from top corporate posts in recent years reads like a *Who's Who* of America's managerial elite: Morgan Hunter served as president of Scott Paper from May 1979 to November 1980; Robert Swanson, president of Greyhound, from February 1980 to October 1980; George Arnold, president of Wheeling-Pittsburgh Steel, from October 1979 to August 1980; Jerome Filiciotto, president of Rohr Industries, from June 1978 to February 1980; James Mills, chairman of Sperry & Hutchinson, from April 1980 to November 1980; James Coles, president of the Imperial Corporation of America, from August 1979 to August 1980; Franklin Winnert, chief operating officer of Certain-Teed, from March 1979 to August 1980; O. E. Powers, president of McGraw-Edison, from January 1979 to August 1980. The Kaiser Steel Corporation's recent president, James Will, resigned after four months on the job, apparently as a result of uncertainty over a proposed buy-out by an investor group and an attractive job offer elsewhere; he was the company's eighth president in eight years. Roger Morley was suddenly let go as president of American Express after the widely publicized Amex attempt to take over

McGraw-Hill. The list goes on, the pace quickening in the last two years; Lyman Hamilton, Jr., let go at ITT; William Waltrip, at Pan American; John Backe, at CBS; Wilfred Corrigan, at Fairchild Camera.

Many of these firings have come suddenly, without warning, from disgruntled chairmen or powerful board members. "I know a coup when I see one," said Roy Ash, when he was abruptly ousted as chairman and chief executive of AM International last spring.[24] Occasionally the intrigue reaches deep into the company. One executive vice-president at RCA has a network of personnel managers all over the company (and the world) who report to him on other RCA executives. By keeping track of their expense accounts and such activities as the use of the corporate plane, this executive has built a power base that can make or break careers. His dossiers were instrumental in the board's decision to force out Robert Sarnoff as chairman in 1975 and in convincing another recent chairman to dismiss Maurice Valente as president of NBC.[25]

Since 1976 the rate of corporate firings has doubled. And these exiting executives increasingly have been replaced by executives who have left other firms rather than from within existing corporate staffs. Lee Iacocca, abruptly dismissed at Ford, was hired by Chrysler. Robert Abboud, fired as chairman of First Chicago after repeated rounds of public combat with vice-chairman Harvey Kapnick (who was dismissed simultaneously by the board), almost immediately became president of the Occidental Petroleum Corporation. John Nevin, shunted aside at Zenith, promptly signed on as president at Firestone Rubber.

Executives are circulating among America's largest firms at a velocity that rivals the exchange of paper assets. Fewer than 40 percent of the chief executive officers of the 500 largest industrial companies rose through the ranks of the companies they now head. The rest maneuvered through law firms, accounting firms, or other corporations on their way to the top.[26] GE once had on its payroll a dozen executives who now head other giant firms. The same is true of Ford. Edward Hennessey, Jr., chief executive of the Allied Corp., for example, has been employed by no fewer than six other large firms. He indicated in a recent interview that he learned about acquisitions at Textron, financial controls at ITT, international operations at Colgate-Palmolive, and marketing at Heublein. He went to United Technologies for operating experience and a crack at becoming chief executive but left in 1977 when Allied offered to make him chief executive even faster. The *Wall Street Journal* reports that Allied's recent decision to rescue Bendix from the jaws of United Technologies was likely to have been motivated, at least in part, by Hennessey's desire to get revenge on his former employer for thwarting his earlier ambitions.[27]

Short term management tenure does more damage to the economy than to executives' bank accounts. Fired executives are getting larger and larger settlements along with their pink slips. Amex agreed to keep Roger Morley on its payroll as a consultant for up to two years, an arrangement that could net him almost $300,000. CBS agreed to pay its dismissed chief executive, John Backe, everything due him on a contract that ran to 1983 —$2 million-plus. Indeed, more and more executives are obtaining termination agreements in advance of taking jobs in the first place. CBS reportedly agreed to pay its new president, Thomas Wyman, two years' salary, at $300,000 a year, if he is fired. Fifteen percent of the nation's 1,000 largest companies now have agreements, affectionately known as golden parachutes, specifically providing for continued compensation should the companies be taken over. In the fall of 1982, after United Technologies had made its $1.5 billion takeover bid for Bendix, the Bendix board issued "parachutes" to its top executives in the event that the company succumbed, totaling $16 million in salary and other benefits, including more than $4 million in severance pay for William Agee, the chairman of the board. [28]

Voluntary and involuntary turnover is also occurring at an increasing rate in middle management, and among technical specialists and unskilled workers. The average American holds ten different jobs before retirement. The number of years that an average worker stays put in one job has declined steadily, from 4.6 years in 1963 to 3.6 in 1980. One-third to one-half of all U.S. managerial and office workers leave their jobs each year. This is in marked contrast with companies in Western Europe, where the annual turnover rate averages no more than 12 percent, and in Japan, where the average is 6 percent.[29]

Rearranging employees is analogous to rearranging paper assets. Some such shuffling is useful and often necessary. But when undertaken on a wide scale, when it becomes the automatic response to changes in the firm's environment, it is disastrous. It has made American companies less rather than more adaptable to new systems of production. Like other aspects of paper entrepreneurialism, employee shuffling has served as a short-term substitute for the costly and difficult process of transforming the system of production. By replacing their managers in rapid-fire succession, firms can create the impression of vitality and change. This may help boost stock prices in the short run. But the new managers merely rearrange the same organizational boxes as the old; there is no real change. The firm's underlying decline proceeds apace. By the same token, a high velocity of firings, hirings, layoffs, and rehirings at the lower levels may enable the firm to adjust to short-term market fluctuations and appear to be more "dynamic," but it also serves as a deceptive palliative. It allows the firm to avoid undertaking more basic change. And it demoralizes everyone involved.

Managers who anticipate a short tenure with their firm unsurprisingly have little interest in long-term solutions to its basic problems. Their goal is to make the firm (and themselves) look as good as possible in the immediate future. A vicious circle sets in. Managers who know they will be judged by the standards of paper entrepreneurialism, if not beaten by a better player, resort to paper entrepreneurialism as a defensive measure.

Nor can managers who enter new companies with no direct knowledge of their products or production abilities be expected to contribute much to long-term product development. They would not know where to start. Their skills are in paper, not in product; that is how they made their reputations and why they were hired in the first place. The only general knowledge which they carry around in their heads, from one executive suite to another, concerns the manipulation of symbols and the abstract scrutiny of disembodied measures of firm performance. RCA has had four chief executive officers in the past seven years. Each has had a very different view of the company and the direction it should take. Robert Sarnoff sought to build a conglomerate around the electronics company he inherited. Sarnoff's successor, Anthony Conrad, emphasized satellite communications. The next, Edgar Griffiths, sought to squeeze more money out of operations; he tried to dismantle the conglomerate and replace it with five operating units and to move into financial services. None has been with RCA long enough really to understand the company, let alone to set it on a constructive course.[30]

For similar reasons, turnover makes it difficult for employees to learn from one another. One of the strengths of the American semiconductor industry in the early 1970's, for example, was the rapidity with which high technology was diffused within it, as professional engineers moved from company to company. But as semiconductor technology has become more complex, there has been a greater need for continuity and teamwork. Competitive success in creating a low-cost 64K Random Access Memories (RAMs) has depended less on maverick geniuses than on highly skilled teams, for the simple reason that no maverick genius is capable of the range of complex and interrelated tasks the chip's production entails. But rapid turnover has hindered semiconductor manufacturers in achieving the organizational learning they need to become truly flexible-system producers. Only Motorola and Texas Instruments have been able to preserve their teams for any length of time, but to do so, they have had to locate their memory divisions in the relative isolation of Texas. In California's "Silicon Valley," on the other hand, there are so many chip producers and so much job hopping that it is said, only half in jest, that many engineers change companies but keep the same parking lots.[31]

More and more, our productive processes are marked by suspicion, distrust, insecurity, and opportunism. Managers fear for their jobs. They worry that valued employees will suddenly leave the company. Employees, in turn, fear that they may be sacked without warning. This fearful atmosphere inhibits cooperation at all levels. Employees are not entrusted with trade secrets lest they take them to a competitor after they quit or are fired. They are not trained in general skills on the assumption that such an investment by the firm will be lost when they leave. Fear of job loss also inhibits the flow of accurate information up the corporate hierarchy. Bad news is buried layers down until—months or years later —it erupts into a major crisis or scandal, often long after those who were responsible have moved on to other jobs. Job insecurity discourages cooperation even among employees at roughly the same level. Why help your junior colleague if there is a risk he will displace you when he learns to perform his job better?

Because of the high mobility of capital and management, those who have the strongest economic stake in the long-term health of an enterprise are apt to be its lowest-level employees, whose mobility is most limited. Because they cannot merely hop to another job, such employees must live with the consequences of declining long-term productivity within an industry and a region. Investors and managers are generally better placed to reverse the decline, but they have less incentive—they can simply withdraw. (It is significant that in Japan trade unions are among the most vocal advocates of long-term investment strategies that emphasize productivity and growth.)

6.

Perhaps most troubling is that the atmosphere of insecurity and impermanence which characterizes all levels of American business has bred a selfish attitude among directors, managers, and employees, an egoistic mentality which is seriously undermining American enterprise. Within a productive system that increasingly depends on cooperation, good faith, and team spirit, the dominant ethic is coming to be cynical indifference and opportunism. The paper entrepreneurialism pursued by the firm as a whole inevitably finds reflection in personal manipulation among people within the firm. "Beggar-thy-neighbor" tactics which impose losses on groups outside the firm for the sake of short-term paper gains are mirrored by similar tactics inside—a pattern of behavior best described by the legal term "self-dealing."

We are witnessing an extraordinary increase in self-dealing within American enterprise. It is difficult to measure, of course, because much of it is covert. But the signs are everywhere, and they help explain some of the more bizarre paper entrepreneurial maneuvers of recent years. The reason many professional managers fight off unfriendly acquirers—even when they offer huge premiums over the market value of the stock—is that the managers are more concerned with keeping their jobs than with the value of the shareholders' stock, and they are free to act on this priority. (Indeed, the generous "golden parachutes" awarded by boards of directors to managers under threat of takeover are best understood as attempts by boards to reduce the likelihood of such self-dealing.) By the same token, when professional managers plunge their companies deeply into debt in order to acquire totally unrelated businesses, they are apt to be motivated by the fact that their personal salaries and bonuses are tied to the volume of business their newly enlarged enterprise will generate rather than to the potential for any added returns to shareholders. (Acquiring firms' stock has not gained any value in the wake of the latest wave of acquisitions; many have plummeted on the very day the takeovers are proposed.[32])

The special "consulting" fees often enjoyed by the directors of giant firms are another symptom of self-dealing. RCA, whose stock price has declined steadily since 1967, recently awarded one of its outside directors $250,000 to negotiate the retirement of one chairman and the hiring of another; another director is a partner in RCA's principal investment banker and broker, which collected $6.7 million in fees from 1977 through 1980, as RCA intensively traded corporate assets.[33]

The rapid increase in executive compensation over the last decade—as real returns to shareholders and production workers stagnated—gives rise to an appearance of self-interested behavior. From 1971 to 1981 total compensation of senior management in the Standard & Poor's 400 rose by 10 percent in real dollars. During the same period total shareholder value in the S&P 400—stock price appreciation plus dividends—declined in real dollars by 2 percent. In 1981 (hardly a banner year for investors or production workers) executive salaries scored their largest increase (15.9 percent) in seventeen years.[34] Fifteen corporate leaders now award themselves more than $1 million annually. Last year the median compensation for the chairmen of America's 500 largest corporations was $445,158—approximately thirty times that of the average factory worker. These figures exclude executive perquisites: In a recent survey 69 percent of corporate executives indicated that they have use of company cars; 53 percent have company-financed country club memberships; 55 percent, luncheon club memberships; 79 percent of the companies surveyed paid for the travelers' spouses when the executives travel on company business.[35] Even if corporate executives are somehow worth these extraordinary sums—as seems doubtful—the dramatic gulf between this level of compensation and what an average production worker earns creates a strong impression of unfairness.

The very mechanisms of paper entrepreneurialism create enormous opportunities for self-dealing. Executives, lawyers, and financial experts (or their relatives) who have inside information that their company is about to be acquired or to make a bid for another can reap extraordinary profits on the stock market. On July 1, 1980, for example, trading in the Fidelity Financial Corporation's common stock soared to 126,000 shares, a 900 percent jump from the day before, and the price of a share rose $1, to $12.50 a share. Ten days later volume in the Crocker National Corporation common surged 630 percent, and the price of a share rose

10 percent. Both instances of increased trading came just before public announcements that the companies were to be acquired. Profiting on the basis of inside information is illegal, of course, but it is almost impossible to detect or to control. Since 1978 the Securities and Exchange Commission has filed more insider trading charges than it did in its prior forty-four-year history. SEC enforcement staff members estimate that the volume of insider trading in recent years has reached "phenomenal levels." The new, flourishing market in stock options has enhanced the profitability of insider trading, while making it even more difficult to uncover. The SEC is now investigating allegations that some insiders are using secret Swiss bank accounts to buy stock options after receiving advanced information of takeovers.[36]

Along with such practices within companies, paper entrepreneurialism offers lucrative opportunities to external professionals. One has only to consider the vast sums pocketed by the lawyers and investment bankers who orchestrate today's takeovers and other paper transactions to wonder to what extent these groups are responding to a demand and to what extent they create it. The dozen law firms that presided over the recent clash of Mobil and U.S. Steel for control of Marathon Oil together gained more than $10 million from the deal. Du Pont's purchase of Conoco netted $15 million for its investment banker, the First Boston Corporation. (All told, First Boston earned $75 million for its merger work in 1981.) Fees in this range are not unusual in the paper contests of recent years. An antitrust case brought against several manufacturers of fine paper was recently settled for $62 million; lawyers' fees consumed $21 million of this total. Even bankruptcy can be lucrative. Lawyers and other professionals who are nursing Itel, the once high-flying computer leasing company, under Chapter 11 of the Bankruptcy Act, have received $6.7 million from the company for fees and expenses so far.[37]

Cynical self-dealing is not confined to the upper reaches of corporate America. Lower-level employees, perhaps taking to heart the example of top managers, are enriching themselves at their firms' expense. The U.S. Chamber of Commerce estimates that employee theft has grown from $16 billion annually in 1971 to $75 billion in 1980. Theft takes many forms, from simple pilferage to kickbacks, bribes, sale of trade secrets, and outright embezzlement. The insurance premiums companies must pay for coverage against employee theft of all kinds have risen 14 percent a year since 1975, in real terms.[38]

As businesses have become more complicated, and the technologies of accounting and control more intricate, there are more opportunities to subvert the system for personal gain. Bank embezzlement has now become more common and more costly than bank robberies. (The FBI, which is now investigating 800 cases of embezzlement of more than $100,000 each, estimates losses from embezzlement to be at least five times those from robbery.[39]) In "Silicon Valley" losses from thefts of integrated circuits—chips smaller than a fingernail that can sell for $100 each—are more than $20 million a year. Computer crime is one of America's fastest-growing occupations. Losses in the 100 or so cases of computer fraud reported annually now run in the range of $100 million. And the leaps being made in computer technology—costly software programs on microfilm that can be carried off in one's hip pocket, computers with remote units to which large numbers of employees have access—are creating new opportunities for sophisticated fraud. American companies now spend $150 million annually on computer security devices.[40]

In a recent study of employee theft, two researchers from the University of Michigan found that the largest thefts are perpetrated by high-level employees—typically with engineering and technical responsibilities—who have greater knowledge than lower-level workers about the value of things to be taken and have relatively open access to tools, equipment, and materials. The typical industrial thief is a "short-timer," who expects to move on to another firm soon.[41]

Among lower-level employees, self-dealing may mean old-fashioned pilferage. But more often it manifests itself in indirect ways, having more to do with alienation and indifference than with outright dishonesty. Industries are increasingly plagued with chronic absenteeism and work stoppages. In auto-manufacturing plants, unscheduled daily absentees climbed from 3 percent of the work force in the 1950's to 8 percent by 1980, hitting 12 to 15 percent on workdays preceding weekends and holidays. (Interestingly, while Japanese auto-manufacturing plants have an unscheduled absentee rate of only 2.1 percent, their rate of scheduled absentees, 6.2 percent, is much higher than that in U.S. plants, 3.8 percent, suggesting that the American problem is at least partly attributable to failures of communication between workers and managers.[42])

During the 1970's the average number of days lost each year to industrial disputes for every 1,000 employees was 529 in the United States, compared with 32 in Sweden, 38 in West Germany, and 148 in Japan. Britain was a close second, with 481 days lost.[43] As the recession deepened between 1981 and 1982, labor disputes have declined in America, but the decline is due to growing unemployment and fear of job loss rather than to any underlying change of attitude. Should the economy show signs of real recovery, the disputes will surely resume.

The American work force at every level lacks a sense of shared purpose. In a Harris poll conducted in 1978, 70 percent of U.S. workers agreed that management and shareholders benefit from increases in productivity, but less than 20 percent believed that employees also benefit.[44] These beliefs are confirmed when product improvements result in layoffs, as fewer employees are needed to accomplish the same tasks; when cash-rich companies plow their earnings into acquisitions and mergers rather than into expansion and additional jobs; when companies offer their professional managers, directors, and outside consultants startling rewards while seeking wage reductions from their blue-collar work forces.

7.

There are no villains to this piece. We cannot place blame on any single group. Professional managers, middle-level managers, professional specialists, low-level employees, investors, outside lawyers, accountants, and financial brokers—every participant in U.S. enterprise has responded in predictable and understandable ways to the growing problem of America's outmoded industrial base. Nor, sadly, are there any heroes. Every group has taken advantage of opportunities to increase its economic security at the expense of others.

The problem has evolved out of the nation's incapacity to alter its underlying process of production. When the shift in global advantage commenced in the late-1960s, America's professional managers and employees viewed any substantial restructuring out of high-volume, standardized production as risky, costly, and unnecessary. When profits began to decline, managers reflexively sought to tighten the control apparatus they inherited from scientific management, adding rules and reporting requirements. The controls invariably required more layers of managers and staff experts. The additional layers reduced the firms' flexibility still further, they forced senior managers to place even greater reliance on stark, quantitative data, and they distorted communications throughout the enterprise.

As industry stagnates, its financial and legal underpinnings have gradually taken on lives of their own, offering opportunities for manipulation and short-term gains. As a result, U.S. firms have turned toward paper transactions—conglomeration, creative accounting, public relations, speculation, and litigation. And as the firms have turned to paper, they have increasingly called upon the services of lawyers and financial experts, who now dominate executive suites.

Paper shuffling has its correlate in people shuffling. All this rearranging of industrial assets and people in turn has made it more difficult for American enterprise to undertake basic change. It has enforced short-term thinking, discouraged genuine innovation, and consumed the careers of some of our most talented citizens. It also has transformed many American companies into fearful and demoralized places characterized by cynical indifference and opportunism.

The pain of adjustment has been considerably less in continental Europe and Japan simply because their business enterprises have been less wedded than those in the United States to high-volume, standardized production. They have generally avoided paper entrepreneurialism, in large measure because they have lacked the managerial tradition out of which it evolved. Their attitudes toward paper entrepreneurialism are vastly different from American attitudes. The Japanese, for example, tend to view their companies more as collections of people than as accumulations of physical assets. When a Japanese firm diversifies out of an industry, therefore, it may sell off some plant and equipment and purchase new ones, but it keeps together its human network and applies it to the new undertaking. To the Japanese, the notion of purchasing or selling a company seems vaguely immoral, like the purchase or sale of people.

All these nations have suffered economic slowdowns in recent years, at least in part because their economies inevitably rise and fall in tandem with the American economy. But few other industrialized countries have had slowdowns as severe as the U.S. decline because our leading competitors have been shifting into new processes of production as fast as they can. And when the next upturn comes, they will be better positioned for new growth than the American economy.

The rigidities built into American enterprise are only part of the problem and suggest only part of a solution. The U.S. government could have reduced the cost and risk of economic change for American business and labor and thereby forestalled paper entrepreneurialism, but it did not. It did not largely because the superstructures of management in America —around which business, labor, and government have been organized— were themselves designed to support high-volume, standardized production, not to accelerate industrial change. This larger organization of industry has, in fact, retarded America's shift to flexible-system production, in ways that we shall now explore.

IX
HISTORIC
PRESERVATION

1.

America's superstructures of management evolved in response to the needs of individual firms to reduce the risks of high-volume, standardized manufacturing through industry-wide coordination of production and investment. By the 1960's many of the nation's basic industries—steel, automobiles, rubber, petrochemicals, consumer electronics, electrical and nonelectrical machinery—had become stable oligopolies of three or four major firms, led by the largest and most entrenched. Government indirectly encouraged these arrangements through its regulatory agencies, advisory boards, and procurement processes. In its time, as we have seen, this system worked reasonably well. American industry achieved unprecedented productivity by taking to their limits its core principles of standardized mass production. But as the terms of global competition began to change in the late-1960's, and as the competitive advantage of industrialized countries shifted to flexible-system products and processes, the superstructures could not respond.

The superstructures of management typically have sought to preserve

America's old industrial base intact, shielding it against foreign incursions, rather than adapting it to the new realities of international competition. They have done for American industry as a whole what paper entrepreneurialism has done for the individual firms that compose it; they have sought to evade the challenge of economic change.

2.

By the mid-1960's America's basic industries had lost the habit of competing. U.S. Steel was setting the pattern of industry-wide investment, production, and prices in steel; General Motors, in automobiles; Du Pont, in many lines of chemicals; RCA, in many electronic products; GE and Westinghouse, in electrical machinery; Caterpillar in farm machinery; Goodyear, in tires; Boeing, in aircraft. Industry-wide unions in each of these industries were negotiating three-year pacts, many including automatic cost of living increases. Some government agencies, like the Department of Defense, were routinely negotiating noncompetitive contracts with industry leaders; other agencies, like the Federal Trade Commission, were guarding against price-cutting to retailers and dealers.

Since profitability was more or less guaranteed, there was no reason to innovate in new products or processes; indeed, too much innovation could destabilize the structure. In the 1950's American steelmakers produced nearly 50 percent of the world's steel. Their steel plants—though most had been built before World War II—were still the world's largest and most efficient. But by the mid-1960's American steelmakers knew that the newly developed basic oxygen furnaces were more efficient than their open-hearth furnaces. New methods of continuous slab or billet casting were superior to standard U.S. techniques. Steel technology had simply progressed since most plants were built—a fact not lost on foreign competitors. But it would have been difficult and costly for U.S. firms to fit the new technology into their old plants without completely suspending production and redesigning the plant site. They saw no reason to go to this trouble and expense since industry profits could be maintained through careful coordination among producers.[1]

America's automobile industry was just as complacent. Three major automakers dominated U.S. highways and, to a large extent, the highways of the world. They knew that newly developed stamping technologies (which had in fact been designed by American machine press manufactur-

ers) could save money over the long term. They were also aware of a wide range of more efficient pollution-control devices. Some industry experts even predicted the trend toward smaller cars. But the industry balked at investing in basic change. It did not have to.[2]

The electronics industry was equally comfortable. America had invented television. In 1964 television manufacturers produced more than 1 million sets. In 1968 Motorola replaced the vacuum tubes in its televisions with solid-state printed circuit boards. But RCA and Zenith, the industry leaders, were slow to follow. They did not produce a full line of solid-state TVs until five years later, by which time Japanese manufacturers were already flooding the market with them.[3]

The new videocassette industry traces a similar story of complacency and competitive decline. Videocassette recorders were invented in America in 1956 by the Ampex Corporation. But RCA, Zenith, and all other American manufacturers were not interested in trying to produce a low-cost model for the average consumer. The industry assumed that television manufacturing was a mature and stable business with few opportunities for technological leadership. It largely emphasized marketing and style instead.[4]

Other U.S. industries also concentrated on high-volume and standardization to the exclusion of major innovations. America's tire manufacturers, seeking only to increase volume and reduce unit costs, disregarded advances in radial tires; its appliance companies ignored technical advances in microwave ovens; its makers of machine tools disregarded the development of numerical controls.

Foreign competition came as a rude shock to this stable system. When the first wave of low-priced Japanese steel, automobiles, and television sets hit America's shores in the late 1960's, producers complained that the competitive success of foreign goods was based on cheap labor, dumping, and other unfair trade practices. Japan's wage rates at the time were significantly lower than those in America, but this gap could not account for the differences in price. In fact, Japan's competitive success was based largely on technological superiority. While American steelmakers clung to their open hearths and ingot casting, Japanese steelmakers were investing heavily in basic oxygen furnaces and continuous casting. By 1978, 78 percent of Japanese steel was being produced in basic oxygen furnaces, compared with 58 percent of American steel; 51 percent of Japanese steel

was continuously cast, compared with 15 percent of American steel. Similarly, while American automakers toyed with style changes, Japanese automakers were investing in the new stamping technologies and were experimenting with more efficient engines and pollution control devices. And just two years after Motorola had introduced solid-state circuitry, Japanese television manufacturers fully commercialized the new technology. By 1971, 90 percent of Japanese-made televisions were solid-state. And by 1979 the Japanese were flooding the American market with videocassette recorders. They had no competition.[5]

But it was not just Japanese companies that posed a competitive threat. It was also West German machine tool companies, French manufacturers of radial tires, Swedish manufacturers of precision instruments, and textile manufacturers from developing countries.

Nor was the problem solely a reluctance to innovate. Unaccustomed to price competition, American industry often refused to let prices respond to market conditions. The steel industry, for example, was addicted to regular price increases set by the industry leader, U.S. Steel. When Japan's steelmakers reduced their prices in response to the steel glut of the late 1960's, American steelmakers were unable to respond in kind. Their system of administered prices and guaranteed wage increases had rendered their pricing policies far less flexible than those of the Japanese.[6]

The technological backwardness and inflexible pricing policies of key U.S. industries let imports continue to mount. By 1969 foreign steel was claiming more than 9 percent of the American market, and Japanese-made black-and-white television sets were taking 31 percent of the American television market. By 1976 steel imports had increased to 18 percent, imports of Japanese-made color televisions had claimed 35, and automobile imports were rising beyond 20 percent of the American market.

3.

American producers, unready to compete on technology or price, instead turned to the superstructures of management, seeking protection from imports. Dominant producers within steel, automobiles, consumer electronics, and other industries formed political coalitions with organized labor. They petitioned the executive branch. They lobbied Congress. They sought support through the federal courts. In 1969, for example, major steel producers and the United Steelworkers together

obtained a voluntary restraint agreement, limiting the tonnage of steel that could be imported into the United States. When these restrictions failed to stem the tide, the industry filed "antidumping" petitions, seeking countervailing duties on steel imports that allegedly had been dumped into the American market at prices below their "fair market price." In 1978 the Carter administration agreed to impose a trigger-price mechanism on foreign steel, which effectively barred imported steel at any price below the computed cost of producing it by Japan's most efficient steel producer, plus transport charges, overhead, and a stipulated profit margin. The trigger price was increased by 12 percent in 1980, after the steel industry agreed to withdraw its antidumping petitions. In 1982 U.S. Steel once again filed petitions alleging that foreign steel producers were dumping steel in the American market, and the trigger-price system was suspended. The steel industry has now obtained a formal quota on European steel imports.

Other industries have followed the same pattern. Facing competitive decline, firms have responded to the challenge not with product or process innovations but with paper competition, commencing with dumping complaints and litigation and ending with various sorts of trade restrictions. In 1968 the U.S. Electronic Industries Association, representing television manufacturers, filed complaints with the government alleging that the Japanese were dumping television sets in the American market. In 1974 Zenith filed a countervailing duty case, claiming that rebates of Japan's commodity tax on its exported television sets constituted a subsidy (that case eventually went to the United States Supreme Court, which decided against Zenith). The U.S. television manufacturers thereafter commenced an antitrust case against several Japanese television manufacturers, claiming that they were engaged in a conspiracy to destroy the American consumer electronics industry. (This case was eventually dismissed.) Finally, in 1977, the U.S. government negotiated a marketing agreement with Japan, which limited imports of Japanese color televisions to just under 1.6 million sets annually. Similar agreements subsequently were negotiated with Taiwan and South Korea.

Between 1972 and 1977 the Treasury Department initiated 122 antidumping investigations at the behest of various other American industries. In 34 of them, the government found that American manufacturers had in fact been injured by imports. (There had been only 13 such findings in all of the preceding eleven years.[7]) The dumping cases were followed by formal trade restrictions. In 1978 the U.S. government substantially increased tariffs on CB radio transceivers. In April 1981 the Reagan administration forced Japan to restrict its auto exports to America. At about the same time the administration quietly reimposed duties on $3.8 billion worth of imports from Hong Kong, South Korea, Taiwan, Brazil, and Mexico, thereby substantially increasing the protection accorded American manufacturers of car parts, electrical goods, fertilizer, and chemicals. The Reagan administration even put quotas on imported clothespins. There are now special duties on 132 products, ranging from South Korean bicycles to Italian shoes. And pressure is mounting for new legislation to require that a certain percentage of the content of autos sold in America be American-produced.

U.S. industries threatened by foreign competition have also gained protection through a wide assortment of government subsidies, special tax provisions, and subsidized loans and loan guarantees. These forms of assistance have mushroomed since the late 1960's, as global competitive pressures have increased. In 1950, for example, the total cost to the federal government of special tax credits and tax depreciation allowances going to specific industries amounted to only $7.9 billion (or approximately 1 percent of the nation's gross national product). By 1980 the cost had grown to a staggering $62.4 billion (almost 3 percent of that year's GNP). In 1950 the cost to the government of subsidized loans and loan guarantees to specific industries (measured in terms of interest charges and loan defaults) was only $300 million. By 1980 the annual cost had grown to $3.6 billion. Outstanding federal loan guarantees targeted to specific industries now total over $221.6 billion. Taken together, government subsidies and tax expenditures to promote certain industries have risen from $77.1 billion (or 9.2 percent of the GNP) in 1950 to $303.7 billion (13.9 percent of the GNP) in 1980.[8]

Industries that have lost their competitive edge have fared well in these sweepstakes. The Chrysler Corporation now has $1.5 billion in loan guarantees. America's steelmakers have more than $550 million in outstanding loans and loan guarantees, and they receive approximately $50 million a year in special tax benefits. The ailing shipbuilding industry receives more than $500 million in subsidies each year and has more than

$6.3 billion in outstanding loans and loan guarantees. Until recently price controls on oil and gas yielded cheap feedstocks for America's synthetic fiber manufacturers (desperately competing against textile manufacturers in Southeast Asia and Europe), giving them 23 percent lower mill costs than their international competitors. And in 1981 America's ailing airlines received $3.6 billion in new loans and loan guarantees.[9]

The list of government benefits and beneficiaries gets longer year by year as the global competition intensifies. The benefits also become better hidden. Unlike direct government spending, the public cost of these loans, loan guarantees, and tax benefits is difficult to measure because most of these items do not show up in the annual federal budget. Most do not require explicit congressional authorization and appropriation. Public officials, therefore, find it easy to manipulate these programs in ways that create the appearance of lower public spending than is actually taking place and to avoid acknowledging the massive government assistance going to industry. In 1982, for example, the Reagan administration merely removed from the 1983 federal budget 87 percent of the cost of direct loans to industry that it planned to make in 1983. By judicious budget editing, the administration conjured the appearance of frugality.[10]

By the same token, the supposedly voluntary export agreements that have become popular in recent years are less visible, and therefore more politically expedient, than outright tariffs and quotas. They allow administrations to stick to their free trade rhetoric. In the wake of the voluntary agreement to limit Japanese auto imports, Vice President Bush noted that the Reagan administration "stopped short of asking the Japanese" to take such steps and that the administration would not "go down the slippery slope of protectionism." Technically he was telling the truth. It was not necessary for the United States to make a formal, explicit demand—the Japanese were made well aware of legislation pending in Congress to limit auto imports.

Hidden subsidies and trade agreements are especially costly to America since they let higher taxes and consumer prices be imposed without the check of public scrutiny. They are perfect devices for a government that wants protection from imports but does not want to admit it. Precisely because indirect subsidies and hidden trade barriers are hard to identify, control, or measure, they may also ultimately pose the most serious threat to the entire fragile system of international free trade, which is dependent on informal policing and goodwill.

4.

American industry has used import protection and subsidies in order to maintain profits and provide cash for paper entrepreneurial exploits, rather than to build new plants, improve equipment, undertake new research and product development, or upgrade the work force. In other words, government assistance has supported a rearguard action to preserve America's old industrial base of high-volume, standardized production, and not a campaign to meet world competition by shifting its industry toward flexible-system production.

Major U.S. steel producers, for example, declined to invest in new plant and equipment during the "breathing space" they enjoyed after voluntary restrictions had been imposed on imported steel. The restrictions, meant to sustain the steel industry while it retooled to meet foreign competition, went into effect in 1969. But the industry's capital expenditures for each of the next six years were below the 1968 level. At the same time Japanese steel producers were increasing their assets by more than 23 percent per year. Nor did the American steel industry undertake any major restructuring after the trigger-price system was initiated in 1978.[11]

Most firms in the American apparel, textile, footwear, and color television industries have displayed the same failure to retool once the government has offered a shield of protection. The recent restriction on the export of Japanese automobiles to the United States was founded on the American automobile industry's implicit agreement to use the opportunity to retool. But because this agreement was never made formal, the government and the public have no recourse now that the investment plans are falling short of their original targets.

To be sure, government programs to encourage new investment themselves have often been poorly targeted or inadequate to the task of shifting America's productive base. Industries in dire straits typically have difficulty raising the capital necessary for major restructuring since banks and investors are understandably reluctant to sink money into enterprises that show so little promise of profitability in the short run. Policies based on quotas, trigger-price systems, and other forms of import protection have, at most, provided declining industries with a respite from further erosion of their profits rather than with a surge of new cash.

Loans and loan guarantees have carried no conditions that firms use them to retool rather than to retrench. Nor have they been specifically targeted to those segments of declining industries that have the best chance of becoming internationally competitive. The Trade Act of 1974 authorized the U.S. government to provide limited loans and loan guarantees to companies injured by foreign competition, but it restricted eligibility to firms that had already experienced an absolute decrease in sales or production. As a result, these funds have come too late, after firms have already been seriously weakened, and the help has gone to the most feeble companies in the industry rather than to those with the best chance of regaining a share of the world market. In any event, the funding has been too limited. In the apparel industry, for example, the average grant has been approximately $1 million—far too little for any kind of major retooling. It is not surprising that few companies have taken advantage of the program. By 1978 only about 200 firms had applied for assistance, out of the estimated 14,000 that were eligible.

When government subsidies have come in the form of *ad hoc* bailouts to particular failing firms like Lockheed and Chrysler, the government has imposed an ongoing, cumbersome form of review. Indeed, there are strong parallels between the government's role in these programs and the roles assumed by creditors and judges under the reorganization provisions of the bankruptcy code. But this process of reorganization is far too particularized and administratively unwieldy to form the basis of a broad adjustment program.

The other recent policy to promote industry restructuring has been the negative one of rolling back health, safety, and environmental regulations. In response to claims by the auto, steel, and textile industries that such relief was necessary for their competitive survival, recent administrations have trimmed, rescinded, or delayed various regulations. The Reagan administration has taken on this task with a vengeance. In conjunction with its push for Japanese restraint on auto exports, for example, it decided to relax or rescind thirty-four auto-related environmental and safety regulations. The administration also announced that it would relax future water pollution standards for steel plants.

Regulatory rollbacks will not restore America's industrial edge since regulations are demonstrably not responsible for American industry's competitive decline. During the 1970's the U.S. steel industry spent an average of $365 million annually to reduce pollution and improve worker safety—about 17 percent of its annual capital investment during the decade. Of this cost, 48 percent was subsidized by state and local governments through industrial development bonds.[12] During the same period Japanese steel manufacturers spent almost twice that amount for the same purposes.[13] Spending for pollution control and safety by European steelmakers was of the same magnitude as in the United States. And even if the American auto industry retains all the money it hopes to save by avoiding regulations—an estimated $1.4 billion over the next five years—it will not come close to raising the $80 billion it needs to retool sufficiently to regain competitiveness with Japan.

Industry savings from regulatory rollbacks rarely have been translated into new plant and equipment or new research and development. When U.S. Steel entered into consent decrees with the Environmental Protection Agency in 1979, giving the company extra time to comply with pollution requirements, for example, its chairman announced that the firm could "now act aggressively to revitalize [its] Pittsburgh area operations." But it has made no major steel investments in Pittsburgh since then. Similarly, the Steel Compliance Act of 1981, amending the Clean Air Act to allow steel companies to defer compliance for three years, did not require them to restructure their operations; not surprisingly, little restructuring has followed. Steel industry investment in new plant and equipment is now running more than $1 billion short of what its spokesmen say they need to modernize.[14]

Indeed, notwithstanding substantial import barriers to protect domestic steel producers, tax incentives, and assorted regulatory rollbacks—all designed to encourage new steel investment—the American steel industry has been enthusiastically diversifying out of steel. In 1979 U.S. Steel walked away from thirteen steelmaking and fabricating facilities while investing in a new shopping center near Pittsburgh and announcing that it would build major chemical facilities in Houston. In its 1980 strategic plan, U.S. Steel publicly committed itself to shrinking its steel business as a percentage of its total business, from 63 percent of the company's assets in 1975 to under 50 percent by 1980. That timetable has since been accelerated. From 1976 to 1979 U.S. Steel's nonsteel assets grew 80 percent while its steel assets grew only 13 percent. Its steel operations now represent only 40 percent of its assets. Its recent $6.4 billion purchase of the Marathon Oil Company will all but exhaust U.S. Steel's $2.5 billion cash reserve and load its balance sheet with added debt. Indeed, the merger will more than triple the company's 1982 interest expense, to $840 million. It will, however, offer several important tax advantages, of the sort already considered.[15]

Other steel companies are following the same route. National Steel, disdaining steel expansion, has decided instead to acquire three large savings and loan companies, worth $6.9 billion. LTV, the corporate parent of Jones & Laughlin Steel, recently made an unsuccessful multimillion-dollar bid for Grumman Aircraft. Republic Steel has moved into the insurance business. And Armco has diversified itself so extensively in the last three years that it has now dropped the word "steel" from its corporate title.

This is not to suggest that steel or any other industry in distress should necessarily invest in its original product. Diversification into a more promising business may be a far superior way to adapt to new competitive conditions. But distressed industries base their pleas for public assistance on the claim that they need it to regain competitiveness and avoid further layoffs, rather than simply to maintain overall corporate profitability. The specter of unemployment haunts these negotiations. It seems disingenuous, to say the least, for businesses to use the assistance in order to diversify out of industries and leave their workers behind. Despite massive layoffs and plant closings, the American steel industry has been unwilling to place any substantial burden on its investors. Between 1972 and 1979 dividend payments averaged 49 percent of U.S. Steel's earnings, and 53 percent of Bethlehem's earnings. Like all skillful paper entrepreneurs, steel executives have kept their eyes sharply fixed on the short-term bottom line.

5.

Policies to protect declining industries are not only failing to promote new investment but in fact are dragging down the rest of the American economy. Like all devices that artificially maintain the price of domestic goods, import restrictions send costly ripples through the economy, undermining other domestic industries that depend on the restricted goods. In an economy increasingly subject to foreign trade, any import barrier is apt to jeopardize the competitiveness of related industries. For example, the protection accorded U.S. textile manufacturers put clothing manufacturers at a competitive disadvantage in world trade, since they had to pay higher prices for the textiles they used. To compound the damage, these restraints encouraged foreign textile manufacturers to shift their production to apparel, thereby channeling their cheap textiles into the U.S. market through finished goods. Hong Kong, Korea, and Taiwan soon were flooding the U.S. market with cheap clothes, causing American apparel manufacturers in turn to seek protection.[16]

The U.S. steel industry's protectionist trigger-price system not only has cost American consumers more than $1 billion annually in the form of higher prices for U.S. products that contain steel but has also penalized all U.S. firms that use steel—manufacturers of automobiles, farm machinery, appliances, and machine tools—which must now pay 25 to 35 percent more for steel than their European and Japanese competitors. Their plight is in some ways more serious than that of the American consumer, who can still at least purchase many foreign products made with cheaper steel. American steel-based industries are rapidly losing ground in world markets to foreign competitors whose costs are lower. One could have confidently predicted that ten years after voluntary import controls were first placed on steel, the U.S. automobile industry would be seeking protection for itself.

Ironically, these efforts to preserve America's old industrial base have actually tended to make the economies of Japan and several developing nations more flexible and dynamic than they otherwise would be, precisely because they have been forced to adapt to U.S. protectionist policies. Voluntary import restrictions have invited foreign manufacturers to upgrade their products in order to maintain their foreign earnings with the limited quantity they can export. Thus, the restrictions have pushed foreign producers into the more expensive and specialized end of the U.S. market, where American manufacturers otherwise have their best chance of maintaining competitiveness.

Since the onset of the trigger-price mechanism Japanese steelmakers have duly limited shipments of steel to the United States to between 6 and 6.5 million tons annually. But the per ton value of Japanese steel has more than doubled. The restrictions have encouraged Japanese and other foreign manufacturers to shift their production to higher-valued specialty steel products, such as stainless steel bars and alloy tool steel. Specialty steel had previously been the most dynamic segment of the American steel industry, relatively secure against imports. Since this shift in foreign production, however, specialty steel manufacturers have found themselves directly challenged by Asian and European producers who are now intent on gaining a larger share of the U.S. market.

The recent voluntary restriction on Japanese auto imports has had a similar effect, encouraging Japanese automakers to produce slightly larger cars with more sophisticated engineering, which command higher prices in America. As Japanese cars become precision instruments, American auto manufacturers find themselves losing competitive ground in the upper end of their product lines, where they used to have the advantage.

Indeed, precisely because foreign nations have so readily adapted themselves to American attempts at protecting the old industrial base, each protective device has lasted only a short time until additional protectionist measures have become necessary. Exporters from countries not subject to the agreements have rushed in to take advantage of whatever marketing opportunities the restrictions create, while manufacturers from restricted countries have shifted their operations to nonrestricted countries, thus circumventing the agreements. Some foreign manufacturers have simply altered their products so that they fall outside the agreements. In response to a flood of imported shoes from Korea and Taiwan, voluntary export agreements were negotiated with these countries in 1977. One year later footwear imports from Hong Kong, Italy, and Brazil had more than filled the gap. And because the 1977 agreements had not covered rubber footwear, Korean and Taiwanese manufacturers merely changed the composition of their products, substituting rubber for certain parts. In no time millions of Americans were wearing rubber shoes from Korea and Taiwan.[17]

The same result followed a 1977 agreement voluntarily limiting Japan's export of color television receivers. By 1978 color sets were streaming into the United States from Taiwan, Korea, and Singapore. After agreements had been reached with these countries, the TVs began entering the United States in the form of subassemblies and components, which were not restricted by the agreements. Since by this time most U.S.

television manufacturers already had established overseas operations to produce their own subassemblies and components, they were in no position to seek yet another round of agreements restricting these imports as well.[18]

Only when protectionist measures have become extremely broad have they had any lasting effect. But besides inflating consumer prices in America, these broad measures have had devastating effects on developing countries that desperately need foreign trade. Under the latest Multi-Fiber Agreement, for example, the United States will impose new restrictions on textile imports from Hong Kong, South Korea, and Taiwan, limiting them to an annual increase of half a percent over the next four years. The bilateral deals that America will soon sign with Mexico, Pakistan, and Brazil will hold these countries to the same export levels permitted under the Multi-Fiber Agreement between 1978 and 1981. Other developing countries, including India, Sri Lanka, and the Philippines, will have to accept cuts in their quotas of textiles to America. Such restrictions brutally retard these nations' economic growth, perpetuating poverty and perhaps even threatening world peace.

Not even comprehensive protectionist measures can halt the decline of an industry losing in international competition. Anticipating further American protectionism, Japanese and West German firms are already rushing to establish manufacturing facilities within the United States. (For example, Volkswagens are now produced in Pennsylvania; Hondas, in Ohio.) But these facilities are, for the most part, assembly operations. Advanced components, made elsewhere, are merely put together by relatively unskilled American workers. They constitute the lowest-valued end of the production process, an area where America could retain long-term advantage only if wages fell drastically. Most of these are dead-end jobs, which count for very little in the emerging system of international trade. Those who perform them will be consigned to a relatively low standard of living, measured against the rest of the industrialized world.

6.

Efforts to preserve America's old industrial base have also taken the form, in recent years, of various schemes to reduce the real wages of blue-collar workers. Firms have relocated (or threatened to relocate) in southern and western states, where average wage rates are somewhat lower, and unions less pervasive, than in the Midwest or Northeast. They have sought to discourage firms that pay higher wages from locating in their areas, for fear that prevailing wage rates would be bid upward. They have mounted intensive campaigns to discourage their employees from joining unions. (The number of unfair labor practice complaints, alleging discrimination in employment to discourage unions and dismissals of employees for union activities, has skyrocketed in recent years, from 18,651 in 1970 to 41,259 in 1980.[19]) They have lobbied to reduce the federal minimum wage and to allow school-aged children to work longer hours. (The Reagan administration is proving receptive to both overtures.) And in some industries, like textiles and apparel, they have hired workers illegally, at wages below the federal minimum.

The most recent variation on this theme comes in the form of union agreements to roll back scheduled wage increases, in return for management's commitment to maintain employment. In 1981 members of the United Auto Workers union employed by Chrysler accepted pay cuts to protect their jobs. The same year members of the United Rubber Workers at one Firestone facility accepted pay cuts in return for company assurances to refrain from layoffs. Members of the United Steelworkers union agreed to a three-year wage freeze to keep two Pennsylvania U.S. Steel plants in operation. In 1982 the United Auto Workers agreed to roll back scheduled wage increases at Ford and General Motors plants in return for greater job security for senior workers and shares in future company profits. The steel industry is now seeking similar agreements from the United Steelworkers.

More painful still are the cases where workers have sacrificed to no avail. In 1979 workers at the General Tire & Rubber Company's Akron tire plant voted to accept a 4 percent pay cut and changes in work rules because the company said that these concessions could "pave the way" for a replacement plant in Akron. Now, nearly four years later, there is still no plant. On the very day that General Motors and the UAW agreed to a package of wage concessions, GM disclosed that it was enlarging its bonus plan for top executives. (One week later the company was forced to rescind the bonus plan.)

To the extent that the American work force depends on industries in competition with low-wage countries, wages will be pushed down toward third world levels. Workers in America's basic industries are being forced to abandon master contracts and automatic cost of living increases in order to save their jobs. They understand all too well that failure to agree to wage concessions will result in additional plant closings. In what is becoming a typical sequence of events, General Motors, operator since 1938 of the Hyatt Bearing Plant in Clark, New Jersey, announced recently that it would close the factory and buy less costly parts elsewhere, including Japan. Leaders of the local UAW union responded with a proposal to slash their pay by 30 percent and buy the plant. General Motors accepted the proposal. On the other hand, Ford decided recently to close its Sheffield, Alabama, aluminum casting plant after employees declined either to buy the plant or to take a 50 percent wage and benefits cut.

But like the other schemes to save America's industrial base—tariffs, quotas, orderly marketing agreements, tax breaks, loans and loan guarantees, and regulatory rollbacks—wage reductions can only stall the decline. They will not make American industry more competitive over the long term because they are not addressed to the imperatives of industrial progress. American workers are obtaining little of real value in exchange for their agreements to take wage cuts. Profit-sharing schemes are empty concessions from companies that are unlikely to have any profits to share for some time to come. Guarantees of job security are of questionable value from firms that may be bankrupt within the decade. And promises of future investment in plant and equipment—even if kept—make little sense in an industry that has no real competitive future.

True, workers who now stand to benefit directly from productivity improvements because of new profit-sharing or worker ownership provisions may be inspired to greater productivity. In the six months since workers have owned GM's old Hyatt Bearing Plant, productivity has improved by 80 percent and the number of defective products has declined from 10 percent to 7 percent.[20] But so long as the system in which they work continues to be based on long runs of standardized products, productivity improvements like these will seldom suffice to overcome America's growing competitive disadvantage in routine, high-volume manufacturing. No amount of energy or goodwill can make up for the substantially lower wages, cheap sources of raw materials, and closer proximity to the most rapidly developing mass markets enjoyed by many other nations. Wage concessions—even coupled with profit sharing, assurances of employment security, or employee buy-outs of outmoded facilities—are simply the mechanisms by which Americans accept a gradually declining standard of living.

7.

America's defense policy has also served to preserve the nation's outmoded industrial base, instead of adapting it to international competition. At a superficial level there is a striking similarity between America's defense-related and aerospace programs and other nations' policies designed to accelerate the development of emerging industries. The Pentagon is now promoting in the United States many of the same industries that are being promoted in Japan by the Ministry of International Trade and Industry (MITI). Since 1975 MITI has financed one-third of the development costs of very-large-scale integrated circuits—the next major stage in the evolution of semiconductors. The project involves four leading Japanese semiconductor and computer manufacturers.[21] In 1979 the Defense Department launched its own very-large-scale integrated circuit project, involving nine American semiconductor and computer manufacturers. The Pentagon has budgeted $300 million for the project over a ten-year period.[22] Similarly, MITI has embarked on a program to spur the Japanese robotics industry, entailing an expenditure of $140 million over the next seven years.[23] The U.S. Air Force and NASA have their own version of the same endeavor: a $75 million program to develop an automated "factory of the future," built around integrated computer-aided manufacturing technology.[24]

MITI and the Defense Department also are squaring off in fiber optic communications. MITI is investing approximately $30 million over the next few years, and Nippon Telephone & Telegraph, a Japanese public corporation, is providing a major market. The Pentagon, meanwhile, is spending about $40 million annually on this technology.[25] In the laser industry MITI is coordinating and subsidizing research; the Pentagon is providing $243 million in research funds in 1981 and accounting for more than 50 percent of U.S. laser sales.[26] In computer software MITI has launched a three-year $180-million program for new applications software packages; the Pentagon is about to launch a $20 million software program applicable to missile guidance and radar. The list could be continued.

Although farther behind in the development of many of these technologies, France and West Germany are also helping their emerging industries become internationally competitive. The French government, for example, is supporting the development of very-large-scale integrated circuits by encouraging joint ventures with American companies and simultaneously providing $140 million in direct subsidies. West Germany is taking a similar approach, with subsidies of approximately $150 million.[27]

Here, however, the similarities with the United States end. Although U.S. defense and aerospace programs have spurred industrial development, they have not spurred it in the direction of commercial success. Apart from the Pentagon's broad concern for the economic health of U.S. defense contractors and NASA's recent flirtation with commercial applications for its space shuttle, the Department of Defense and NASA have no interest in the successful marketing of new products. Their primary interest is in preserving the stability of defense contractors. Indeed, the huge amount of talent and resources locked up in specialized defense and aerospace programs is jeopardizing the international competitiveness of American manufacturers. By contrast, the efforts of our trading partners, particularly Japan, have been focused directly on competing internationally for commercial markets.

The marketing of new commercial products is stimulated by domestic competition, which forces firms to improve their performance and aggressively to seek foreign outlets. Although MITI allows firms to cooperate on specific basic research projects, it promotes fierce competition in marketing. For example, thirty-two Japanese companies now produce semiconductors, and the competition is intense. The rivalry is equally strong in the computer industry, with Nippon Electric, Hitachi, and Fujitsu each trying to gain the lead. Sony and Matsushita are archrivals in consumer electronics.

The U.S. Defense Department, however, has been relatively unconcerned about competition within American industry. More than 65 percent of the dollar volume of U.S. defense contracts is awarded without competitive bidding.[28] Routine cost overruns undermine the bidding process in many other nominally competitive contract awards. The Pentagon is most comfortable with large, stable contractors that are immune to the uncertainties of competition. Most of the early defense contracts for integrated circuits, for example, went to well-established manufacturers that were producing soon-to-be-outmoded vacuum tubes (like Western Electric, General Electric, Raytheon, Sylvania, and RCA) instead of innovators like Texas Instruments, Motorola, and Transitron. Even as late as 1959 the old-line vacuum tube companies were awarded 78 percent of the federal research and development funds devoted to improving the performance and reducing the cost of the transistor, although these established firms then accounted for only 37 percent of the commercial market.[29] (The innovators did eventually penetrate and then dominate the market despite the Department of Defense.) On occasion the Pentagon actually seems hostile to competition, particularly when it threatens the stability of a prime contractor. Secretary of Defense Caspar Weinberger recently argued that the government's antitrust suit against the American Telephone & Telegraph Company should be dropped on the ground that, if successful, it would threaten the viability of AT&T and hence jeopardize communications facilities necessary for national security.

Successfully marketing new products also requires that technology be transferable to commercial uses at relatively low cost. MITI sees to it that new technologies are diffused rapidly into the economy and incorporated into commercial products. Japanese firms bid to participate in MITI projects, agreeing to absorb some of the cost of the research projects. Not only does this competitive process help ensure that government subsidies are as low as necessary to spur the private sector into action, but it also helps guarantee that the Japanese companies acquiring the new technologies are the ones willing and able to apply them profitably, since the firms base their bids on expected profits.

The advanced technologies developed for the next generation of elaborate military hardware—precision-guided munitions, air-to-air missiles, cruise missiles, night-vision equipment, and missile-tracking devices—will not be as easily applicable to commercial uses as were the more basic technologies produced during the defense and aerospace programs of the late 1950's and early 1960's. Precisely because America's commercial semiconductor industry is not likely to be geared to defense needs in the years ahead, for example, the Defense Department has launched its own research and development program for the "chip of the future." In explaining the program, William J. Perry, then undersecretary of defense for research and engineering, told the Senate that while the department has "an outstanding ability to direct technology resident in the defense industry to high priority programs . . . [it has] little ability to influence those companies whose sales are predominantly commercial." Perry continued:

> Therefore we have initiated a new technology program intended to direct the next generation of large-scale circuits to those characteristics most significant to Defense applications. . . . This program will ensure that the U.S. maintains a commanding lead in semiconductor technology and that this technology will achieve its full potential in our next full generation of weapon systems.[30]

But this lead, if achieved, will be in specialized semiconductor technology —specialized away from commercial applications. Far from encouraging commercial development, defense spending on emerging high technologies will have the opposite effect over the long term, diverting American scientists and engineers away from developing marketable applications.

The problems posed by the disjuncture between defense policies and economic needs are likely to loom larger in the next few years, as the Reagan administration's defense buildup gets under way. In total, planned military spending will exceed $1.5 trillion over the next six years. This will profoundly affect several emerging industries. Between now and 1987, for example, defense spending for semiconductors is expected to increase by more than 18 percent, while commercial semiconductor purchases will increase only about 12 percent. A similarly divergent growth pattern is expected for computer sales (16.4 percent for defense, 11.8 percent for commercial purposes), engineering and scientific equipment sales (9 percent for defense, 5.6 percent for commercial purposes), and sales of communications technologies (11.6 percent for defense, 5.3 percent for commercial purposes). Meanwhile, the Defense Department's share of government research and development outlays is expected to rise to more than 60 percent in FY 1983.[31]

The Pentagon's overriding concern for the stability of defense contractors is also manifested by its support for tariffs and quotas on "strategic" industrial supplies, like steel and semiconductors. The Defense Department recently invoked national security arguments to support a quota on imports of 64K RAM semiconductor chips from Japan. The department fears that Japan's capture of 70 percent of the U.S. market for 64K RAMs would leave the military vulnerable if war broke out.

In short, U.S. defense and aerospace programs have become lucrative diversions from international commercial competition. The programs, while profoundly affecting America's industrial development, have failed to promote economic adjustment. Indeed, they have retarded it. This is not to suggest that the goal of economic adjustment should necessarily take precedence over national defense. But defense and other policies should at least be made as compatible with adjustment as possible. We should recognize and explicitly weigh trade-offs and linkages among national goals. It could well be argued, for example, that national security depends as much on the health of the national economy as on defense expenditures. To pursue these two goals in isolation, with no appreciation of either conflicts between them or opportunities to integrate them and serve both simultaneously, is wrongheaded and wasteful.

8.

The superstructures of management in America were designed for stability, not adaptability. They made high-volume, standardized production predictable and thus, during the management era, supported most Americans' prosperity and security. But America's economic future depends on adjustment to a sharply different world economy. The superstructures of management—organized along industry lines and dominated by the largest and most entrenched producers within each industry—are inappropriate to this new task.

When threatened by international competition, the superstructures of management have reacted as they have always to threats to stability: They have closed ranks. Managers of firms imperiled by imports have joined with organized labor to obtain import restrictions, government loans and loan guarantees, special tax benefits, and relief from environmental regulations—all designed to preserve the least competitive segments of the industry. At the same time managers have sought to reduce real wages by threatening to close plants unless unions agree to wage concessions. Organized labor has responded to layoffs and plant closings not by supporting industrial adjustment but by joining management in calling for protection. The nation's defense and aerospace programs, meanwhile, have favored not the most dynamic but the older and most entrenched firms.

In the early 1960's, when only 8 percent of the American economy was subject to foreign competition and America still enjoyed rapid growth, a decline in one high-volume industry was typically offset by increases in another. Capital and labor could shift fairly easily out of old enterprises and into new, because production processes were similar across the economy. But today, with more than 70 percent of American industry exposed to foreign trade, with much slower domestic growth, and with the only real opportunities for future growth located in a very different system of skill-intensive production, these adjustments are far more difficult. Declines are not automatically offset by growing industries that readily absorb the newly freed capital and labor. Instead, the declines are marked by plant closings and rising unemployment. This gives a simple fact of political life enormous importance: America's old industries and their workers carry far more political power than emerging flexible-system industries. Whole cities or regions are often dependent on declining industries' networks of suppliers, distributors, independent contractors, and service businesses as well as on the industries' own employees. Through the superstructures of management, these groups exercise their political influence and exploit well-established connections.

By contrast, flexible-system producers, almost by definition, are small and new. Although they may offer great potential for future jobs in the region, few people are now dependent on them for their livelihoods. A job lost is felt far more painfully than a potential job that never develops.

This disparity in political power between declining high-volume producers and emerging flexible-system producers makes it risky for politicians to advocate policies promoting adjustment rather than protection. Declining industries and their dependents prefer protection for the simple reason that adjustment subjects them to an uncertain future, while protection at least temporarily preserves the status quo. The emerging industries cannot match this political appeal.

Adjustment policies can in principle be designed to compensate citizens dependent on declining industries for the risks to which economic change subjects them and thus to gain their political assent. But to implement such policies, America must have the institutional capacity to marshal precise information about the needs of the declining industries and their dependents and to negotiate adjustment agreements that preserve the interests of emerging industries. In both these aspects of industrial policy making—acquiring strategic business information and negotiating adjustment agreements—the superstructures of management are sorely lacking.

Because these superstructures are organized by industry, no agency of the U.S. government has overall responsibility for gathering detailed information about world market trends, the competitive strategies of trading partners, and the long-term outlook for particular segments and firms within global markets. Instead, the information is gathered piecemeal within the Commerce Department, the State Department, the Treasury, the Internal Revenue Service, the Securities and Exchange Commission, the Federal Trade Commission, and other agencies and boards concerned with particular industries, and it is gathered in such broad aggregates or idiosyncratic detail that it is of little use for making industrial policy. For example, when the U.S. government was faced with pleas for loan guarantees from the Chrysler Corporation, no government agency was prepared to evaluate Chrysler's position. Congress was forced to rely on a perfunctory study of the industry supplied by a private consulting firm.

Although management superstructures traditionally have facilitated industry-wide exchanges of company data on investment and production, American business managers have been reluctant to release information to the public about their firms' competitive prospects. This reluctance has been due, in part, to their concern that inadvertent public disclosure of these data might forewarn suppliers, employees, creditors, or investors about pending changes in the firms and thereby jeopardize the firms' paper entrepreneurial strategies. Managers of declining firms rarely want to admit that their businesses are in trouble for fear that they will thereby create a self-fulfilling prophecy; managers who are plotting takeovers or new tax avoidance schemes rarely want to reveal their plans for fear that others will rush in to take advantage of the opportunities first. Thus, to the extent that the paper strategies of American firms are dependent on secrecy and surprise, information will not be forthcoming—except in the extreme circumstances when a declining firm faces imminent collapse (as with Chrysler) or a declining industry is in immediate peril of losing a large share of its market to foreign competitors. But by that time protection in one form or another is typically the only public policy that can be invoked. Adjustment simply takes too long.

Short of the competitive strategies of American firms' turning on real improvements in products and processes rather than on paper entrepreneurialism, and therefore becoming less dependent on surprise, there seems little hope of eliciting from the private sector the quality of information that industrial policy makers would need. One is struck, for example, by how readily Japanese, West German, and French officials gain access to data from their domestic firms. Apart from the possibility that these governments are better able to maintain the confidentiality of the data they receive than is the U.S. government and have thereby earned a greater degree of business confidence (a possibility that should not be too quickly dismissed), the only explanation for the far greater openness of foreign firms seems to lie in long and accepted traditions within these nations of government leadership in economic development and in the fact that they are far less dependent than American firms on paper strategies turning on the tactic of surprise.

Nor do America's superstructures of management permit adjustment policies to be negotiated across industries. Instead, each major industry maintains its own trade association, with Washington offices staffed by public relations professionals, lobbyists, and lawyers. There are now an estimated 8,000 trade association offices in the capital; they directly employ 42,000 people, and farm out additional work to 8,000 public relations specialists, 12,000 Washington-based lawyers, and 9,000 lobbyists.[32] These people plead on behalf of their industry in many public arenas: congressional committees and subcommittees, independent regulatory agencies, grant-making agencies in the executive branch, executive agencies that are responsible for fiscal and monetary policies, the federal courts, and the media. Although they implicitly trade upon past votes or campaign contributions—or upon the veiled threat to withhold these benefits in the future—they generally base their arguments for government assistance on the importance to the economy of maintaining their industry's profitability.

In this system of industry-centered bargaining it is relatively easy to impose costs on those who are unrepresented—typically consumers, emerging industries, and other major industries that bargain in different forums. The costs of industrial decline cascade down through the economy until they come to rest on groups too unorganized or too politically weak to pass them on to someone else.

Rather than fight such protectionist measures directly, industries that bear the costs often find it politically easier to use their own management superstructures in order to impose offsetting costs elsewhere in the economy. Instead of seeking to modify or eliminate the trigger-price system —a strategy that would entail a direct confrontation with the steel industry—American automakers have sought to improve their position by limiting Japanese import competition. Similarly, the trigger-price system has injured American specialty steel manufacturers as foreign producers of basic steel have switched to specialty steel in order to maintain their foreign earnings. But instead of opposing the trigger-price system, specialty steel manufacturers are lobbying to extend the system to their products as well. In precisely the same manner, the American semiconductor industry lobbied Congress in the spring of 1982 for import restrictions on Japanese semiconductors. American computer manufacturers, whose competitive position would be hurt by any such restrictions, were reluctant to lobby against their sister industry.

The most competitive businesses within each of America's major industries and their industrial customers have seldom sought protection but have often had it thrust upon them. This has been the case for much of the textile industry as import barriers raised raw-fiber costs; for a significant portion of the clothing industry, agreements of which limited fabric imports; for parts of the shoe industry—particularly dealers and retailers —as footwear manufacturers obtained protection; and for specialty steel producers and automakers in the wake of the protection given to carbon-steel manufacturers. Similarly, it was no accident that in 1979 a robust General Motors opposed tariff protection against Japanese imports, while Ford clamored for it. Seeing its own profits threatened from abroad, a less confident GM has now joined the pro-protection chorus.

The American government could have recognized and responded positively to these differences within industries by strengthening the most competitive businesses and helping workers prepare for and find new jobs. Instead, it has watched passively as one industry after another has lost its market share to foreign producers. Inevitably the least competitive businesses within each industry have been able to form strong political coalitions, with the support of organized labor, to demand and obtain protection.

9.

America is trying to preserve its old industrial base, but at the price of a gradually declining standard of living for its citizens. Barriers against imports are forcing Americans to pay higher prices—restrictions on steel imports have increased the prices of steel goods by more than $1.3 billion a year, and tariffs on apparel cost consumers $1.9 billion annually.[33] Subsidized loans, loan guarantees, and tax benefits are forcing Americans to pay higher taxes in order to finance these benefits. Rollbacks of environmental regulations are forcing Americans to breathe dirtier air and drink dirtier water. Wage reductions and tacit reductions in the minimum wage are forcing Americans to accept less take-home pay.

These declines in the U.S. standard of living would be more bearable if they resulted from positive steps toward a stronger industrial base and a higher standard of living in the future. But they will lead to nothing but further declines because they are conditioned on preserving American dominance in high-volume, standardized production, rather than on adapting American industry to flexible-system production. The super-structures of management continue to seek preservation over adaptation because preservation is viewed as a safer strategy in the short term. And because America has no institutional means of reducing the insecurity from, or compensating the short-term losers for, major economic change, preservation will continue to be the politically attractive alternative.

Other nations, meanwhile, are struggling to adapt their economies to changing patterns of world trade. Sometimes this has required the tempo-rary use of tariffs or quotas in order to protect "infant industries" until they reach a scale where they can compete internationally. Sometimes subsidies, government-financed loans and loan guarantees, and targeted tax benefits are used to boost emerging industries. The tools are similar to those used in America, but their purposes and effects are diametrically opposite. Rather than preserve an outmoded industrial base, these nations use such tools to guide their economies into high-valued production.

Since the 1973 oil crisis and subsequent recession both West Germany and Japan have moved capital and labor out of industries with little promise of long-term competitiveness, leaving behind smaller, more streamlined industry segments better able to compete. For example, while other governments were busy promoting investment in basic steel in the mid-1970's, both West Germany and Japan anticipated the competitive decline of their basic steel industries and smoothed the movement of resources out of steel.[34] They have undertaken similar, although not uniformly successful, efforts in shipbuilding, fibers, aluminum, and petrochemicals.

Under Japan's Structurally Depressed Industries Law, the Ministry of International Trade and Industry (MITI) can form "recession cartels" within depressed industries, temporarily restricting output and thereby driving up prices. The key to the success of the program lies in the explicit subsidies given to firms that agree to scrap excess capacity and in the firms' use of these subsidies to retrain and relocate their workers for more profitable endeavors. The subsidies for scrapping thereby accomplish two related objectives: They induce the least competitive firms to exit from the industry, thereby improving the profitability of more competitive firms; and they provide workers with adjustment assistance that is geared to cushion and accelerate industrial change.

West Germany has instituted a similar program, but one somewhat less explicit and administered primarily through banks and regional labor boards rather than through subsidized cartels. Industries in distress receive bank loans and regional subsidies in exchange for their pledges to reduce capacity. The loans and subsidies are used expressly to shift resources into growing industries in the same areas. Germany's regional programs are substantial, averaging $4 billion annually since 1970 (in 1980 dollars), or 15 percent of total industrial investment.

This is not to imply that these other countries are innocent of politically expedient protectionism. Political coalitions in their own declining industries occasionally are so strong and so threatened by economic change that they seek and get protection. This is particularly true of the agricultural sector in Japan and the European Common Market countries and of textile workers in Western Europe. Under the Multi-Fiber Agreement just completed, the European Economic Community is planning to cut textile quotas for Hong Kong, South Korea, and Taiwan by 10 percent in 1983. Since 1978 Sweden and Belgium have been pouring huge sums of money into their dying steel industries. In no democratic industrial country can protectionism be avoided entirely. But nations that have made adjustment a centerpiece of their economic strategies—that have developed programs designed to move capital and labor into higher-valued industries—are more likely to avoid protectionist policies which seek merely to preserve the past.

Adjustment has not been the central theme of American industrial policy. Instead, over the last fifteen years the superstructures of management in America have opted for historic preservation of an increasingly outmoded industrial base. Every major participant in the U.S. economy is afraid to risk change in his economic status for fear that the burden of change in the economy as a whole will fall disproportionately upon him. But the unwillingness of all participants to risk economic change is dooming everyone.

A collective willingness to endure major economic change can come about only when citizens trust that the burdens and the benefits of such change will be shared equitably. That challenge must be met through a nation's social policies. Lurking beneath the issues of economic growth and adjustment are deeper issues of social justice—issues to which we will return.

X
DEAD-END LABOR

1.

America's prosperity and its place in the world economy ultimately depend on the value of the work Americans can do. Our future hinges on specific citizens, with specific skills, working at specific jobs. But public policies have so far failed to smooth the shift by American workers to flexible-system production. Indeed, these policies have too often retarded adjustment, in ways this chapter relates. The problem, broadly, is that neither macroeconomic manipulations nor social welfare programs have been designed for the transition we now face. Macroeconomic policies view the citizenry as an abstract "pool" of labor, one that flows along well-worn channels in response to the changes in taxes, government spending, and the money supply. Social welfare policies, in turn, deal only with the demonstrably "needy"; they are addressed almost exclusively to the immediate unmet needs of our most unfortunate citizens, not to helping an entire labor force enhance its productive capacities. This cleavage between economic and social policies means that neither can be fully effective; the ultimate result is that only a small share of the world's new high-value jobs is going to Americans and that a growing proportion of America's work force is unemployed or—more insidiously—locked into dead-end employment.

Macroeconomic policies—manipulating the supply of money and the level of taxes and government spending—are too broad and too blunt. When these policies have been aimed at stimulating the economy in an effort to cure unemployment, they have resulted in higher and higher levels of inflation. When they have sought to "wring" inflation out of the economy by restricting the money supply and reducing demand, they have brought on higher and higher rates of unemployment. In the early 1960's inflation could be tamed with a relatively low rate of unemployment (3.5 percent). By 1976 the "normal" unemployment rate compatible with modest inflation had risen to 6 percent. By 1980 it was 7 percent. In the most recent attack on inflation the Reagan administration has pushed unemployment to over 10 percent.

As the skills of America's labor force have become more obsolete, the problem of unemployment has become less open to amelioration through fiscal and monetary policies. Greater deficits must be endured, and more money put into circulation, to achieve the same level of economic stimulation. But in order to cope with the resulting inflation, more draconian policies must then be invoked in the opposite direction, causing still higher rates of unemployment. The downward spiral gathers momentum. Prior to 1969, an increase in unemployment resulted in a substantial decline in help-wanted advertising as employers hired the highest-skilled unemployed workers. But since then help-wanted advertising has stayed high even when unemployment rises, indicating a decreasing demand for the skills held by laid-off workers.[1] In short, we are beyond economic "fine tuning."

Similarly, social policies have traditionally made no reference to the goal of economic evolution. Programs that have been designed as temporary or permanent aids to the disadvantaged or as sorters and trainers for preexisting jobs at best perpetuate the ongoing process of production. They may promote the upward mobility of exceptionally gifted or ambitious individuals. But they do not encourage the evolution of an entire work force within a dynamic industrial system.

Programs of unemployment compensation, welfare, education and training, housing, health, mass transit, and day care in America have been based on the same principles of high volume and standardization that shape the organization of firms and industries. These principles have influenced both the form and the substance of American social programs. In form, the programs have been packaged and delivered in standardized units that fail to reflect recipients' individual circumstances and have been fragmented into separate payments and services issued to applicants like standardized parts. Whatever the nature, severity, or duration of their needs, Americans are limited to "off-the-shelf" social services.

The substance of these programs has also been shaped by America's system of high-volume, standardized production. They have sought either to prepare people for preexisting jobs within that system or to acclimate them to dependent lives outside it. They have involved no efforts to adapt the labor force to new roles in an evolving system of production.

This bias is unsurprising; these programs grew out of an economy centered on stable mass-production industries. Programs that were part of the New Deal (Social Security, unemployment compensation) were designed to soften the blow of unforeseen, temporary job loss—to tide people over until they could obtain the same or a similar job elsewhere —and to provide for workers' subsistence after old age or infirmity had retired them from the labor force. Social programs that originated in the 1960's (Medicaid, food stamps, and so on) were intended to preserve the unfortunate from the worst effects of long-term poverty unless or until they could be integrated into the system of production. Meanwhile, throughout the management era public education has served to sort and train children for preexisting professional or blue-collar occupations. And publicly supported job training programs have assumed a stable set of well-defined jobs for which the individual is to be fitted, like a standardized part for a giant machine.

The existence of the giant machine itself has been taken for granted. To be sure, there have been cycles of boom and recession. But the basic nature of the production process—its stable job categories, rules, and routines—has been taken to be an immutable feature of modern industrial life. Social programs have been built around this process, helping people get into it, sustaining them when they could not get into it, and providing a sort of safety net when the process occasionally failed.

Because adaptation was not the issue when these programs were designed, America has failed to appreciate the potential of public programs for easing the transition of its work force into skill-intensive production. The consequences have been severe. Unemployment and the fear of unemployment are exacting a heavy toll. In any given year, 1 American family in 6 is temporarily impoverished. In 1979 alone—not a recession year—22 million Americans, or about 20 percent of the working population, were unemployed for at least one week.[2] Not even senior, relatively secure workers can confidently expect their life's work to be tied up with their current firm. In many large American firms 30 percent of the work force is comprised of production workers with at least ten years' seniority; although they are unlikely to be laid off, they are still "hourly workers," with no guarantee against dismissal on short notice.

One researcher has found that every time the rate of unemployment rises by 1 percent, deaths in America from all causes rise by 1.9 percent. When a person becomes unemployed, he is likely to have more gastrointestinal problems, more infections, and higher blood pressure than when he was employed.[3] Ironically, most workers receive health insurance coverage through schemes sponsored by their employers; once they lose their jobs, they also lose their health insurance—precisely when they need it most. Thus, 36 percent of America's unemployed workers and their families are without health insurance.[4] Nor do unemployed workers immediately or automatically become eligible for Medicaid.

These problems are compounded when an entire community or region, like Detroit or the industrial Midwest, suffers rapid economic decline. The infrastructure of roads, hospitals, sewers, educational institutions, and other public goods depends on a steady stream of tax revenue; the sudden demise of industry often leaves the community without any alternative means of support, just when the demands on public services by the newly unemployed are at their peak.

Even though the more immediate burden falls on specific people and communities, all America bears the cost of unemployment. Every 1 percent increase in the jobless rate costs roughly $75 billion in lost production of goods and services, $25 billion in lost taxes, and $5 billion in unemployment compensation.[5] And when unemployment hits minority youth especially heavily, the nation also loses an irreplaceable part of its future. Two out of every five black teenagers are now out of school and out of a job. America has never before had a period when so much unemployment was concentrated in minority youth. These young people are not learning how to contribute to America's future growth and well-being. They are learning, instead, that their country has no opportunities for them. Some are learning about drugs and crime. The future cost to America of these disaffected young people is incalculable.

The official unemployment figures in fact mask a much larger employment problem. Almost as many Americans again as are actually counted among the unemployed are jobless but have given up looking for work, and these discouraged workers are not included in the unemployment statistics. In 1982, 11 million Americans were counted as unemployed; an additional 6.5 million wanted jobs but were too discouraged to look for them.[6] And many Americans who do have jobs suffer from the mismatch between their capabilities and available work. Many work part time, although they would prefer full-time jobs. Many work for less than the minimum wage. Many work in menial, dead-end jobs that do not fully use their skills, training, or education. And many working Americans have cause to worry that their jobs will not last. The growing obsolescence of the American labor force manifests itself in all these ways.

At the same time the demand for skilled and semiskilled machine operators, engineers, computer programmers and operators, skilled assemblers, optical workers, elementary software designers, and personnel to maintain, repair, and service complex machinery continues to grow. There are now about 1 million unfilled skilled or semiskilled jobs. America is already short an estimated 60,000 skilled machinists, and 22,000 more will be needed annually over the next decade. Yet only about 2,800 skilled machinists are graduated each year from various apprenticeship programs. The average age of America's tool- and diemakers is approaching fifty years; if present trends continue, within the next decade this vital reservoir of skills—central to many flexible-system processes and already in short supply—threatens to dry up. The precipitous rise in U.S. defense spending planned for the next five years will create additional shortages of engineers, scientists, and machine operators. Evidence of these tightening bottlenecks is found in the average earnings of skilled and semiskilled workers in America, which have risen relative to every other occupational group—from 72 percent of the average earnings of professional workers in 1972 to 80 percent of professional workers' earnings in 1978.[7]

How can unemployment and labor shortages exist at the same time?

The answer is that the signals of supply and demand are inadequate to shift workers smoothly into the best jobs. A large part of the problem is that much of the American work force is now immobile. Workers feel too insecure to leave family, friends, and familiar territory; they are unable to finance their own retraining; and they are uncertain about where new jobs are located and for what jobs training should be sought. Demographic trends suggest the employment problem will worsen. Women and minorities, mostly unskilled, will account for 74 percent of the growth of the labor force in the next decade.[8] Most people who are unemployed are unskilled. Others simply have the wrong skills. In the absence of effective programs to prepare people for high-value employment, the simultaneous existence of jobless people and unfilled jobs is no mystery. Of course, the problem is not just obstacles which block dead-end workers from moving automatically into these skilled and semiskilled jobs. At this point, even if these barriers were overcome, there would not be enough of these higher-valued jobs to go around. The American economy is not yet evolving quickly enough to gain an adequate share of the world's flexible-system industries.

Finally, not only have social programs been inadequate or inappropriate, but they have also been the first targets of periodic campaigns to reduce government expenditures. The assumption that their purpose can be only to prepare economic laggards for traditional employment—or to save the unemployable from utter destitution—has relegated these programs to a subordinate position, dependent for their legitimacy and funding on the overall health of the economy. They are seen as forms of collective consumption—analogous to charity—affordable only when resources can be spared from more pressing tasks. Between 1965 and 1975 the percentage of municipal bond issues that were voted down in referenda nearly doubled, resulting in cutbacks in local education and social services.[9] The "tax revolt" (represented by California's Proposition 13 and Massachusetts's Proposition 2½) has starved local school systems. And the Reagan administration's deep budget cuts in education aids and loans, job training and retraining, and nutrition benefits for expectant mothers are seriously jeopardizing America's future stock of human capital.

The idea that education, job training, health, housing, and nutrition programs are social luxuries, to be indulged in if and when the American economy is strong enough to afford them, stands the true relationship on its head. It is precisely because these programs have not been properly conceived and adequately funded that the work force is now stymied. American workers cannot shift into flexible-system production because they lack the training and skills to do so; they cannot obtain the necessary training because public schools, colleges, and job-training programs are inadequate to the task; they cannot physically move to places where they have the best chance of obtaining on-the-job training because they lack the housing, health care, and income insurance necessary to make that transition bearable.

2.

Persistent unemployment and pervasive mismatches between skills and job opportunities are symptoms of a basic problem: America's labor force is not participating in the growing segments of the world economy. One out of every six jobs in the American economy now depends on the automobile industry. One out of every five unskilled manufacturing jobs in America is in the textile industry. All told, one out of every three American workers now depends for his or her livelihood, directly or indirectly, on American industries that are losing rapidly in international competition.[10]

True, the economy performed extraordinarily well during the last decade in terms of creating 21 million new jobs for the surge of young people and married women who entered the labor force. But a large percentage of these jobs were dead ends. Seventy percent of them (outside government) were in services and retailing; almost all these jobs are sheltered from international trade. Thirty percent of the new jobs (employing almost 7 million people) were in eating and drinking places (mostly as waiters, waitresses, cooks, and kitchen helpers), health services (hospital orderlies and attendants), and business services (typists, clerks, messengers, deliverymen, security guards, low-paid salesclerks, cashiers, janitors). Since 1973 the increase in employment in eating and drinking places alone has been greater than the total employment in America's auto and steel industries combined. Employment in finance, insurance, and real estate has increased substantially, but most of the new jobs in these industries also have been in low-level clerical and sales positions. Some new jobs also have been created in the shoe, textile, and tanning industries, but many of these have gone to illegal immigrants (an estimated 6 million of them are now working in the United States), who work for sub-minimum wages in order to compete with workers doing much the same tasks in Southeast Asia.[11]

Even America's high-technology industries are filling almost as many dead-end jobs as skill-intensive ones. Low-skill production workers now constitute 45 percent of the American electronics industry work force. They do such things as assemble integrated circuits, stuff circuits into printed boards, and transfer silicon wafers from ovens to acid baths and electroplating tanks—unskilled and tedious work. And because these production workers compete directly with workers in Taiwan, South Korea, and China, their pay is low, and declining in real terms. Between 1972 and 1978 their average salary increased by only 7 percent. By 1979 they were earning $4.52 an hour, or about $9,000 a year. (In contrast, between 1972 and 1978 the average salary of electronics engineers increased 33 percent; by 1979 they were earning an average of $48,000 yearly.[12])

Most of these new jobs in the American economy—in menial occupations sheltered from international trade or in low-paying assembly operations in direct competition with foreign workers—have no futures. Wages do not increase with experience. Few or no benefits attach to these jobs. There is almost no job security. The majority of Americans in jobs like these are unprotected against an incapacitating accident, a heart attack, an illness, or a sudden layoff.

It is true that even if America were to adapt itself to flexible-system production, there still would be some routine jobs to be filled by relatively unskilled workers. Not everyone is capable of maintaining precision machinery, developing software, or participating on a problem-solving team. But it seems a safe guess that among the millions of Americans now locked into dead-end jobs, there are vast numbers whose latent talents and untapped capacities for learning could be put to far more productive uses.

3.

America has no mechanisms to shift its work force out of unemployment and dead-end jobs into the kinds of flexible-system industries where Americans can gain and maintain competitive advantage while preserving or increasing their real wages.

Unemployment insurance is the main public program for Americans out of work. But it is designed to tide people over during temporary periods of unemployment, not to help the large numbers of workers who are unemployable because they have no marketable skill. Coverage is limited, providing only a fraction of the worker's previous earnings (usually one-half) for only twenty-six weeks. It is not available at all to people who have not yet entered the work force. And there are wide variations among the states in eligibility and benefits. Six states and the District of Columbia provide benefits which extend slightly beyond twenty-six weeks. Another thirteen weeks are available under a federally mandated scheme applying to states where unemployment has been particularly severe. Most states also place a ceiling on the amount of weekly benefits that can be obtained; where the ceiling is low, as in New York, Texas, and California, workers who before had held relatively high-paying jobs may have to get by on only a small fraction of their previous salaries. Given these restrictions and inconsistencies, it is not surprising that only one-half of America's unemployed receive unemployment insurance at any given time.[13]

Public welfare, in the form of Aid to Families with Dependent Children, is of little help. In half the states the program is available only to single-parent families; in the other twenty-five states it also applies to two-parent families in which the principal wage earner is unemployed. But in order to qualify, the family's assets (including house and car) must not exceed $1,000. At most, the program reaches only the hard core of America's poor.

The United States does have job-training programs, but they are generally restricted to the unskilled. There are no programs to retrain people with obsolete skills or those who wish to improve their skills. America's publicly financed job-training programs do not prepare even the unskilled for real careers. They are oriented primarily toward "public service" jobs rather than toward new jobs in the private sector. In 1980, $6 billion of $11 billion in job-training money was spent on public service employment. Many states and localities have used these job-training programs to hire people they would have hired anyway. And even these public service jobs have been temporary. In 1980, 40 percent of the job trainees were unemployed after leaving the program.[14] In any event, the Reagan administration is cutting back these programs severely:

Department of Labor outlays for job-training programs declined to $4.5 billion in 1982 from $7.8 billion in 1981, despite the addition of almost 2 million men and women to the unemployment rolls.

The private sector does provide some training. In 1981 American firms spent more than $30 billion on courses for their employees, affecting about 6 percent of the labor force.[15] (This is roughly half the cost of higher education in America.) The Bell System, for example, spent $1.7 billion conducting 12,000 courses for up to 30,000 employees daily at 1,300 training sites around the country. Xerox opened a $75 million training and management center, where it trains 12,000 employees a year.

The vast majority of these programs, however, provide training in narrow jobs or in processes unique to the company rather than in broadly applicable skills. There is an obvious reason for this. Broader training would render employees much more marketable, and therefore require that the firm pay them a higher wage in order to retain them. Few firms are so generous (or foolish) as to want to bid up the wages of their work force in this way. In any event, companies are now spending about the same amount on training per employee that they were in 1969—even though the need for such training is much greater now that America's competitive position is in jeopardy.

Special government assistance has been available to workers and communities injured by foreign trade—to provide relocation, retraining, and extended unemployment insurance to workers whose jobs have been eliminated because of imports, and to aid communities facing economic decline. But like unemployment compensation and job training, these "trade adjustment" programs have been disconnected from the process of industrial change in America. As a result, they, too, have failed to help ease the transition of the labor force to flexible-system production. Administered by the Department of Labor and far removed from forums like Treasury, Commerce, and the office of the U.S. Trade Representative, where tariffs, quotas, and bailouts for industry are formulated, worker adjustment programs have been encumbered by administrative problems of determining whether imports are to blame for job loss and of deciding where workers should relocate and for what jobs they should seek retraining. In practice, these programs have provided workers with little more than extended unemployment compensation. Since 1975, 1.2 million

American workers have received cash payments under these programs, totaling $4 billion. Yet only 36,000 workers have obtained any training, and only 4,000 have received job search allowances. In 1981 cash benefits totaled $1.5 billion, but the training budget was only $17 million. A survey of laid-off workers who had exhausted their unemployment benefits revealed that only 20 percent had received counseling, only 8 percent had received job referrals, and only 7 percent job training. (The Reagan administration has also targeted trade adjustment assistance for substantial reductions.[16])

The only job-training programs with direct ties to the nation's economic development have been conducted by the Defense Department. Since World War II the military has trained generations of Americans. A survey undertaken in 1964 showed that 18 percent of all nuclear power workers and 45 percent of all licensed nuclear operators learned their skills in the U.S. Navy.[17] Many of the nation's skilled machinists, electricians, machine operators, and computer programmers also received their training while in military service. Defense-related education programs spawned new skills: The GI Bill following the war enabled 7.5 million veterans to attend college or technical school. The National Defense Education Act of 1958, inspired by Sputnik, provided low-interest education loans, teacher training, and funds for doctoral research. All these programs, in turn, helped ensure a well-trained work force, which contributed to America's economic development well into the 1960's.

But defense-related job-training and education programs can no longer be relied upon to shift America's labor force into higher-valued production. These programs have been reduced in recent years, as more defense resources have been channeled to advanced weapons systems and other sorts of military hardware. Because new weapons technology is so specialized, the training that is provided has tended to be less broadly applicable to civilian occupations than before.

Most community and regional development programs have been similarly irrelevant to real economic progress. Firms seeking to diversify or to develop new products in an effort to regain competitiveness seldom, if ever, base their location decisions on the financial lures offered by needy communities—such as tax abatements, low-interest financing, or transportation facilities, most of which are made possible by federal grants. For one thing, the real value of these offerings constitutes, at most, a very small fraction of the costs of starting and operating a new enterprise, particularly when compared with factors such as prevailing wage rates, the availability of workers with particular skills, access to raw materials and suppliers, and local energy costs. Perhaps more significantly, so many jurisdictions now offer these inducements that they largely offset one another. As communities bid to attract businesses, one city's gain is another's loss, and little or no additional investment occurs. Federal programs finance much of this competition. For example, program eligibility standards have been drawn so loosely for grants from the Commerce Department's Economic Development Administration that 80 percent of American communities are now eligible; more than half the nation's locales have been deemed eligible for urban development action grant programs administered by the Department of Housing and Urban Development; and as a practical matter, every community in America can offer low-interest loans financed by federally subsidized industrial development bonds.

The problems of worker and community adjustment are exacerbated by other public policies. The tax code, for example, effectively subsidizes capital mobility, but not the use of unemployed labor or underused public infrastructures. Firms in declining industries can typically take a tax loss on the plant and equipment that they leave behind, treat the cost of moving their headquarters as a deductible business expense, and take advantage of accelerated depreciation and tax credits for their investments in new plant and equipment elsewhere. But they reap no tax advantage from keeping their former employees or from utilizing the infrastructures of their former communities. Thus, the tax code biases firms' incentives against staying put.

Similarly, American antitrust laws recognize that restrictions on mergers should be relaxed for failing firms, which otherwise might be deprived of the capital they need to regain competitive strength. But businesses that have been granted such antitrust immunity have not been required to accept even limited responsibility for their workers or communities. On the contrary, the resulting mergers have often meant closing or relocating the failing firm's facilities, with no provisions for labor or community adjustment.

The net result of all these programs has been the continued atrophy of the American labor force. Workers' skills are not upgraded to fit them for flexible-system production.

4.

America's system of public education is similarly inadequate to the task of preparing citizens for skill-intensive production. Because public schools are financed largely by local property taxes, schools in the poorest neighborhoods and in regions particularly hard hit by economic decline are least able to provide their students with the basic skills necessary for job mobility. In America's largest cities the middle class has all but abandoned the public school system, sending its children to private schools instead; left behind, in underfunded, decaying facilities, are the working class and the poor. The decay of American public education resembles other facets of the current impasse. In response to America's economic decline, public schools have been starved of resources. And as its public education degenerates, the erosion of its economic base accelerates.

The result is hardly surprising. Nearly 13 percent of the young in New York City are now functionally illiterate.[18] Between 1963 and 1982 the median score on the verbal Scholastic Aptitude Test declined from 478 (out of a possible 800) to 426; on the mathematics SAT, from 502 to 467.[19] The National Assessment of Education Progress reports that today's high school students are less able than their counterparts of a decade ago to understand and analyze what they read.[20]

In fields of knowledge directly related to America's competitive position in the world economy, the decline in educational quality has been particularly dramatic. Fewer than one-fifth of the nation's high school students now study a foreign language, and only 4 percent study one for more than two years. Only 8 percent of American colleges and universities require some minimal competence in a foreign language for admission (down from 34 percent just fifteen years ago). Only one out of six high school students has any math or science training beyond tenth grade. Fewer than 10 percent of U.S. high school students study physics. Only 3 percent study calculus. While in 1960, 59 percent of American high school students took at least one science course, by 1977 the proportion was only 48 percent.[21]

Part of the problem is the scarcity of suitable teachers. There are only

10,000 high school physics teachers to cover 17,000 American school districts. Chicago has only one physics teacher for every two high schools. High school mathematics and science teachers are fleeing the schools for higher-paying jobs in industry. Public schools have been denied the resources to come anywhere close to matching industrial salaries, and scarce talent is drawn into immediate production at the expense of the future. In 1981 alone 1,000 physics teachers—10 percent of the total—left the classroom for jobs in industry.[22] Many of those who remain are unqualified to teach math or science: More than half the 2,000 high school principals surveyed in 1981 by the National Science Teachers Association judged their math teachers to be unqualified. In the same survey officials from 600 teacher-training schools reported a 77 percent decline since 1971 in the number of high school mathematics teachers they graduated, and a 65 percent decline in the number of science teachers.[23]

The same "brain drain" is occurring in U.S. universities. American engineering schools in particular are badly understaffed. Across America, 2,500 of 20,000 faculty positions in engineering remain unfilled. Even prestigious MIT cannot fill faculty positions in microelectronics and computer engineering. At San Jose State University, in the heart of California's "Silicon Valley," one-third of the engineering faculty positions are unfilled, and the department must turn away half of the qualified applicants. Nearby electronics companies, meanwhile, suffer from shortages of engineers—shortages that current trends promise to worsen.[24] (It is ironic that both California and Massachusetts, the two states that have most successfully parlayed first-rate public health and educational systems into regional centers of skill-intensive industries, have succumbed to tax revolts that starve the sources of the skilled workers these industries will need in the future.) And as a result of reductions in federal funding, university science and engineering laboratories are grossly outdated. In sum, American students are not obtaining the education they need for leadership in flexible-system production.

Neglecting public education has the most damaging results for the children of less affluent Americans. Local school districts in the poorest areas of the country now have even fewer resources. Proposed tax credits for parents who send their children to private schools would further erode middle-class support for public education. And many American universities face pressure to accept students on the basis of their ability to pay.

America's future work force is being doomed to start out handicapped.

Underlying these disturbing trends is another factor, having more to do with the way American education is designed and administered than with its funding. Even if America were to devote more resources to education, simply more of the same would not prepare its youth for roles in flexible-system enterprises. At best, the current system of education prepares young people for preexisting jobs in high-volume, standardized production. Some students are sorted into professional ranks and trained in the manipulation of abstract symbols. Others are prepared for lower-level routine tasks in production or sales. Few students are taught how to work collaboratively to solve novel real-world problems—the essence of flexible-system production.

U.S. education has been modeled on scientific management. Students are sorted, programmed, and controlled in a high-volume, standardized production process essentially like any other. Knowledge is divided and subdivided into discrete units, delivered according to preset instructions, and monitored at regular intervals through standardized examinations—precisely Frederick Taylor's prescription of specialization by simplification, preestablished rules, and feedback information. Students move through high schools and universities as if they were on a conveyor belt.

American education has followed the form of American business. As businesses have merged and consolidated, so, too, have schools and universities—into centralized "comprehensive" school districts and giant university campuses. Increasingly America's educational curriculum is planned and monitored by professional administrators and delivered by teachers whose low salaries and tedious, repetitive jobs are coming to resemble those of production workers in a traditional American factory.

These trends toward consolidating physical plant and separating the planners and providers of education have had predictable results: Professional education administrators now spend a large portion of their time dealing in abstract rules and numbers, distilled to the point of being disconnected from the real processes of learning. Countless efforts are made to measure and quantify educational achievement. Professional administrators start from these measures to devise standard rules and procedures for teachers and students. Success in American education is coming to be measured largely by the degree of order and management control in the classroom.

Collaborative and innovative problem-solving skills simply cannot easily be learned in a routine and tightly controlled environment. People cannot be trained to participate in flexible-system enterprises when their daily lives are dominated by high-volume, standardized institutions. Children cannot learn to take responsibility and to work creatively within an atmosphere that discourages personal responsibility and rewards rote responses. America's schools and universities have come to mirror American firms—rigid systems for achieving economies of scale, impressively efficient but incapable of imaginative responses.

The value of education transcends its economic dimension, of course. Knowledge does not need to be justified in instrumental terms. But in our present period of fiscal belt tightening, it is well to remind ourselves of the connection between education and our collective well-being. A decline in our citizens' capacity to analyze, innovate, create, and communicate will condemn us all to a meager existence as it impoverishes our cultural and civic life together.

5.

Other social policies (or their absence) have conspired to render much of America's labor force physically immobile. The fragmented administration of welfare and unemployment insurance, imposing different requirements and offering different benefits in every state, itself has discouraged mobility. Many unemployed Americans are reluctant to look for work in another part of the country for fear that they will lose the minimal assistance they have.

Federal housing policies have locked the labor force into stricken communities and regions. Generous credit assistance to homeowners (available through the Farmers Home Administration, the Federal National Mortgage Assistance Administration, and the Veterans Administration), coupled with tax breaks (in the form of mortgage interest deductions and the ability to "roll over" proceeds from the sale of one's old house to purchase a new house without paying any tax on the transaction) have transformed the nation's housing stock into many middle-class Americans' primary form of savings. With so much at stake in one's home, the financial and psychological costs of moving are extremely high. This is particularly true if local housing prices are depressed as a result of a plant closing or any other manifestation of local economic decline, while housing prices in growing areas of the country are driven up by the increasing demand.

Those who cannot afford to own their own homes are often even more trapped. The nation's stock of low-cost rental housing units is decreasing rapidly. In Washington, D.C., alone, 13,600 housing units have been converted to condominiums in the last five years. Only 2 percent of Washington's rental units are available for occupancy at any given time. More than 10,000 area residents are now on the waiting list for public housing. For America's poor, it takes a long time to obtain adequate accommodation. Once a rental unit is obtained, the occupants are understandably reluctant to leave. Rent control laws in many jurisdictions further discourage the unemployed or underemployed from looking for jobs elsewhere since the laws deter private builders from erecting other low-cost housing while allowing rents on existing units to shoot up if the current tenant forays out in search of work in another city.

Other social policies also are rendering the nation's labor force less adaptable. America's fragmented and expensive system of health care causes many Americans to fear that a debilitating illness will use up their savings and impoverish their families. Planned cutbacks in Medicare will only heighten this fear. Medical insecurity discourages people from searching for new jobs in locations far removed from family and friends who might sustain them in times of hardship.

Mass transit and day care represent other failed opportunities for helping American labor shift into new production. If adequately funded, both sorts of programs would allow workers to search for work within a large radius of their homes. But mass transit and day care are becoming among the first victims of America's economic decline. Subway systems in Boston, New York, Philadelphia, and Chicago are in near collapse, plagued by aging equipment, vandalism, and frequent breakdowns and derailments. Bus systems in other major cities are experiencing periodic shutdowns because of insufficient funding. And the demand for day care facilities is far outrunning their availability.

In all these ways America is inadvertently accelerating its economic decline. By failing to appreciate and act on the link between these social programs and future productivity, America is condemning itself to a long and painful economic transition. Insecurity born of the fear of sudden, arbitrary, and unanticipated loss—whether of job, home, or health—does not inspire people to new productive feats. To the contrary, insecurities like these discourage risk taking and constrain adaptability. People who feel insecure want to keep what they have, even at the cost of some hardship and discomfort; the unknown could be far worse. In the face of such insecurity, people will seek better lives for themselves and their families only when their situation is truly desperate—as generations of immigrants will attest.

6.

America's social policies have been disconnected from its economic development. The design and administration of social programs have tended to replicate the organization of high-volume, standardized production. Programs have focused on the delivery of standardized commodities—years of education, months of training, weeks of unemployment assistance, units of housing, or numbers of hospital beds. This quantitative, production-oriented approach to social services is wastefully inappropriate to the needs of a labor force in transition.

The design and administration of these programs also reinforce the ideology of charity: Because the programs are evaluated on the basis of the number of "units" delivered, rather than their broader physical and psychological effects and the attitudes and commitments they engender, social policy in America has created a sharp distinction between the donors and recipients of public services. In times of economic decline, citizens who view themselves as donors are likely to resent the taxes they must pay to finance these programs, while citizens who view themselves as recipients are apt to feel the stigma that attaches to their dependent status.

This ideology of charity and the rigid bureaucratization of social services that accompanies it were perhaps appropriate to an America with a stable industrial base that progressed not by evolving but by becoming steadily bigger and more efficient. During the management era unemployment, inadequate education or training, substandard housing, and poor health were considered the problems of specific afflicted individuals, upon whom the community at large took the affordable degree of pity. The charitable ideals behind these programs were not entirely selfless, of course, since any person could fall victim to misfortune, and most people wanted some form of insurance against these risks. And because these programs were intimately tied to major industries (like housing construction, hospital construction, pharmaceuticals, and agriculture), they could be justified as providing a useful stimulus to the economy. But they were not viewed as instruments of economic development.

Since around 1970, however, the ideology of charity and its rigid systems, which "deliver" social services to identifiable "recipients," have been inappropriate to the nation's needs. America's economic future now depends, in large part, on the speed and efficiency with which its labor force can be shifted into flexible-system production. Social programs that prepare Americans to meet the challenges and accept the insecurity of adaptation are central to this transformation. Generous unemployment. compensation, well-endowed education and training programs, an adequate supply of housing, and comprehensive health care—if administered in ways that mesh with the opportunities in emerging flexible-system enterprises—should promote adjustment within the labor force. They would give people the will and ability to learn new skills, to discover new job opportunities, and to relocate. They would support economic change.

Such social programs would not be public charities. They would be aspects of a nation's strategy for economic development. Nor would they forge sharp distinctions between donors and recipients; they would be designed more to accelerate adjustment than merely to ameliorate specific misfortune. They would be broadly based and broadly visible. No stigma would be attached to them. On the contrary, citizens would be urged to participate in them, for the benefit of the community at large. For the faster and more efficiently the labor force shifts to higher-valued production, the greater the wealth of society as a whole.

The connection between social policy and economic development is understood by many of our international competitors. Job security and relatively full employment have been built into their organization of production. Between 1959 and 1976 unemployment in the United States averaged 5.4 percent of the labor force. But in France it averaged only 2.4 percent; in Sweden, 1.9 percent; in Japan, 1.4 percent; and in West Germany, 1.2 percent. Since 1977 unemployment in America has averaged 6.5 percent. But in France it has averaged 5.8 percent; in West Germany, 3.5 percent; in Japan, 2.1 percent; and in Sweden, 2.2 percent.[25] In continental Europe and Japan, an unemployment rate over 6 percent is a national scandal, causing governments to topple and labor unions, banks, and business associations to develop concerted strategies to find new jobs. In America, by contrast, an unemployment rate of 7 percent has become an accepted fact of economic life.

All these nations have elaborate programs of job training and retraining, both within and outside firms. At any given time between 1 and 2 percent of the labor forces in West Germany, France, Sweden, and Japan are training for new jobs. (Only one-tenth of 1 percent of America's labor force is in training or retraining.) Nor is job training limited to the lower rungs of the employment ladder. All workers are encouraged to upgrade their skills, even if they already have jobs.[26] Since 1969, for example, West Germany has offered every adult up to two years of full-time training or retraining. More than half the people who take advantage of this program are already employed but want to improve their skills for better jobs. The government pays all training costs and also provides the recipient with an income subsidy, which may be as high as 90 percent of his or her last wage. The subsidy rate is highest for low-wage workers, who therefore sacrifice very little present income in order to upgrade their skills.[27]

For the past thirty years Sweden has had a reemployment plan, developed by one of its trade union leaders, Gösta Rehn. Companies notify "Rehn boards," located throughout the country, of their future employment needs. The boards match these anticipated needs to workers who are looking for new jobs by providing them with training and relocation assistance. The Swedish government finances much of the boards' activities, but Swedish business and labor also participate.

A number of continental European countries also provide workers with vouchers that can be cashed in for on-the-job training. The government repays the employer a percentage of the employee's wage for a certain period of time. The voucher system thereby matches training to specific industrial needs, guarantees that companies undertake some portion of the investment to demonstrate their intent to employ the newly trained workers, and creates incentives for companies to locate in high-unemployment regions.

Japan provides its unemployed workers in designated "structurally depressed industries" with generous job-training and placement assistance, linked to unemployment benefits. Bank loans and government subsidies to Japan's larger companies encourage them to maintain and retrain their work forces and also help their smaller subcontractors maintain full employment by anticipating economic changes and retraining their workers in advance.[28]

Workers in these nations cannot be fired from their jobs arbitrarily, while the vast majority of American employees can be dismissed without notice or reason. When a plant is to close, workers receive at least two months' prior notice, so that they can prepare themselves for another job; many American workers receive no notice at all. When an employer becomes insolvent, workers in most of these nations continue to receive wages from the government for at least one year; American workers enjoy no such wage insurance.[29]

Social Security and unemployment insurance are also more generous in continental Europe and Japan than in America. If we take 1978 as a typical year, 21.1 percent of Sweden's annual income goes to Social Security, while 90 percent of its unemployed receive substantial compensation. In Japan, 9.7 percent of national income goes to Social Security, and 81 percent of the unemployed receive compensation. (The larger Japanese companies provide additional unemployment and retirement benefits that bring the total much higher.) And in West Germany 19.9 percent of the national income goes to Social Security, and 75 percent of the unemployed receive compensation. In the United States, on the other hand, only 9.3 percent of national income goes to pay Social Security, and only 34 percent of those who are unemployed receive compensation. Even those Americans who get compensation receive on average only 50 percent of their previous earnings. In Sweden, West Germany, and Japan, unemployment compensation ranges from 60 to 75 percent of previous earnings.[30]

Unlike America, each of these nations has a substantial national health insurance program. Sweden spends $883 per person per year on health care; West Germany, $591 per person; Japan, $389 per person. U.S. public spending for health care is only $341 per person.[31] Infant mortality (a measure of public health) is substantially lower in Sweden (8 per 1,000 live births), Japan (8.9), and West Germany (9) than it is in the United States (14.1). Life expectancy is longer in Sweden (72.1 years for men and

77.8 for women), Japan (72.2 years for men and 77.4 for women), and West Germany (68.8 for men and 77.2 for women) than it is in the United States (68.7 for men and 76.5 for women).[32]

These other industrial nations spend a larger portion of their yearly gross national products on all forms of social services for their citizens —unemployment benefits, workmen's compensation, benefits for children and the physically handicapped, health care, old age, and disability —than does America. Sweden spends 33.8 percent of its GNP on these sorts of social services; West Germany, 30.6 percent; the Netherlands, 27.7 percent; France, 22 percent; Japan, 17 percent (not including substantial contributions by Japanese companies). The United States spends only 14.2 percent.[33]

It would be a mistake to conclude from these examples that American social policies lag behind in all respects. The U.S. school system surely is more egalitarian than public schools in Europe and Japan. More than 75 percent of American pupils now graduate from high schools, and more than half enter college. In most other industrialized nations less than 30 percent of the young people are graduated from high school, and many go on to technical and vocational programs instead of college.[34]

Nor does America seek to deport its unemployment problem, as do some Western European countries. In 1975 there were 5.9 million foreign workers in Western Europe; since then, as unemployment has risen, many have been induced to leave. The United States occasionally rounds up a few illegal aliens, but this effort is not a major part of the fight against unemployment.

The real difference is that in continental Europe and Japan social services are perceived to be central agents of economic change. They are also, of course, lively political issues, but in general their successes and shortcomings are measured not by the static tallies of the quantity of services delivered but by how adaptable and well utilized their labor forces have become as a result. These programs are, by design, helping to ease the transition of their workers out of high-volume, standardized production into flexible-system production.

In America and Britain, by contrast, public assistance is explicitly and almost exclusively linked with poverty. Income maintenance schemes typically are based on means tests, with eligibility limited to those at the very bottom rungs of the economic ladder. (For example, one in three elderly British citizens needs means-tested supplementary welfare benefits; one in four elderly Americans falls into the same category. But the West German basic pension scheme is sufficiently generous that only 5 percent of retired Germans need means-tested aid.) While in America and Britain recipients of public assistance carry the stigma of failure in the competitive struggle, a rise in the welfare roles in continental Europe or Japan is seen instead as an economic indicator, signaling adjustments that are occurring (or need to occur) in the national economy. In America using social services is often considered symptomatic of moral failure; in other industrial nations public social programs are justified as a collective commitment to sharing the burdens of economic adjustment.

Because they have been disconnected from the nation's economic development, social services in America also have lacked a unifying vision of their purpose, their desired effect, their relation to one another, and their place within the national life. They have been fragmented into hundreds of assistance programs, financed by separate appropriations, and administered by different departments and agencies at every level of government. They have been used as conduits for political payoffs and bailouts to selected industries, like housing construction and pharmaceuticals. They have been confused in the public's mind with specific efforts designed to overcome the vestiges of American racism, like school busing, affirmative action, and minority quotas. Without any explicit link to national progress, they have become vulnerable to the divisive rhetoric of belt tightening. Underlying many of the inadequacies of American social programs, in short, is the fact that they have not been directed in any explicit or coherent way toward the large task of adapting America's labor force.

7.

America's work force is stymied. Its inability to shift to flexible-system production has accelerated the nation's economic decline and has aggravated problems stemming both from management strategies of paper entrepreneurialism and from political strategies of historic preservation. Indeed, the stagnation of America's work force has driven many workers to join in political coalition with managers who seek protection from imports. At the same time the lack of adequate job training and basic education among America's workers has made it difficult for firms to find and keep the skilled labor they need for flexible-system production and thus has encouraged the sterile substitution of paper entrepreneurialism. These three manifestations of the nation's economic impasse—paper entrepreneurialism, historic preservation, and dead-end labor—are mutually reinforcing. Business, government, and labor in the United States all are trapped within a rigid set of institutional relationships that inhibit economic adjustment.

America will eventually adapt to the new realities of global competition. It has no choice; adaptation will be forced upon it. Indeed, there are signs that such adaptation is beginning in a few places within American business and government. Some of America's most farseeing companies—IBM, Hewlett-Packard, and Control Data—are actively pushing their capital and labor into higher-valued production. High-technology firms in general find it more profitable to refrain from pleas for historic preservation because they know they have much to gain from rapid adjustment and much to lose from policies that seek to maintain the status quo. Several state governments are also trying to encourage movement into flexible-system production. California is now launching a $22 million package of subsidies aimed at invigorating the state's high-technology firms and retraining its workers for skill-intensive industries. Both Minnesota and North Carolina are financing large microelectronics research centers. Ohio is establishing a $5 million fund to aid high-technology companies and to retrain its work force. And in a few instances, business, labor, and state governments have pooled their resources: General Motors, the United Auto Workers, and California recently launched a $10 million training program designed to help 8,400 unemployed automobile workers find new jobs.

But these isolated efforts are scarcely significant when weighed against the magnitude of the shift that must occur. By and large, America's transition to flexible-system production continues to be halting, painful, and fraught with inequities. Managers' attention continues to be fixed on rearranging industrial assets and on manipulating abstract numbers and rules. Lawyers and financiers proliferate and prosper. Pressures mount for protective tariffs, quotas, marketing agreements, and rollbacks of health, safety, and environmental regulations. Blue-collar workers are forced to make wage concessions without reciprocal guarantees of job security or reinvestment. There is continued political pressure to reduce the minimum wage. Social services are cut. And the poor are disproportionately burdened by unemployment. Had America perversely set out to block the adjustment of its economy and society, it would have done little differently.

THE ERA OF HUMAN CAPITAL

Part Four

XI
SOCIAL CHANGE

1.

Human organizations are subject to evolutionary pressures. Organizations are alliances of individuals, who accept an institutional structure to shape their work together as long as that structure continues to serve their common needs. Organizations of whatever scale that cease to meet their members' needs eventually give way to new institutions that meet their members' needs more effectively. Cultures whose most pressing needs are material may call on their organizations to compete primarily for markets. But people look to their organizations to meet other needs, including the articulation of social values and a sense of civic life, in which case organizational evolution is driven by a subtle kind of competition for cultural legitimacy. Since no society's priorities, at any stage, are only social or only material, these forms of organizational competition—the one conducted in the economic realm, the other in the civic realm—are inextricably linked.

In America's first era of rapidly increasing productivity, spanning roughly 1870 to 1920, the dominant pattern of organization was a loose network of institutions for quickly mobilizing vast reservoirs of readily applied resources. Workers poured into American cities from overseas and from the farm; capital, from overseas and from thousands of new American shareholders; and basic inventions, from Britain and from a generation of American mechanics and tinkerers. Raw supplies and finished products moved in and out of America's factories over newly built railroad lines. No overarching institutional structure directed or constrained this mobilization. The cultural ideal that gave force to this vast mobilization was the myth of the self-made man, whose foresight and strength of character enabled him almost single-handedly to amass a fortune. The saga of rags to riches gave hope and meaning to Americans, as it propelled unprecedented occupational and geographic mobility.

But the momentum could not last. The loose pattern of organization that had encouraged mobility became too unpredictable and inconsistent to sustain the new demands that were being placed upon it. To synchronize the flow of goods within the individual firm, managers needed to replace skilled craftsmen with foremen—but in a manner that did not give the foremen arbitrary authority over the workplace. To guard against ruinous competition and inadequate demand, managers needed to coordinate their investment and production with one another—but in ways that were politically acceptable. And to soften the social impact of industrialization, a different group of managers needed to develop the capability to provide municipal services—but in a way that did not encourage bribery, embezzlement, and bossism. Within each of these concentric spheres of organization extending out from the core process of industrialization, America needed a new pattern of organization that would provide both stability and legitimacy.

The managerial organization met these requirements. Between 1920 and 1970 American business, labor, and government hewed to a new set of organizing principles in which tasks were simplified, ordered according to preestablished rules, and carefully monitored. These principles were put into effect by a new class of professional managers who controlled individual firms, coordinated investment and production across whole industries, and found their way into government. High-volume production, featuring long runs of standardized products, generated vast economies of scale and new levels of wealth.

The social vision that underlay this process was rooted in the ideals of large-scale efficiency and of rules to constrain arbitrary authority—ideals as applicable to curing social ills as to defending the nation against foreign aggressors. The principles were those of scientific management, symbolized by the well-oiled machine and suggesting a pattern of organization by which Americans' aspirations could be achieved without political rancor.

But once again the economic context has changed, and our institutions are coming under pressure to evolve. The rigid management-centered organization has become inappropriate to an America now linked to an integrated world economy. That pattern of organization can be duplicated anywhere on the globe, including areas with lower-wage labor and cheaper access to raw materials and emerging markets. Since 1970, therefore, the economies of America and every other industrialized nation have undergone a profound structural change, as the high-volume industries that underpinned these economies in the previous half century—steel, textiles, automobiles, rubber, shipbuilding, and chemicals—have become less competitive in world markets. The only way industrialized nations can increase their citizens' standards of living in the future is to concentrate on the high-value niches within these industries and to seize and keep world leadership in new industries based on advanced and emerging technologies. This requires a different form of organization, one far more flexible and adaptable than the structures designed to support high-volume, standardized production.

Japan understands this future. So, to a lesser extent, do West Germany and France. They also know that economic success will depend upon the speed and appropriateness of their shift in production, not simply on the scope of new investment. Governments and businesses in these nations therefore are racing to gain sophistication in these new sectors and to prepare their labor forces—their stores of human capital—to participate in them. The current world recession has slowed their progress, to be sure, but they are at least moving toward economic adaptation. Britain and America, trapped by an ideology that cannot accommodate such a change or acknowledge the need for a national strategy to respond quickly to it, are experiencing massive unemployment and declining real incomes.

America and in a similar sense Britain are victims of their own past success. The pattern of organization on which high-volume, standardized production was based is difficult to uproot. Other industrialized nations, less bound to that pattern, are evolving more smoothly. The myth of an efficient and apolitical society—whose wealth derives from efficient high-volume manufacturing, whose capacity to defend both its wealth and its freedoms requires a stable and predictable economic system, and whose dependent citizens can survive contentedly on the surplus of that productive system—is so firmly rooted in America that its adaptation to the new global market has been stymied.

2.

This ideology has sidetracked Americans into endless debate over the relative merits of two highly artificial concepts: the "free market" and "national planning." The real choice facing America is rather between evading the new global context or engaging it—between protecting the American economy from the international market while generating paper profits, or adapting it to meet international competition. Either way, government will be actively involved. And though the form of government involvement may be different, the fact of its involvement will be nothing new.

Many Americans feel that government should—and, but for regrettable lapses, does—refrain from interfering with the market. We may even acknowledge that the market itself is a product of public institutions that establish property rights and liability rules and determine how contracts are to be enforced. But we see these as neutral "rules of the game" which do not selectively affect specific industries or groups.

The enduring myth of the unmanaged market illustrates the power of ideology over political reality. The subtlety of the transformation has obscured the extent to which America's once-dynamic industry has degenerated into a vast system of paper entrepreneurialism. We cling to the fiction of an economy based on transactions in real goods and services when, in fact, a significant portion of economic activity is purely symbolic—founded upon the manipulation of abstract rules and numbers. America's free market has been supplanted by interlocking networks of subsidiaries, conglomerate headquarters, and financial institutions, through which industrial assets are rearranged and managers are recirculated, but from which new products and processes rarely emerge. Government manages the casino, so to speak, through its tax laws and rulings, antitrust judgments, and securities regulations, all of which form the financial environment within which paper entrepreneurialism flourishes.

By the same token, the broad array of tariffs, quotas, voluntary export agreements, and bailouts for declining businesses that now pervade our economic system is somehow considered an isolated exception to the government's normal role of benign neglect, while our defense-related contracts, targeted tax breaks, and assorted subsidies for particular industries are seen as separate issues, unrelated to industrial development or to the dynamics of the market. Many Americans object to the subsidies foreign governments offer their emerging industries but then fail to acknowledge the seminal role defense and aerospace projects play in the development of our own emerging industries. We demand that foreign governments reduce the procurement preferences they give certain of their domestic industries but then demand that our own large, regulated manufacturers buy only from American producers. In short, our mythic assumptions lag behind our economic reality: Every major industry in America is deeply involved with and dependent on government. The competitive position of every American firm is affected by government policy. No sharp distinction can validly be drawn between private and public sectors within this or any other advanced industrialized country; the economic effects of public policies and corporate decisions are completely intertwined. But so long as this pattern of government involvement is hidden from public view, the result will continue to be historic preservation of an outmoded industrial base.

Nor do we acknowledge the potentially critical role of America's social programs for adapting our labor force to a new era of production. Many Americans tend to view all government expenditures, including those on health and education, as forms of collective consumption that periodically must be reduced in order to free resources for productive investment. We fail to appreciate that sums spent by government on health and education are investments in America's future productivity, no less important to that future than private investments. The government deficits that result from productive social investments should cause us no more concern than the debt that private businesses incur in order to invest in productive assets.

These disjunctures between ideology and reality make it doubly difficult for policy makers to choose adjustment over protection. So long as all government assistance to businesses and to individual citizens is seen as somehow illegitimate, the government is forced to respond to each industry's plea for assistance as if it were an exceptional case and to respond to all such requests with special emergency interventions. Industry participates in this charade, disguising its long-term strategies to obtain government supports through targeted benefits embedded within particular tax laws, appropriations, agency regulations, court rulings, and executive orders. Because neither government nor business can admit to the intimacy of their relationship, both sides treat it as an illicit affair, hiding it from public view and thereby undermining the chances for those aspects of the relationship that do promote positive adjustment to earn cultural legitimacy.

Programs of assistance to individuals, meanwhile, are seen as handouts to segments of the population that have failed in the competitive race. Because we have little familiarity with the relationship between social welfare and economic development, social services remain understaffed and underfunded, suspected of fostering "waste, fraud, and abuse" and organized in ways that perpetuate dependence rather than promote social change.

Much of the American public, unaccustomed to considering the ongoing process of industrial evolution or the role of public policies in promoting it, is likely to think in caricatures. Any mention of industrial policies summons the specter of national planning, in which bureaucrats —ignorant of or indifferent to market forces—shift capital from industry to industry to nurture their favorite future "winners." Our inability to distinguish between this caricature and the realities of well-designed adjustment policies—through which government seeks to *promote* market forces rather than to supplant them—has confounded political dialogue.

Many American economists, meanwhile, comfort themselves with the assumption that any inefficient allocation of human or capital resources will eventually be corrected as the economy moves toward a new "equilibrium." But equilibrium is a vanishing mirage on a constantly shifting horizon. America *will* adjust; the questions are how painful the adjustment will be and whether or not American adjustment will keep pace with world economic change. The process of adjustment is the stuff of economic and political history. There are many routes that the adjustment can take—some far easier, more socially equitable, and more efficient than others.

For all these reasons it has been difficult for Americans to think strategically about their country's economic development. Their only experience with national strategy derives from national defense. It is hardly surprising that many adjustment policies over the years have been presented as aspects of national security: The Eisenhower administration's highway building program—called the National Defense Highway Act of 1956 and justified on national security grounds—provided an infrastructure that guided and accelerated postwar industrial development, particularly for the automobile and housing industries. Similarly, educational programs and subsidies embodied in the GI Bill and, later, in the National Defense Education Act spurred great advances in Americans' store of human capital, which in turn contributed to our economic development well into the 1960's; but once again, the effort had to be justified by the rhetoric of national security.

National security has also supplied a pretext for our assorted energy programs, providing, at various times, price supports, loan guarantees, tax breaks, and direct subsidies to the oil, coal, nuclear, and synthetic fuels industries. And our bulwark of tariffs and orderly marketing agreements has been justified as necessary to national security, lest we grow dependent on foreign sources of strategic goods like steel.

This reasoning has impoverished the political dialogue, preventing us from confronting long-term economic issues that require strategic thinking. It also has distorted policy by giving disproportionate weight to mercantilist goals, such as gaining "independence" in energy and strategic materials, and by glossing over the problems of coordinating our industrial policies with those of other nations so as to discover the most advantageous and workable American role in the world economy.

3.

Above all, this false choice—the free market versus central planning, business culture versus civic culture—has prevented us from understanding the central importance of human capital to America's future.

Unlike high-volume production, where most of a firm's value is represented by physical assets, the principal stores of value in flexible-system enterprises are human assets. Specialized machines and unskilled workers cannot adapt easily to new situations. Flexible machines and teams of skilled workers can. Only people can recognize and solve novel problems; machines can merely repeat solutions already programmed within them. The future prosperity of America and every other industrialized country will depend on their citizens' ability to recognize and solve new problems, for the simple reason that processes which make routine the solution to older problems are coming to be the special province of developing nations. Industries of the future will not depend on physical "hardware," which can be duplicated anywhere, but on the human "software," which can retain a technological edge.

Financial capital formation is becoming a less important determinant of a nation's well-being than human capital formation. Financial capital is highly mobile. It crosses international borders with the speed of an electronic impulse. International savings are flowing around the globe to wherever they can be put to use. The eagerness of Western bankers to recycle petrodollars to Poland and other high-risk countries is evidence enough. But a nation's store of human capital is relatively immobile internationally, apart from a few high-flying scientists and engineers. The skills, knowledge, and capacity for teamwork within a nation's labor force will determine that nation's collective standard of living.

The preeminence of human capital in flexible-system production gives new urgency to the old problem that markets alone fail to generate enough investment in human skills. Incentives to invest in human capital differ fundamentally from incentives to invest in physical capital because human capital investment, and the productivity that flows from it, are necessarily social. A firm contemplating worker training knows that some employees, once trained, will leave the company. It invests less in human capital than it would if it could somehow ensure that the workers would stay on and apply their new productivity to benefit the firm. Meanwhile, the next company neglects developing its own work force, confident that luring qualified workers away from the other firm will be cheaper than setting up its own training program. Because companies cannot force their workers to remain in their jobs and pay off the investment in increased productivity, no firm spends as much on human capital as it should (and would, if it could only reap the full benefits).

Even individual workers are apt to underinvest in their own training.

When a person decides how much and what kind of training to get, he is usually ill-informed about the value of a certain skill since that value is determined in the context of a job. He is uncertain about how well the investment will pay off for him, and the uncertainty makes him reluctant to spend much of his time or money on learning new skills. And even if he could be certain of the future value of investing in his own human capital (in terms of increased earnings), he may not be able to afford a year or two of training in new skills. While loans are available for investments in physical capital, many workers are forced to finance their human capital investments themselves. They cannot offer lenders an interest in their more productive future selves as collateral against a training loan. The lesson is that unaided market forces lead workers, like firms, to underinvest in human capital.

This pattern of "market failures" is complicated by the fact that in flexible-system enterprises the real value of a worker's skill depends not solely on his own training but also on how his abilities complement and enhance the skills of his co-workers. When productivity gains flow over time from an integrated working unit, it makes no sense to depend wholly on individuals' cost-and-return calculations to set the level of human capital investment.

In short, we are entering a new era of productivity in which the costs, the process, and the return from investments in human capital all are inescapably social. In the era of human capital and flexible-system production, failing to recognize this and to respond with the right mechanisms to supplement the market means stifling the sources of future economic growth.

But the fact is that America is now doing little to build new human capital, and the nation is wasting its present stock. We have organized production in a way that squanders our talents. Some of America's most gifted citizens are engaged in manipulating abstract symbols, with no result other than the rearrangement of industrial assets and the replacement of names on organization charts. Other citizens are unemployed or working in dead-end jobs that are sheltered from international competition. America displays great ingenuity in revitalizing its old physical assets: A Procter & Gamble factory that once made the ill-fated Pringle's potato chips now produces Pampers; many of bankrupt Braniff's jets now fly the "friendly skies." But America is sadly neglectful of its human assets. All too often, when a company fails, its plant and equipment are quickly redeployed, but its workers are—in effect—scrapped.

Unless America moves quickly into a new era in which upgrading and using our human capital become a central concern, however, our future wealth will come primarily from extracting coal, timber, and grain from our lands, from assembling advanced components that have been designed and fabricated elsewhere, and from distributing the resulting products to our own citizens. We will become a nation of extractors, assemblers, and retailers—poor by the standards of the rest of the world.

Already America's gross national product per person (a crude measure of economic well-being, to be sure) is lower than it is in several other industrialized countries. Our average life expectancy is lower than in fourteen other industrialized countries, and our unemployment higher. We have higher rates of infant mortality. We enjoy less job security. These are illustrations of long-term trends that had already begun fifteen years ago. They will worsen unless we act deliberately and strategically to speed the movement of capital and labor into higher-valued production.

But ideologies resist change, particularly when change seems to threaten people's economic security. The process of long-term decline, once under way, has a self-perpetuating quality. It rigidifies old ideologies and engenders a widespread conservatism. It also breeds divisiveness as each group discovers it can preserve its own standard of living only by appropriating a portion of another group's declining wealth.

The dilemma is that the groups seeking to seize assets from each other are often the very ones that must collaborate if real growth is to occur. The clearest example is in labor-management relations. Here the portion of the pie shared by workers has been declining as inflation has outstripped wage hikes. Trying to recoup, unions demand catch-up raises, only to find that other unions do the same, generating another round of inflation. And as corporate managers harden their positions in the face of declining profits, they are apt to resort to hostile counterstrategies: hiring consultants to "bust" their unions; moving factories to other states or countries. The result is likely to be a breakdown in cooperation between unions and management, possibly sparking crippling rounds of strikes, that will ensure there will be even less product to spread around. Only when an entire industry faces collapse—as is now the case with automobiles, steel, and rubber—do labor and management begin to recognize their common interests, and by then it is usually too late for affirmative change. There is only time enough to make wage concessions and to form political coalitions seeking protection against imports, both of which merely perpetuate the underlying problems or pass them on to consumers and other industries.

American society is now rife with other "beggar-thy-neighbor" tactics, many of which are rational from the standpoint of the individual actor but are tragically irrational for society as a whole: the asset rearranging undertaken through conglomerate merger, manipulation of balance sheets, and schemes of tax avoidance; the exorbitant salaries and bonuses provided to executives in America's largest companies; the rising incidence of employee theft and insider dealings; the political demands for tariffs, quotas, and bailouts to protect companies against foreign competitors; and the refusal by many middle-income taxpayers to foot any longer the bill for social services. The vicious circle has closed: As the economy continues to decline, Americans grow more cynical about collective endeavor. Their consequential retreat into egoism merely accelerates the decline since collaboration is the only way to reverse it.

Altering the ideological lenses through which many Americans have come to view government, business, and the economy will be difficult. It ultimately will depend on the quality of U.S. politics (a subject to which we will return). But in the short term several changes can be made at least to slow the decline and reduce the fear and insecurity that are fueling it.

4.

America could take several immediate steps to help shift into higher-valued production. These steps could overcome bottlenecks and constraints that now retard economic change and also serve to ameliorate the burdens that make change disproportionately painful to certain groups. They could be accomplished by merely altering the mix of tax incentives and subsidies flowing to American business, which now encourage paper entrepreneurialism and historic preservation and discourage investments in human capital.

For example, in place of public service job-training programs that merely perpetuate dead-end labor, we could provide unemployed workers with vouchers that they could cash in at companies for on-the-job training. Firms that accepted the vouchers would have half their training costs paid by the government, for up to three years. The program could be financed by a payroll tax paid by employees and employers. Any workers unemployed longer than three months would be eligible. The virtue of such a program is that it would match training to specific industrial needs and, by ensuring that companies themselves finance part of the training, help target program funds to firms that are serious about employing the newly trained workers. The program also would create incentives for companies to locate in high-unemployment, low-skilled regions, the work forces of which would collectively represent a substantial subsidy.

One variation on the same theme would feature retraining vouchers. These would be available to any worker who has been employed for more than two years at his present job and wishes to upgrade his skills. The vouchers could be cashed in at universities or accredited training facilities, which would be reimbursed by the government.

Programs like these would quickly pay for themselves. In West Germany, which has similar programs, the cost per participant is approximately $14,000 per year, once savings from reduced unemployment costs are netted out. This sum is likely to be far smaller than the new productivity benefits that are generated. Also, empirical evidence suggests that companies do respond to wage subsidies by increasing employment as well as by reducing their rate of price increases.[1]

In addition to such direct subsidies, tax incentives could be used to encourage companies to invest in upgrading their work forces and communities. The tax code now provides incentives leading in just the opposite direction: Companies that wish to desert their workers and communities in pursuit of greener pastures can now deduct their costs of moving as a business expense, write off the plant and machinery left behind, and obtain tax credits and accelerated depreciation against new plant and machinery purchased at the new location. On the other hand, education and training costs that expect to be incurred for the purpose of preparing employees for new jobs in which they are not currently engaged cannot be deducted from current income. This policy preference generates large social costs as workers and communities are left stranded within vast pockets of unemployment.

To reverse this policy preference, the tax code might permit companies to claim tax benefits for retraining their older workers for new jobs. Just as a tax depreciation now can be taken against machines which are gradually becoming obsolete, the tax code might also permit employers to set aside an annual tax-deductible reserve fund for human capital development, based on the number of workers on the payroll. The accumulated funds would be used for retraining and upgrading the work force within a certain number of years of their being set aside, or else the deduction would be lost. The tax code also might reward companies for remaining in their communities by giving them deductions proportional to their length of stay. In effect, this would be a kind of reverse depreciation—recognizing that the social benefits of remaining within a community (and the social costs of leaving it) often increase with the duration of a company's stay.

Tax reform might also eliminate the inconsistencies that invite paper entrepreneurialism. As of now, the tax code rewards corporations and individuals for rearranging assets and speculating on their future value. The code confuses economically sterile transactions and productive investments in new wealth. It does this by, among other things, making interest payments on loans for *any* investment tax-deductible. One avenue of reform would be to allow interest deductions to be taken only for the purchase of new assets or the modernization of old ones. Under this rule, mergers and acquisitions would not qualify for tax deductions. Nor would speculation in commodity futures, paintings by old masters, or real estate. Lest millions of middle-class homeowners suddenly be impoverished by this measure, however, mortgage interest payments on one's principal residence would still be deductible even for older houses, but the deduction would be limited to, say, $5,000 per year.

There are many other ways in which incentives could be restructured to encourage human capital investment. For example, companies now have little to lose by laying off their employees during downturns. By foisting their payroll expenses onto the states' unemployment insurance funds, they reduce their fixed costs. Then, when the economy improves, the companies hire back their employees. This merely encourages employers to consider their employees as fungible commodities and discourages them (and their employees) from making long-term investments in training. It also promotes needless unemployment.

An alternative scheme would be to make companies' payroll contributions to the unemployment insurance system depend on the extent to which their former employees have been forced to use the system in the past. If a company's practice was to lay off many of its employees every time there was a downturn in the business cycle—shifting the carrying costs for its labor "stock" onto the community—its unemployment insurance premium would be higher than that of an identical company that had kept its workers employed. Like any other insured entity, the former company would be deemed a relatively bad risk and would pay accordingly. If unemployment insurance rates were directly pegged to a company's employment history in this way, companies would have more of an incentive to maintain their work forces intact and to invest in their long-term development.

A final change in the tax system might encourage savings (so that there is more money to invest) without giving a windfall to the rich or placing a disproportionate burden on the poor. The Reagan administration has sought to spur savings by cutting taxes for the rich. It claims that rich people invariably save more and spend less of any extra earnings than do poor people, for the simple reason that the poor are more likely to need that extra dollar for basic necessities. But this argument is highly questionable. It is no secret that the rich are likely to spend large chunks of any new income on Persian carpets, rare paintings, antiques, yachts, luxury cars, and vacations. Conspicuous consumption like this makes many middle-class and lower-middle-class people feel even poorer and convinces them that they alone bear the burden of fighting inflation and financing economic growth.

A straightforward alternative would be to replace the personal income tax with a progressive tax on consumption. Under this system, income would not be taxed so long as it remained as savings. But money withdrawn from savings during the course of a year would be taxable, as would sums borrowed for consumption. The tax rate would be greater the more money was spent. To ensure against the possibility that vast accumulations of wealth will merely be passed down to future generations, the new tax system would need to be accompanied by increased inheritance and gift taxes.

A personal consumption tax would not be difficult to administer. Banks and other savings institutions would keep records of annual personal savings deposits. A copy would be attached to a taxpayer's return, documenting his or her deduction of savings from yearly earnings for the purpose of computing taxes due. And the consumption tax schedule could be designed to yield the same overall revenue as the income tax now yields. The only difference is that the progressive consumption tax would encourage more savings, more equitably.

Other changes could be made in programs that use business subsidies to attract investment to various regions of the country. America's economy has come to be based on distinct economic regions, each with its own climate, raw materials, demographics, and special needs. Major business investments ripple throughout a region, fostering skills, spinning off new innovations (consider "Silicon Valley" around Stanford University and Route 128 around Harvard and MIT), and spawning networks of suppliers that are dependent on the region's major industries. Similarly, a region's special problems—traffic congestion, inadequate sewage treatment, disposal of toxic wastes, water shortages—are largely a function of the regional pattern of industry. Within these regional economies, public and private investments are inextricably linked. But as capital markets have become national and even international, bank lenders and institutional investors have become almost oblivious to these linkages. National capital markets focus narrowly on an individual company's bottom line. Across America, money that used to remain within regions is now pouring out. Money market funds have grown to more than $200 billion, from only $11 billion at the end of 1978; most of this growth has been at the expense of financial institutions, mainly in small towns. The public response to this problem has been a welter of local tax abatement schemes, industrial development bonds, urban development action grants, and Economic Development Administration loans—all of which are spread so widely and so thinly across the land that their net effects cancel one another out, burdening taxpayers and granting companies pure windfalls that fail to influence location decisions.

Instead of this patchwork, the federal government might establish regional banks to provide low-interest long-term loans to industries that agree to restructure themselves to become more competitive. The banks would also supply cities and towns in the region with low-interest financing for maintaining and developing infrastructure such as roads and sewage treatment plants. Bank directors would be appointed by state governors. The banks would finance themselves by issuing government-guaranteed bonds and shares of stock.

Some of these bonds and stocks could be made available to union pension funds. Pension funds are rapidly becoming a primary source of industry financing in America. Public employee pension fund assets now exceed $200 billion; private employee funds, $450 billion. AT&T's pension fund alone is up to $31 billion. Indeed, such funds are now America's largest single source of investment, underpinning stock values as individual investors abandon the equity market. While private investors have dumped more than $20 billion worth of stocks since 1978, pension funds have increased their equity holdings by a greater amount. This year pension funds are expected to absorb $11 billion of new corporate debt and most of the new equity issues. But a substantial part of this investment has been unrelated to America's human and economic development. Pension funds now hold $12 billion in foreign securities and another $13 billion in real estate. By 1990, if present trends continue, 22 percent of pension fund assets will be invested in these ways. The potential social benefits flowing from investment in a regional economy have not been considered in these investment decisions. The investment of a given proportion of pension fund assets in regional development banks would help spur the economy and thereby benefit American workers over the long term.

Regional development also could be promoted through regional-based training programs. Participating companies within a geographic region might pool their training activities, with each company paying one-half of 1 percent of their payroll costs into a common training fund. The government would provide matching funds. The resulting training centers would contract with the participating companies to provide employees with appropriate training and retraining. The companies would help in the design of these programs.

Many companies are too small to provide their employees with adequate training and retraining. But through combining their efforts and receiving additional public funding, training programs could reach a scale that would make them worthwhile. With participating companies directly involved, the programs could have a multiplier effect throughout the area, increasing the quality of the regional work force and attracting higher-valued jobs to the area.

Whatever form these programs might take, the government programs flowing to businesses cannot be redirected to economic adjustment unless government has the institutional capacity to view all its programs in light of the nation's long-term economic health. The government now has no way to monitor the aggregate impact of these programs on particular industries. Defense procurement, as we have seen, has a powerful effect on the economic development of the nation, spawning entirely new industries, setting the direction for their future development, enriching or impoverishing regions whose economies depend on defense contracts, employing one-third of the nation's scientists and engineers, contributing more than one-third of its total research and development budget, and training a large number of its skilled machinists. Other policies—tariffs, quotas, marketing orders, price supports, bailouts, federal loans and loan guarantees, subsidized insurance, and special tax breaks—also affect the pattern of industrial development. Government programs that promote certain industries or businesses amount to 13.9 percent of the nation's gross national product.

But as has been shown earlier, these programs have been unrelated to the goal of long-term economic growth. The government now gives $455 million in tax breaks to the timber industry and $2 billion in subsidies to the dairy industry, but offers no special encouragement to the semiconductor industry. It spends five times as much on research and development for commercial fisheries as it does for steel; $6 billion in loans and loan guarantees go to the shipbuilding industry, compared with $940 million to the automobile industry.[2] Without the institutional capacity to focus these programs on the competitive performance of our economy as a whole, government policy will inevitably serve the politically strongest or most active industries and businesses.

One small step toward a more strategic and more publicly accountable approach to national economic policy, therefore, would be to establish a public board to monitor these programs, perhaps located in the White House's Office of Management and Budget. As part of its responsibility, the board would each year recommend to Congress and to the President what changes should be made in programs that may be retarding national economic development.

Taken together, changes like these would constitute a modest start to a dynamic economy. Of course, before we were to launch on any one of them, we would want to know a great deal more about its likely effects on business strategies and possible substantive or administrative difficulties. But even if they all were to be successfully implemented, they would not be a panacea. For America to enter fully into the era of human capital will require more dramatic changes in the way we organize ourselves—the subject to which we now turn.

5.

In the era of human capital, an era that all industrialized nations are entering, high-volume, standardized production will to a great extent be replaced by flexible-system production, in which integrated teams of workers identify and solve problems. This new organization of work necessarily will be more collaborative, participatory, and egalitarian than is high-volume, standardized production, for the simple reason that initiative, responsibility, and discretion must be so much more widely exercised within it. Since its success depends on quickly identifying and responding to opportunities in its rapidly changing environment, the flexible-system enterprise cannot afford rigidly hierarchical chains of authority.

That new organization of work will rest on a new organization of society. Like the superstructures of management that stabilized high-volume, standardized production and the social programs that remedied its failings, flexible-system production will need to be supported and sustained by a broader public framework. But unlike the old management superstructures, these new policies will need to promote adaptability instead of stability, inclusion in the production process rather than exclusion through welfare. We can only speculate on the exact shape that these policies will take. But our government and business institutions, and those of every other advanced industrialized nation, already are evolving in a direction that promises to integrate economic growth with the development of human capital. Economic policy will be linked to social policy.

In broad outline, the system may look like this: Government will assist businesses in modernizing and adapting their production processes. But instead of outright giveaways—like the countless tax abatements, tax credits, accelerated depreciation rules, subsidized loans, loan guarantees, tariffs, quotas, marketing agreements, and price supports that now cushion American business against change—this new form of assistance will be tied explicitly to upgrading capital and labor. Businesses will be contractually obligated to restructure themselves, as a condition for receiving the assistance.

Such restructuring will usually involve new investments in human capital. Businesses that receive restructuring assistance will agree to maintain their old work forces intact. Firms will not be blocked from diversifying into other lines of business as part of their restructuring plans. But whatever business they choose to enter, their obligation to their employees will remain. If the firms diversify, they will have to retrain their workers to take on jobs in the new line of business, to keep them on their old jobs, to find them other employment, or to pay them unemployment benefits comparable with their former salaries until the workers themselves find new jobs. However the workers are employed, it is clear that these firms will have a strong financial incentive to make the most of them —since the employees in any event will remain on their payrolls.

The virtue of this scheme is that it will connect capital adjustment to labor adjustment. We will not need to choose between the social costs of "runaway" plants, on the one hand, and laws that bar plant closings, mergers, and acquisitions, on the other. Capital mobility will be preserved, so that physical and financial assets can be applied to higher and better uses. But the bias against labor mobility will be removed. Firms will have incentives to make new investments in both capital and labor, and the two categories of investments will be coordinated. Had U.S. Steel been required to take responsibility for its work force in this way as a condition for the tax benefits, trigger-price protection from imports, and regulatory rollbacks it received, it surely would have invested in a business to which its workers therefore could more easily adapt than Marathon Oil.

This restructuring process will be extended to cover other forms of human capital investment. For example, we can expect that a significant part of the present welfare system will be replaced by government grants to businesses that agree to hire the chronically unemployed. The grants will pay a portion of the wages of these newly hired workers for a limited period of time, in an extension of the employment voucher concept. Not only will this scheme be less expensive than welfare in the short run, but in the longer run it will help get people off welfare by upgrading their skills. Firms that hire the chronically unemployed will have an incentive to give them on-the-job training because the firms will naturally want to increase the contributions that these workers make to overall productivity.

Other social services—health care, Social Security, day care, disability benefits, unemployment benefits, relocation assistance—will become part of the process of structural adjustment. Public funds now spent directly on these services will instead be made available to businesses, according to the number of people they employ and the number of chronically unemployed they agree to hire. Government bureaucracies that now administer these programs to individuals will be supplanted, to a large extent, by companies that administer them to their employees. These social services will continue to be available to employees unless they attach themselves to another company. In this way, firms will become the agents of their employees, bargaining on behalf of their workers for different packages of government-supported social services and often purchasing them from private providers, who will be competing against one another to offer the best services at least cost.

The firm's employees collectively will run these company-wide human capital programs. They will elect representatives who will select the combination of benefits and choose the providers. Through labor-management councils also comprised of worker representatives, workers will participate in company decisions about physical capital, helping choose the direction and magnitude of new investment in research, plant, and machinery. Such employee participation in company strategy will be necessary to ensure that capital adjustment and labor adjustment are well coordinated and also to take full advantage of the knowledge and skills of the company's work force.

Business enterprises, therefore, will largely replace geographic jurisdictions as conduits of government support for economic and human development. Companies, rather than state and local governments, will be the agents and intermediaries through which such assistance is provided. As a result, economic development programs and social services will be closely linked.

Firms will have strong incentives to upgrade and adapt their work forces and even to train the chronically unemployed and handicapped. And social services themselves will become less fragmented. Decisions about health care needs, for example, will be related to decisions about needs for retirement benefits or for retraining assistance. The total package of benefits in turn will be tied to a firm's specific production plans: A decision to expand into a new technology may require special emphasis on retraining, relocation, and day care assistance, at least until the company's employees have made adjustments to the new technology, schedules, and locations that the work requires. Social services thus will reinforce group learning and workers' interdependence, instead of excluding recipients from the productive process.

In short, rather than two separate systems that interact only incidentally —one geared to production and the other to passive dependency—we will have one system, serving both economic and human development. Government at all levels will continue to provide certain services directly, in response to common needs within a geographic area for such things as basic education, aid to the severely handicapped, and maintenance of roads and sewers. But business enterprises, acting as the agents of their employee members, will become conduits for many other services. And all citizens (and their dependents) will become employee members of some business enterprise.

If all this sounds strangely utopian, consider how far we have already come toward such a system. With the important exceptions that the unemployed are excluded from participation and that no mechanisms exist by which employees can help shape these human capital programs and coordinate them with the firm's decisions about physical capital investment, our present system of government social spending is rapidly evolving toward this model.

For example, because many in-kind benefits that companies provide to their employees are not considered parts of the employees' taxable income, firms and employees now have a strong incentive to substitute such benefits for wages. A wage increase of, say, $1,000 enriches the employee by only $666, if the employee is assumed to be in a 33 percent tax bracket. But an increase in the value of employee benefits (health insurance, life insurance, or whatever) by, say, $833, makes the employee $167 richer than that $1,000 salary increase would and also saves the company $167 ($1,000 less $833). Of course, the $334 that is now divided between the employee and the company is money that otherwise would have been paid in taxes. The result is exactly the same as if the government had offered the employee and company a grant of $334 to split between them. In-kind company benefits that are exempt from income taxes, therefore, are essentially identical to direct government expenditures for social services. They merely follow a different route, through the firm instead of through a government bureaucracy.

Viewed in this light, the federal government already is undertaking massive social service programs administered through American firms. In 1982, for example, the government provided workers with $16.6 billion worth of health insurance (representing the tax-free part of more than $55 billion in medical coverage provided by firms). Direct federal outlays for Medicare and Medicaid were around $80 billion. So the total federal cost of health care in 1982 was approximately $97 billion—one-fifth of which went to American workers through their firms.

In addition, tax-deferred pension plans administered by firms now rival Social Security as mechanisms by which American workers save for their retirements. In 1982 these tax deferrals amounted to $28 billion. Sums going to employer-sponsored group life insurance now constitute more than one-third of the premium dollars flowing to all life insurance. Other tax-free benefits enjoyed by U.S. workers include subsidized cafeteria food, recreational facilities, home mortgage subsidies, relocation assistance, group legal services, and subsidies for children's private schooling. Some companies have constructed town houses for their employees. Today 240 major companies sponsor child care facilities—twice as many as in 1978. An increasing number of companies are assisting employees to adopt children. (Proposed legislation to exempt such payments from taxable income is pending in Congress.) Twenty-five percent of America's 500 largest companies now help the spouses of transferred salaried employees find new jobs. Many companies provide their employees (and employees' families) with psychiatric counseling. Increasingly, industrial social workers are dealing with employees' alcohol, family, and drug problems. And, as has been shown here, American business spends approximately $30 billion per year on employee education and training.[3]

All told, these employee benefits represent about one-fifth of all government expenditures on social services. Such benefits are growing far more rapidly than direct social services (in 1940 they represented only one-tenth of government expenditures on social services). And these benefits are constituting an ever larger proportion of employee compensation. In 1966 employee benefits represented only 17 percent of the total compensation of American workers; by 1982 benefits had reached 28 percent. In large corporations, benefits now represent more than 40 percent of total employee compensation.[4]

The workplace is becoming the center of social services for a large portion of America's population. Although propelled almost arbitrarily by the tax laws, this change is also congruent with changing patterns of social life in America. As an ever-increasing proportion of married women enter the work force and as geographic communities cease to have real social significance for many citizens, workplaces are becoming the center of social relationships. They are places where people experience authority most directly and learn the practical realities of collective action. The shop floor and the office are where the values of privacy, equity, security, and participation are most intimately discovered, and their lack is most painfully felt. In a real sense, the work community is replacing the geographic community as the most tangible American social setting.

The problem is that we have not fully recognized or adapted to this change. Social services administered by companies do not reach the people that need them the most—the unemployed. At the very time that employee benefit programs are being expanded and tax subsidies are flowing to them as never before, direct social services for citizens outside the production system are being reduced. And within industry, social benefits are not provided uniformly over the work force. Smaller companies tend to offer fewer benefits than large ones. And even in larger firms, benefit packages are fullest for white-collar, salaried employees.

Nor are these employee benefit programs administered by employees, who presumably are better able to judge what they need than are the company's professional managers. Finally, these programs are not related to the performance of the business enterprise: They are not coordinated with firms' capital investment strategies, and benefits do not vary with the circumstances of the firm and its employees. In all these respects, the system's evolution is still far from complete.

6.

Business enterprises in Japan and Western Europe have moved farther along this path than we have. Japanese firms spend, on average, nearly three times as much per employee on social service and recreational programs as American firms.[5] One-third of Japan's labor force enjoys guaranteed lifetime employment. And these larger companies take full responsibility for adapting employees to new production processes.

Although there are features of Japanese industrial organization that we would not want to adopt even if we could, there are other aspects that we would do well to emulate. The Japanese understand the crucial importance to a company's future productivity of maintaining intact the unique community of skills and relationships within a work force: The risk of economic downturns is borne primarily by the shareholders of these companies and by government-linked banks rather than by the employees themselves. Workers are not laid off when sales decline because the company's major shareholders and the government come to its aid. And senior managers are expected to take substantial cuts in pay before they force lower-level workers to bear the financial burden of unemployment. We have only to compare how Mazda handled its huge deficit in the early 1970's—cutting the pay of senior managers by 20 percent, freezing the pay of middle-level managers, but maintaining cost of living increases for its lower-level workers and keeping them all employed—with Chrysler's recent decision to lay off 28 percent of its blue-collar force while firing only 7 percent of its middle-level managers and cutting its white-collar salaries by an average of only 5 percent. Is it any wonder that Mazda's work force was committed to restoring the company to competitive health and maintained the skills to do so? Can we expect the same from Chrysler's workers?

In Japan, when workers must be laid off, they do not go on welfare. They go to work. The Japanese government spends large sums (in 1981 one-fourth of the entire budget of the Ministry for International Trade and Industry) on subsidizing small businesses—mostly retail—which function as a kind of human capital safety net for people who otherwise would be chronically unemployed. Workers thereby maintain their skills, pride, and motivation. And day care, training, and other forms of social services continue to be supplied through the firms.

Handicapped workers are integrated into Japanese firms. By law, companies must hire at least 1.5 percent of their workers from among the handicapped. Employers of 300 or more workers must pay the equivalent of $130 a month for each employee short of the 1.5 percent target. These payments, which totaled about $74 million in 1981, go into a fund to pay for specialized equipment needed to make handicapped people productive members of the work force.

Even Japan has a long way to go in fully using its human capital. Several groups continue to be excluded from the process of economic development. Social barriers have blocked the advancement of Japan's 1.2 million *barakumin* ("ghetto people"), descendants of the lowest social order in feudal Japan. The vast majority of them remain trapped in urban ghettos, working in menial jobs and suffering extreme poverty. Also excluded is Japan's population of 700,000 Koreans and the 15,000 Ainu, descendants of the country's earliest inhabitants. Women in Japan face social barriers that effectively bar them from responsible positions in industry, and employees of small manufacturers and retailers do not have the same generous benefits as workers in Japan's largest firms.

Still, the overall organization of Japanese society promotes social and economic adaptation rather than preservation of the status quo. While Japan's social failings should not be glossed over, the direction that it has chosen will put increasing pressure on Japanese society to remove these vestiges of prejudice.

Other nations also are taking steps to merge their social and economic policies. In Sweden a range of social services are delivered through the unions, while Swedish companies provide many additional services. Most general physicians in Sweden, for example, are affiliated with companies. Firms in West Germany also provide generous employee benefits: In 1977, while the average hourly wage of American workers was 15 percent higher than that of West German workers, the latter received benefits that were 63 percent higher than those received by the former; thus, the total "social wage" of West German workers was 6.5 percent higher than that of their American counterparts.[6]

In West Germany the combination of social services delivered through employee benefits and direct social services constitutes 27.8 percent of the nation's gross national product. Combined indirect and direct social service expenditures are of similar magnitudes in other Western European nations and in Japan. But in Great Britain the combined figure represents only 20.6 percent of the GNP, and in the United States it is only 11.1 percent.[7] Social adjustment has not been a high priority in either Britain or America. The sorry states of both economies attest to that failing.

Despite America's relative slowness in integrating its economic development and human development programs, social services are already to a great extent delivered through business enterprises. American workers no longer live by wages alone but depend on social services channeled through both the public and private sectors. Business enterprises are rapidly becoming the central mediating structures in American society, replacing geographic communities as the locus of social services and, indeed, social life.

We should not underestimate the magnitude of the changes that will be entailed in completing this transformation of the American work community, extending its benefits to those who are now excluded and rendering it more democratic. Ultimately the prospects for such changes will depend on how we resolve the political choices that lie before us.

XII
POLITICAL CHOICE

1.

America confronts a choice. We can continue to endure a painful and slow economic transition in which industrial assets and managers are endlessly rearranged through paper entrepreneurialism, political coalitions seek and obtain shelter from foreign competitors, and a growing share of American labor becomes locked into dead-end employment. This kind of transition can lead only to a lower standard of living for many Americans. It will be coupled with political rancor and divisiveness as the steadily shrinking economic pie is divided into ever smaller slices.

The alternative is a dynamic economy in which capital and labor adapt to engage the new realities of international competition. Rapid adjustment offers Americans a rising standard of living. But the politics that must underpin a dynamic economy are far more difficult to achieve. Ultimately America's capacity to respond to economic change will depend on the vitality of its political institutions. Only by acknowledging the powerful links between the social and economic dimensions of our national well-being can we forge a consensus for progress. And only through such a consensus can we craft vigorous institutions and forward-looking strategies to accelerate economic evolution. America's choice is fundamentally a political one.

The burdens and benefits of rapid economic change inevitably fall unevenly in the first instance: Older jobs are threatened; older investments, jeopardized; sacrifices are demanded of some for gains that others reap, at least in the first round. But unless citizens trust that these gains and losses will be shared equitably, the groups that stand to lose disproportionately will resist change with every resource at their command. They will prevail. Economic minorities in America hold the power to veto proposals that jeopardize their well-being. This is an invaluable virtue of our political system—giving force to the guarantee against tyranny by the majority—but under the imperative of economic change it is also a substantial challenge. The wide diffusion of effective veto power requires complex negotiations and creative solutions to the problems of economic "losers" before change can occur. American democracy often makes economic change enormously difficult while ensuring that once brought about, the change will by and large be fair.

There is a further virtue to a fair sharing of the burdens and benefits of industrial change beyond its obvious moral appeal. Such an allocation is necessary if economic responsibility and initiative are to become widely felt and exercised. The nature of flexible-system production makes this perhaps truer today and in the future than at any time in America's past. For as we have seen, productivity in the era of human capital will depend largely on collaboration, group learning, and teamwork.

2.

The political choice is apparent in the microsociety of the business enterprise. Employees who doubt that the burdens and benefits of rapid adaptation will be shared equitably resist change outright or resort to subtle forms of sabotage: Blue-collar workers cling to work rules and rigid job classifications and fight against new technologies and productivity improvements; technical specialists steal company assets and make off with company secrets; managers earn as much money for themselves as they can before deserting the company for more lucrative positions elsewhere. Without a network of mutual obligation within the enterprise none sacrifices for the long term or for the greater good of the work community. All seek to defend their prerogatives. Such is now the case in the typical American and British company.

Flexible-system enterprises depend on participation and thus on security and equity. Wherever such enterprises are found—in many Japanese factories, in the *sogo shosha* (trading companies) of Japan, in a few American companies producing high-technology goods, in Israeli kibbutz industries, in several Swedish and West German firms, in the plants of the Mondragón region of Spain—they share many of the same attributes: The salaries, benefits, and status of senior managers are not vastly different from those of junior employees; employees are relatively secure in their jobs; and important company decisions depend on widespread consultation and negotiation. These features contribute to increased productivity not because they make employees somehow "feel good" about the firm—on the contrary, they sometimes cause strains and frustrations and demand an annoying amount of time and attention —but because they enhance the organization's capacity to adapt quickly to novel situations. Only when skills, knowledge, and responsibility are widely diffused can employees build on one another's strengths in responding to new problems and opportunities; only when employees feel relatively secure from arbitrary job loss and on an equal footing can they collaborate spontaneously. In this setting industrial change does not have to be "sold" to the work force; change is promoted and carried out by the work force.

Flexible-system enterprises exist in large part for the people who work within them. Of course, if the enterprises are successful, they also enrich their customers, suppliers, and stockholders. But one of their central missions is to enhance the lives of their employees. In a real sense they are political communities whose leaders are accountable to their members.

Managers in the typical Japanese company and in many West German and Swedish companies start from the understanding that their enterprises are answerable primarily to their employees, rather than to their stockholders, for the simple reason that private equity markets are relatively insignificant in these nations. But the typical American or

British manager still acts—or at least claims to act—on the notion that the enterprise should exclusively serve the interests of a separately identifiable group of people who hold its shares. This notion carries less and less validity. A half century ago Adolf Berle and Gardiner Means recognized that the technical owners of America's largest corporations —the shareholders—exerted little or no control over these firms and that it was unrealistic to suppose they ever would; managers were in control. Today that observation can be extended: The vast majority of shareholders not only exert no control but also lack any interest in operational control. Shares of stock no longer signify ownership in any functional sense of the term. Once shares are issued, they become something akin to lottery tickets, held purely for the sake of selling them within a short time at a higher price. American shareholders have little more proprietary concern for the companies they briefly "own" than ticket holders have for the administration of the state lotteries they play. The vast majority of shares are held by institutional investors— insurance companies, pension funds, mutual funds—that manage their clients' funds by moving in and out of large blocks of stock at a fast clip, in search of short-term gains.

Finally, if we go a step farther and seek the real interests behind these funds, we come full circle: With employee pension funds and group insurance funds growing at an extraordinary rate, the legal owners of a sizable chunk of American industry turn out to be American workers. (The trend is in the same direction in Britain.) But because the lines of responsibility from manager to employee are so attenuated, filtered through a maze of plans, trustees, institutional investors, and stock portfolios, most employees do not feel that they are in any significant sense owners of American business. Instead, the fiction of a stable and personified group of shareholding owners has come to serve as a screen for managerial autonomy.

The issue is political, not economic. The underlying economic relationships are the same in the typical American company as they are in the typical Japanese and continental European company—employees are the major beneficiaries of industrial success and the major victims of industrial failure. But the political relationships are vastly different. The fates of American workers are not directly linked to the success of the particular companies they work for, and they have no formal means of participating in company decisions. In West Germany employees are directly represented on workers' councils and on supervisory boards. In Japan employees participate through elaborate systems of consultation at all levels of the firm. (Sixteen percent of the board members of Japanese companies have previously been trade union leaders.) In Sweden formal, influential union boards represent workers.[1]

Because the institution of professional management has never taken firm root in continental Europe or Japan, there is not the sharp division of labor between the planning and execution of work that has characterized Anglo-Saxon enterprises. This radical bifurcation of the work force is now having disastrous results in America and Britain. It has defined two distinct corporate cultures that communicate primarily through formal channels of management directives and union complaints. It is keeping the vast repository of information embodied in the work force locked out of the processes of decision. It is sapping workers' sense of common cause with their firms and forcing unions to rely on cumbersome and inefficient shop-floor rules to protect their members' interests. In short, it is destroying the foundation of economic community that now underpins industrial vitality.

This is not to suggest that companies in continental Europe and Japan are models of labor-management harmony. On the contrary, Japanese labor unions annually mount a rhetorically aggressive "spring offensive" against management. Swedish workers are proud of their militancy. Many French workers espouse socialist ideals. And West German labor unions periodically fulminate against their companies. The difference is that these adversarial contests take place within an industrial framework premised on an acknowledgment of equity, job security, and participation as legitimate corporate goals. Workers in these countries understand that their fates are tied to the profitability and competitiveness of their firms. They therefore bargain for change and adaptability—retraining programs; relocation assistance; new investment in plant and equipment. Their counterparts in America and Britain, meanwhile, seek to maintain the status quo because change threatens their economic security.

In Japan and continental Europe labor militancy has become largely symbolic—a periodic ritual through which all elements of the work force reestablish their social compact. Indeed, in many of these countries white-collar employees are themselves union members who duly participate in these rites. Nothing could be farther from the bitter and contentious conflicts that have long separated professional managers from workers in America and Britain.

3.

The same issues of political accountability surround multinational enterprises, only on a different scale. Seventy percent of the value added in American manufacturing currently derives from firms that have branches, subsidiaries, or joint ventures outside the United States; a similar percentage of manufacturing income in Japan, West Germany, Sweden, and Britain is earned by multinational enterprises.[2]

But, importantly, there are now two distinct types of multinational enterprise. The type which includes a growing proportion of American and British industry owes its allegiance to no particular country. Its managers, directors, creditors, shareholders, and employees come from many nations. It is a pure multinational.

The other type, which characterizes much of Japanese industry and a portion of industry in continental Europe, spreads its operations around the globe, as does a pure multinational, but its primary orientation is to the citizens of a particular nation. Regardless of how many of its managers, directors, creditors, shareholders, or employees lie outside the nation, the enterprise nevertheless is pledged to promote the welfare of its home country's citizens. This type may be called a national multinational.

Superficially, pure multinationals and national multinationals look much alike. Both invest all over the world—building plants, setting up assembly operations, entering long-term supply contracts, and establishing local distributors. But their strategies are profoundly different because they are propelled by different presumptions of responsibility.

National multinationals seek to increase the real incomes of their home country's citizens over time. They are agents of their national economies. Thus, their foreign investments are calculated to support their nation's economic progress and to accelerate the development of their citizens' skills and knowledge. They accomplish this by investing abroad in new sources of supply, new distribution outlets, low-skilled assembly operations, and low-wage manufacturing facilities of a kind that their nation has already surpassed.

Japanese multinationals, for example, are even more actively engaged than American-based multinationals in worldwide investment programs. But the underlying strategies of Japan's multinationals are geared to increasing the real wages of Japanese workers over the long term. In what may at first seem a paradoxical approach to serving the interests of its workers, Japan now leads all other industrialized countries in transferring technology to developing nations in Southeast Asia, the Pacific basin, and Latin America and, increasingly, in Africa and the Middle East. Between 1976 and 1978 more than 50 percent of Japan's machinery exports went to developing countries, compared with 30 percent for the United States. In dollar volume Japan now exceeds the United States in exports to developing countries of electrical power machinery, motor vehicle parts, metalworking machinery, and other sophisticated equipment. It also leads in sales of entire plants. For many Japanese firms, developing nations are now more important markets than the United States.[3]

How does this technology transfer raise the real wages of Japanese workers? The answer is simple. Rather than resisting or ignoring the new economic dynamism of the developing world, Japan is actively taking a role in it by pacing its own industrial evolution to accommodate—and lead—world development. The demand for many products is growing more rapidly in developing countries than in industrialized countries. Sales of automobiles, television sets, and home appliances are sluggish in the United States and Western Europe both because of the current recession and because most Americans and Europeans already own these products. But in many developing nations sales of these consumer goods are booming. By building manufacturing facilities there and providing these nations with entire plants of their own, the Japanese are participating directly in that growth. Japanese companies thereby gain outlets for their older technologies, at the same time establishing channels to market their newer technologies all over the globe.

In this way the developing nations have been incorporated into the growth strategies of Japanese companies. They are being groomed to become prosperous markets and suppliers for the Japanese economy. This strategy is realistic because of the continual forward movement of Japanese industry—with public agencies coordinating the pace of change, Japanese companies are willing to discard older technologies as fast as newer ones can be developed. Japanese firms understand that competitive advantage in industrial products is a dynamic phenomenon which depends ultimately on the constantly advancing skills and knowledge of their nation's work force. To stand still is to fall behind. The developing nations provide the impetus.

Meanwhile, Japanese companies are establishing facilities in America and Western Europe for assembling Japanese automobiles, trucks, and appliances. This strategy also enhances the real wages of Japanese workers over the long term. Because these assembly facilities require relatively low-skilled labor, they do not threaten the jobs of progressively more skilled Japanese workers. So long as the highest-value portion of the production process remains behind in Japan, foreign-based assembly facilities contribute to the standard of living of Japanese citizens by increasing the demand for sophisticated components produced in Japan. (These assembly facilities also help forestall protectionist sentiment in the host countries.)

Certain Western European companies—like Volvo, which accounts for almost 5 percent of the Swedish gross national product—pursue similar international strategies. Volvo's foreign investments have the effect of increasing the real wages of Swedish workers over time. Investing in a Brazilian assembly plant does not result in a loss of Swedish jobs; instead, it increases the demand for higher-valued components from Swedish factories. This kind of overseas expansion complements Volvo's investments progressively to upgrade its Swedish work force.[4]

The motives of Japanese and certain Western European multinationals originate more in cultural and informal political ties with their home countries than from direct political controls imposed on them. But state-controlled multinationals are also becoming common. Such companies now turn out 54 percent of the world's steel, 35 percent of its polyethylene, and 20 percent of its automobiles.[5] They are also manufacturing computers, semiconductors, and aircraft. For example, Airbus Industrie, an international aircraft consortium controlled by Britain, France, and West Germany, is already taking a share of world market away from Boeing; but beyond these immediate sales, Airbus Industrie's long-term competitive value lies in the training and experience gained by French, German, and British aircraft designers, engineers, and production technicians.

Pure multinationals, in contrast with national multinationals, are neither formally nor informally bound to the citizens of any particular nation. Their goal is to maximize their own net earnings and thus to increase the return to their most mobile resources—international capital and international management. Because their profitability is not linked to the successful adjustment of any one nation, pure multinationals have no effective incentive to make long-term investments in human capital. Their decisions about where and how to invest depend exclusively upon where they can find the cheapest inputs, the most rapidly growing markets, and a preexisting pool of adequate labor.[6]

Many American companies are fast becoming pure multinationals. Examples abound. The Hughes Tool Company exported 24 percent of the output of its Houston oil-drilling equipment plant in 1980, but only 17.5 percent in 1981; during the interim it increased production at six plants in other countries. Dow, Exxon, and Mobil are now building a mammoth petroleum complex at Jubail, in Saudi Arabia, to produce 500,000 tons of ethylene a year. During the 1970's General Electric expanded its worldwide payroll by 5,000, but it did so by adding 30,000 foreign jobs and reducing its United States employment by 25,000. RCA followed the same strategy, cutting its U.S. employment by 14,000 while increasing its foreign work force by 19,000. The Carlton Machine Tool Company recently moved from Cincinnati to Taiwan, where it now produces radial drills for half the cost of producing them in America. General Motors soon begins production of its new compact J-car in Brazil, where the average hourly earnings of production workers are only $1.70. McGraw-Hill now prints and binds an encyclopedia in Singapore. International Silver recently closed its American cutlery plant and shifted production to Taiwan. General Electric, RCA, Rockwell International, and Samsonite all operate factories along the Mexican border. Singer has just closed its large Elizabeth, New Jersey, plant and is planning to open production facilities abroad. Mobil makes paperboard packaging in Mexico, Venezuela, and Colombia and owns condominiums in Hong Kong. Virtually every major American producer of consumer electronics products, textiles, footwear, sporting goods, and toys has closed its U.S. plants and opened plants in Southeast Asia, to produce for export to America.

From the standpoint of American workers, the problem with this is not so much a net loss of jobs, even if this is how labor unions typically frame the issue, nor is the solution somehow to compel multinationals to preserve every American job regardless of relative labor costs and capabilities throughout the world. In 1981 foreign dollars invested in America exceeded American investments abroad, creating more new jobs than were exported.[7] The problem is that none of these investments is strategically linked to the long-term development of the American work force. U.S. companies setting up foreign operations are not simultaneously moving American workers into higher-value production. They are not using these investments to stimulate flexible-system skills in America. Instead of giving over their older technologies to less developed countries and using these maturing markets and suppliers to spur new human capital investment in America, American-based pure multinationals are merely transplanting high-volume, standardized production abroad. Instead of approaching international competition as a dynamic process in which older skills and techniques must be relinquished and replaced by newer ones, these American companies view their share of the market statically, as a fixed quantity to be defended against potential encroachment. Transplanting their old production processes abroad is merely one means of protecting themselves against low-wage competition from developing countries.

The real threat is not mass unemployment; American workers will find other jobs eventually (including low-wage jobs in foreign-owned assembly plants). But because this pattern of investment is not easing the American work force into higher-value production, American workers will fill secondary roles in the emerging international economy. Over time, the real incomes of U.S. workers will decline against the standard of other nations' workers.

Governments in many other nations recognize the distinction between national multinationals and pure multinationals. They also distinguish between direct investments in their nations which merely create new jobs and those which also increase the quality of their labor force—between investments in physical capital and investments in human capital. They therefore are bargaining with pure multinationals for more human capital investment: Italtel, Italy's state-owned telecommunications equipment manufacturer, recently entered into an agreement with GTE (headquartered in Stamford, Connecticut) to develop an electronic telephone-switching system for the Italian market on condition that the manufacturing facilities be in Italy. GTE gets an inside track on future business in

Italy, but Italtel gets the know-how. France has just invited Motorola to establish a semiconductor division there and has offered investment incentives on condition that Motorola set up a research and development department in France to help train French engineers. Various governments' conditional offers of market access have led IBM to establish nine research laboratories in Europe and Asia. Ireland is offering incentives for multinationals to establish full-scale manufacturing, research and development, and European-wide administrative facilities in that country. And in a bold move, Singapore recently raised its minimum wage, gambling that the higher wages would force the multinationals that locate there to invest more heavily in employee training, in order to justify the higher expenditures, and that these human capital investments would more than offset any lost investment by multinationals dissuaded by higher wages against locating in Singapore. The gamble apparently is paying off— multinationals, including the American-based Hewlett-Packard, are establishing research facilities in Singapore.

Japanese companies, meanwhile, are entering joint ventures with American companies in the emerging fields of biotechnology, "fifth-generation" computers, fiber optics, and advanced integrated circuits. By the terms of these agreements, most advanced research and engineering are to be done in Japan. The U.S. firms thereby gain access to the Japanese market, but Japan reaps the more durable benefit of investments in its human capital. Japanese firms also are producing aircraft under licensing agreements with McDonnell Douglas and Lockheed, rather than buying the aircraft outright; this arrangement enables the Japanese to learn about up-to-date aircraft manufacturing systems and technologies. In the short run these joint ventures and licensing agreements are more expensive than direct purchases would be, but in the long run they will improve the skills and knowledge of Japanese workers and thereby permit Japan to be more competitive in these industries in the future. The extra costs simply represent sound investments in human capital.

Meanwhile, many Japanese producers are supplying American manufacturers with high value-added products and components. Xerox already is producing many of its small copiers in Japan. Motorola operates an integrated-circuit design center and a test center there. Of the sixteen American firms that built manufacturing facilities in Japan during the first half of 1982, ten were in the business of making advanced semiconductors, and four in biotechnology and fine chemicals.[8] Beginning in 1984, both General Motors and Ford will be importing subcompacts and diesel engines from Japan. All these arrangements also serve to develop Japanese know-how, at the expense of the long-term skills of the American work force.

The issue is a political one, but not in the manner it is usually cast. The question is not how many of a nation's dollars are invested abroad. It is not whether foreign investors are state-owned enterprises. Nor is national security a valid concern in the vast majority of these investment decisions. The real issue concerns the fact that human beings are relatively immobile on the globe compared to financial capital. Because of this, investments in skills, knowledge, and team learning are coming to be the key determinants of national well-being.

By 1988, if present trends continue, 300 giant firms will produce half of the world's goods and services. Their production processes will be fragmented across the globe, with specialized components produced and assembled in dozens of locations. There no longer will be such things as "American" automobiles or "American" computers—only parts of automobiles and computers that are produced in America and specific assembly operations that are undertaken in America. Some of these giant companies will be national multinationals, whose mission will be to increase the value of their home country workers' role in the system. Others will be pure multinationals, dedicated only to maximizing their net earnings. Many national governments will directly influence national multinationals and negotiate with pure multinationals, in an attempt to steer high-valued parts of the production process to their own countries, so that their citizens can improve their skills and increase their real earnings. National governments will thus become bargaining agents for the least mobile factor of international production—human capital.

America has no national multinationals. Instead, it has many companies that are becoming pure multinationals. And the United States government has so far shown itself unwilling or unable to bargain either with foreign-based or with American-based multinationals, for human capital investments in this country.

The political choice is clear. It is the same choice that must be faced within the microsociety of America's business enterprises. It is the choice that underlies the problems of paper entrepreneurialism, historic preservation, and dead-end labor in America. Either the United States adjusts to the new realities of international competition and shifts its human capital resources to higher-valued productivity, or it consigns itself to a gradually declining standard of living, relative to the rest of the industrialized world. Adjustment means ending the nation's total dependence on macroeconomic "fine tuning" or the romance of supply-side economics and turning, instead, to more strategic policies to shift citizens to higher-valued production. Such policies include explicit bargaining with multinational corporations for increased investment in America's store of human capital.

4.

At bottom the political issue is one of social membership. What does it mean to be a member of a work community within a business enterprise? To be a member of an economic community within a nation? For whom does the business enterprise exist?

The concept of membership can, of course, be distorted into crass, exclusionary terms that find their expression in jingoism and mercantilism. The largest Japanese companies, for example, elevate the sense of membership to the point where it threatens employees' privacy and autonomy and excludes many women, minorities, and foreign nationals from its benefits. In America the ubiquitous rationale of "national security" often distorts the concept of national membership into an exaggerated fear of foreign domination. But the concept of membership also can find positive political expression, fostering mutual obligation and respect and encouraging cooperation among citizens. It can form a cultural basis for inclusion rather than exclusion, rendering a nation and its productive enterprises more sensitive to the needs of all people to improve their quality of life.

The lesson is usually left out of economic discussions. It is not only poverty that the disadvantaged find unbearable, but also their exclusion from political participation and membership in a larger community. This is as true for America's poor as it is for the poor of other nations. This sense of isolation and abandonment often breeds real misery, resentment, and sometimes violence. The implication is twofold. Economic development is meaningful only when coupled with social membership. And—in any sort of democracy—rapid adjustment to economic change is possible only when founded upon collective trust that its burdens and benefits will be fairly shared.

But the management era in America has bequeathed us an inappropriate political legacy. Public goals were so uncontroversial through most of the era, especially in the decades following World War II—to win at the arms race and the moon race; to maintain economic growth by "fine-tuning" the money supply, taxes, and public expenditures; to eliminate poverty by transferring the "social surplus" to the poor—that political debate was largely supplanted by questions of managerial efficiency. And since the "right" decision could be established unambiguously by reference to how efficiently each option promised to advance these goals, there was very little public concern with the process of political choice. America merely declared "war" on its most intractable problems—be they poverty, inflation, or energy—on the assumption that all that was needed to solve them was fierce determination, sufficient intelligence, and adequate financial and technical resources mustered and directed by efficient management. Managerial government was adept at finding efficient solutions, but not at engaging the political process by which they were made. It relied on value-blind policy analysis and methods borrowed from business.

Meanwhile, America's political institutions withered. Organizations that had once promoted political participation and negotiation—civic and charitable groups, political clubs, political parties, and trade unions —either atrophied or were transformed into managerial organizations devoted to the efficient delivery of benefits to their members.

So long as the American economy expanded vigorously, overt political choices could be avoided. Public goals were assumed without question. Prosperity smothered potential conflicts and lubricated change as nearly everyone reaped some share of the ever-expanding wealth.

But America's economic decline has exposed the limits of managerial government—its inability to allocate fairly the burdens and benefits of structural change. When faced with hard political choices from which some citizens gain while others initially lose, managerial government has been impotent. It has lacked the legitimacy to orchestrate consensus. Political decisions, when they have been made, have typically been submerged under complex and seemingly neutral issues of economic policy. As a result of this incapacity or unwillingness to engage political choices, many decisions have been made—awkwardly and by default—in the federal courts. These manifestations of political failure deserve a closer look.

Paralysis in the face of political choice has been the bane of many of America's recent liberal administrations. The administration of Mayor John V. Lindsay in New York City exemplified the pattern. This administration was a well-designed managerial system, engineered to process efficiently the various demands placed upon it. But it was incapable of ranking these demands or choosing among them because it had no legitimate mechanism for deciding how the burdens and benefits of public decisions were to be allocated. The result was preordained by the limits of the process: New York City ran out of money in April 1975. The city's bankruptcy resulted in the Emergency Financial Control Board and the Municipal Assistance Corporation's being granted authority to review and reject any proposed spending plans. By failing to deal with painful political choices, the city's officials forfeited control over public decisions. Political issues, unresolved in the political forum, were submerged in the deliberations of nonelected bodies. Other cities have followed the same route.

Jimmy Carter's administration was also plagued by an inability to engage political choices. President Carter entered office promising the American people a federal government that was competently managed. But without any political means for ranking national goals, the administration quickly became mired in dozens of separate initiatives. Few of these claimed deep public support. Most had meager results. "Efficiency" was an empty concept without a political debate to shape proposals and vest them with legitimacy. Liberal governments—trying to be all things to all people, leery of engaging the public in the uncomfortable process of political choice—have ended in predictable deadlock.

When political choices have been made, it has been in the guise of economic policy. One example is the debate over the environmental effects of energy development. Decisions to embark on large-scale energy projects have benefited those who gain access to cheap power while simultaneously imposing losses on citizens who live near nuclear generators or hazardous waste sites or who care deeply about protecting America's beaches from oil spills and its wilderness from strip mining. Yet these political decisions, submerged in the regulatory process, have come increasingly to be based on an abstract tally of costs and benefits—an analytical exercise that cannot engage and thus ignores the distributive issues.

A more pervasive and insidious example of how economic policy embodies and obscures political choice is found in continued attempts to "fine-tune" the nation's economy, using fiscal and monetary manipulation to control inflation. The economy is squeezed and twisted until those citizens in the most precarious position lose their footing. Invariably the poorest among us have been drafted into the inflation fight through unemployment. Inflation is the monetary manifestation of an unacknowledged struggle over how to allocate the losses from economic decline. Organized groups that understand this consistently win the struggle. Other groups lose. Over the past decade the burden of fighting inflation has been borne by young blacks in central cities (86 percent of whom are unemployed), by women (36 percent more likely than men to be unemployed), and by Hispanics (75 percent more likely than whites). It is ever more obvious that the only way inflation can be controlled equitably is through national agreements on overall wage and price increases. Otherwise, the burden of fighting inflation falls almost entirely on those least able to bear it.

Wage and price increases in every other industrialized nation follow guidelines established in national negotiations. In Norway, Sweden, and Denmark economy-wide "framework" agreements are formally negotiated between employer and labor federations; in Austria, Belgium, the Netherlands, and Japan representatives of the major business and labor confederations conduct ongoing negotiations. The national bargaining arenas in these countries provide all segments of the population with highly visible opportunities to clarify goals, articulate demands, and negotiate precise trade-offs among inflation, unemployment, and structural adjustment.[9]

But America and Britain cling to the fiction of a "managed economy," in which government merely applies neutral principles of fiscal and monetary policy. Structural adjustment cannot be a part of this managerial agenda because there is no consensus about the direction adjustment should take and no organizational arena for forging such a consensus.

Economic managers in America and Britain have come to measure the health of their national economies in terms of abstract rates of inflation, interest, unemployment, trade balances, investment, and productivity. They view the world through the eyes of bankers and traders—wedded to abstraction and thus prone to sacrifice the real to the symbolic and the future to the present. They ignore the importance of structural change and adaptability to the nation's economic health and the central role of political choice and compromise in making such change possible.

In their obsession with economic aggregates, these economic managers confuse means with ends. Proximate goals become disconnected from ultimate goals and take precedence over them. The only sensible end of a nation's economic policy should be improving its citizens' standard of living. The concept of "standard of living" is, of course, vague and subjective. But most people probably would agree that it is comprised of at least three elements: the goods and services bought by the nation's citizens; the availability of goods that are not purchased directly but that weigh heavily in most people's sense of well-being, such as clean air and water, protection from crime and accident, and security against medical or financial disaster; and, finally, the sense that these goods and services, both private and public, are justly shared among citizens. Such economic goals as growth, higher productivity, lower inflation, and a strong currency are means of achieving a higher standard of living, but they are not ends in themselves. Policies that sacrifice the real substance of social welfare in the service of these aggregate, proximate goals are justifiable, therefore, only as means to achieve an even higher standard of living in the future. The debate over economic abstractions in America and Britain has obscured this most fundamental premise.

A further symptom of America's political failure is the nation's increasing reliance on courts and judges to allocate the burdens and benefits of economic change. In recent years political dialogue has been supplanted to an extraordinary degree by adversarial litigation. Courts are now called upon to decide such things as where power plants should be located, how the burdens of a certain bankruptcy should be shared among shareholders and workers, how many trees can be cut from watersheds, how many salmon can be caught by American Indians, which workers should be laid off when a certain factory is automated, who should pay compensation to victims of asbestosis, which large mergers and acquisitions should be barred because they lessen competition, and who should bear the costs of Love Canal and Three Mile Island.

Suffering that at one time would have been deemed a personal misfortune—the random consequence of fate—is now perceived as injustice open to redress through the legal process. The reason is simple. The dynamic behind economic change in America is now understood to be neither the benign neutrality of the free market nor efficient management. The forces propelling economic change in modern America, even if unacknowledged, are the same as in every other advanced industrial nation: the highly discretionary decisions of executives in giant companies and administrators in giant government agencies. By virtue of these decisions, some people lose and others gain. But lacking political forums in which these benefits and burdens can be acknowledged and negotiated directly, the losers in America have taken to the courts. Litigation is the only way most citizens can bring officials of large corporations and government agencies to account for their decisions clearly, directly, and truthfully.

But the courts are ill-equipped to settle such issues. These controversies are not so much disputes among individuals as they are political contests among whole segments of the population. Their resolution depends less on findings of fact or interpretations of law than it does on widespread public discussion, negotiation, and consensus. Legal battles do not settle these conflicts; they merely prolong and intensify them, forcing them into an endless sequence of skirmishes, each in a slightly different legal configuration.

There is a danger that the law itself will lose its legitimacy in the process. Legal judgments cannot create social consensus. Quite the reverse: Law can resolve conflicts only through reference to shared principles. Law derives its ethical authority from that reference. Where legal controversy comes to be viewed as a mechanistic and arbitrary device for allocating the burdens and benefits of economic change, law comes to be regarded with cynicism. Under these circumstances, people will obey law only to the extent that they fear being caught and punished for their disobedience. As evidenced by the $86 billion in taxes which the Internal Revenue Service estimates were unpaid in 1981, we have already moved a considerable distance down this perilous road.

These manifestations of America's political failure have a common message. Managerial government, the presumptive neutrality of macro-economic policy, and even the logic of judicial law cannot substitute for political dialogue and choice. There is no "best" solution to how the gains and losses from economic change should be allocated and rearranged. There is an almost infinite range of solutions. And the fairest among them —the one that will generate the broadest commitment to active adjust-ment—is discoverable only through the messy process of political debate and choice.

Political choices pervade economic policy. They are embedded in issues of regulation, inflation, unemployment, and investment. But the ethos of economic management often relegates these choices to an insignificant place in its debates. For politicians it is often much safer to blame our ills on impersonal economic forces and to look for technical solutions than to make explicit the hard choices that otherwise will be made implicitly. Politicians flee from political controversy, perpetuating the American tradition of flight from social problems. The historical path of escape, detoured by the closing of the frontier, tracks straight into the abstractions of economic policy. By describing the economy in mechani-cal terms, policy makers can promise renewal through steps to get the economy "moving again," as if it were a distinct entity only loosely linked to what American citizens do when they go to work.

This is not to suggest that America should seek to politicize every economic issue. The point is that any important economic choice is by nature political, but the political dimension is often systematically ob-scured. This submergence of politics results in economic policies whose burdens and benefits are allocated in ways that many people ultimately consider unfair. Americans, like most people, reject or resist painful decisions that they have had no part in making. Efforts to submerge politics serve only to pervert it. America's accelerating slide into indus-trial preservation is the most obvious but by no means the only illustra-tion of this fact. Only when political considerations are dealt with openly can we avoid the dilemma of inefficient special-interest policies or institu-tional paralysis. Adjustment cannot proceed without mechanisms for explicit bargaining among economic groups and without institutions with the authority to monitor and guarantee the consensus. Again, the real choice is not between the free market or national economic planning, the business culture or the civic culture. The choice is between a covert politics that stymies economic and social progress and an open politics that promotes it.

An explicit incomes policy, for example, would bring into the open all the ways in which government policies to control inflation now work to enrich some people while impoverishing others. Facing the political dimension would require aboveboard choices about how the burden of fighting inflation should be allocated. Similarly, an explicit industrial policy to spur economic growth would require an open debate about the multifarious ways in which large corporations and the government now plan the allocation of capital. An explicit regulatory policy would let Americans deal sensibly with the hard choices about the social costs of a given path of economic development—the concrete sacrifices of health, safety, and the environment that it would entail and upon whom the burdens would fall. An explicit training and retraining policy would give workers in declining industries an alternative to desperate attempts to block change and would let us begin to compensate for the failure of the unaided market to generate enough of the right kind of human capital investments. We have only to imagine the hue and cry that would go up if Congress were to deal expressly with any one of these issues to understand how much political controversy is now submerged within "economic policy."

The notion that the economic and political spheres of our lives can be separated is relatively new. The very word "economics" was not firmly established until Alfred Marshall wrote his *Principles of Economics* in 1890. Before then the term was "political economy"—with the adjective serving as a constant reminder of the "economy's" origins and effects. The entire field branched off in the late eighteenth century from moral philosophy, the study of citizens' rights, duties, and social obligations. In earlier eras it seemed nonsensical to consider economic relationships in isolation from their specific political and social contexts. Which functions society would entrust to markets and how trade was to be structured were explicitly political issues.

The modern intellectual separation of economics from politics has made both spheres strangely unbalanced. The study of politics views people as intensely social animals—forming coalitions, interest groups, and political parties, sometimes exercising statesmanship and solidarity and sometimes colluding against the rest of the public, but always acting

collectively. The study of economics assumes away the social and historical setting and views people as individual "maximizers" who rationally
pursue unambiguously self-interested goals. There is truth in both visions.
We are the products of our societies, yet at the same time we are
fundamentally alone. It is the *interaction* between our public and our
private selves that shapes the nature of our politics and the character of
our economics and determines our capacity to adapt to the changing
conditions we confront as a nation. It is in the balance between the two
that we simultaneously preserve our individuality and cultivate our social
membership. Neither sphere—public or private, political or economic—
must be allowed exclusive claim to our loyalties, or we risk falling victim
to either mass tyranny or solipsism.

5.

At this point in American history we need a political revitalization as
badly as—and in large measure because—we need an economic one. But
there is no simple route to such a civic renaissance. Much will depend
on the quality of America's future political leadership—not only in our
federal, state, and local governments but also in our labor unions, political
parties, corporations and business associations, and civic groups. We will
need leaders who are not afraid to recognize frankly the political choices
that are entailed in major economic change and who are willing to
choreograph openly the bargaining about them. American statesmanship
must rise above both the myth of the unmanaged market and the myth
of neutral management. It must devote itself instead to helping our
citizens perceive the consequence of public choices about economic
change and to hold accountable those who make these choices in the first
instance.

As citizens we must transcend the old categories of civic culture and
business culture and recognize the relationship between the nation's social
and economic development. Americans concerned with social justice must
become familiar with the subtleties of American business and recognize
the importance of profit seeking and investment in economic growth.
American businessmen must accept that claims for participation and
fairness are not obstacles to their mission, but ultimately its very substance.

Finally, we will need political institutions capable of generating large-scale compromise and adaptation. Some of these institutions will be at local and regional levels. But we will also need a national bargaining arena for allocating the burdens and benefits of major adjustment strategies. Such an arena would enable the nation to achieve a broad-based consensus about adjustment. It would enable government, business, and labor to fashion explicit agreements to restructure American industry. Protectionist measures and bailouts to preserve the status quo would be difficult to elicit from government if they were demanded and debated in full view of industrial purchasers, emerging industries, and other groups on whom their costs would fall. Companies seeking financial support or import protection would enter restructuring agreements to ensure that the measures would be temporary and would serve to benefit the overall economy. By the same token, labor and management facing industrial decline would be in a position to negotiate a package of public adjustment assistance designed explicitly to buttress their most competitive operations, retrain their work force, and shift other resources to more profitable uses. Perhaps most important, the single arena could provide a focus for an ongoing national debate about human capital investment and the appropriate allocation of the gains and losses from such change.

To a limited extent, this idea lay behind the establishment of a U.S. Trade Representative's office in the White House. But its jurisdiction is far too limited, its powers too circumscribed and advisory, and the bargaining over which it presides is too covert for this office to become a forum for building a consensus about structural change in America. We have only to compare the USTR with the comprehensive bargaining arena in which West German structural policy is formulated—where many levels of industry, labor, financial, and government leaders thrash out workable agreements on wage rates, selective credit policies, and adjustment—or with the structure and influence of Japan's MITI to comprehend the scale and effort that is implied.

This is not to suggest that either West Germany or Japan provides the United States with an appropriate model. The relative ease with which a consensus about structural policy has been achieved in both countries may have more to do with their recently feudal (and more recently totalitarian) histories than with institutional design.

Japan, in particular, is hardly a model of robust politics. Japan's conservative Liberal Democratic party has dominated the Diet, the parliament, since 1955, and the Diet merely confirms as prime minister the man party leaders select in back-room political deals. Japan's powerful economic ministries, in turn, are run by permanent administrative vice-ministers. These senior bureaucrats and the business leaders who were their old Tokyo University classmates form an impenetrable "old boy" network that in effect governs Japan.

Groups outside this system occasionally shout their disaffection. The violent demonstrations against the new Tokyo airport and the government's nuclear ship project and the ongoing campaign against industrial pollution are cases in point. But these are isolated episodes. They may result in occasional concessions—as when the city of Tokyo abruptly decided in favor of cleaner air—but the routine process of Japanese politics and economic administration is generally secure against such inconvenient outbursts.

America is blessed with a highly contentious political system in which disorder, opportunism, and *ad hoc* arrangements abound and in which hierarchical mass organizations have never found much support. But this by no means rules out the possibility of a more open, more public debate about economic change, in which bargains can be struck "wholesale" in place of the covert "retailing" that now dominates the cloakrooms of Congress, the boardrooms of America's giant corporations, and the courtrooms of every judicial district.

The answer is not "national planning," if we take that term to mean the centralized drafting of detailed blueprints for future economic management. We already have that sort of planning. We have had managerial planning for decades—within our giant corporations and government agencies. Managerial planning depends on stability, predictability, and control. It seeks to be apolitical—a legacy of the management era in America. It is becoming dangerously obsolete as America is caught up in the unpredictable dynamic of international competition. Instead, we need political institutions that are as versatile as flexible-system enterprises—less concerned with making "correct" decisions than with making correctable ones; less obsessed with avoiding error than with detecting and correcting for error; more devoted to responding to changing conditions and encouraging new enterprises than to stabilizing the environment for old enterprises. The instruments for implementing active adjustment will not be the blunt tools of historic preservation—broad-gauge tariffs, desperate corporate bailouts, and prayerful macroeconomics—but more supple tools like restructuring agreements, training and employment vouchers, regional development funds, and tax and financial codes that guide and accelerate market forces while discouraging paper entrepreneurialism. If we are to become a truly adaptable society, our political choices need to be flexible and experimental. They must be compatible with evolving approaches to emerging problems and opportunities. Change and adaptability must be built into our public and private institutions; rigid planning must be avoided.

6.

Economists wisely teach us that the competitive struggle can be a powerful spur to innovation and progress, as each contestant fears that failure to adapt will allow a competitor to gain dominance. Greed and fear are potent evolutionary forces. But the exclusive faith in markets that periodically becomes fashionable in American politics perverts this insight. In the modern world, economic change and adjustment are coming to be driven by competition between complex *organizations*—between business enterprises and between national economies—rather than by competition between individuals. In order to succeed, these complex organizations must be composed of people who can easily and securely cooperate, collaborate, and reach collective judgments. Teamwork and group commitment give organizations their competitive edge; personal conflict and competition within these organizations render them incapable of quick and effective adaptation.

In American society the competitive struggle is occurring at precisely the wrong level—among the American people instead of among America's large business enterprises and between the American economy and the economies of other nations. While America's superstructures of industrial management and import barriers shield firms from competitive pressures, work within those companies is shackled by self-dealing and intrigue. Our government is tainted by back-room deals in which well-connected parties try to pass losses on to someone else. A society so ridden with cynical indifference to public goals and the manipulation of rules for personal gain is simply incapable of fostering enterprises in which workers willingly collaborate for common ends. We are losing the competitive struggle because we cannot work together.

The conservative vision of a market economy in which people are propelled solely by greed and fear is crippling the U.S. economy. A society that simultaneously offers its members both the prospect of substantial wealth and the threat of severe poverty will no doubt inspire occasional feats of dazzling entrepreneurialism. But just as surely, it will reduce the capacity of its members to work together to a common end and to adapt themselves collectively to new conditions. The ideology of wealth and poverty, to which some Americans still cling, is suited to a simple frontier economy in which social progress depends on personal daring. It may well have been a fitting ideology for America's early era of mobilization. But a social ethos shaped in a virgin continent is the wrong vision to guide and motivate the members of an increasingly complex industrial economy.

It is becoming clear that America's economic future depends less on lonely geniuses and backyard inventors than on versatile organizations. Our abundance of Nobel laureates attests to American cleverness. Technical advances originate disproportionately in America—semiconductors, videocassette recorders, and automobile stamping technologies, to name only a few. Our problem is that we are not consolidating this technological leadership into enduring commercial leadership because our industrial organization is not adaptable enough.

The kinds of productive systems that will sustain America's future prosperity are technically intricate. They demand an exacting degree of teamwork. They are vulnerable to individual sabotage in the form of active resistance, the stagnant inefficiency of resentful time servers, or the cynical manipulation of legal and financial symbols. Likewise, our national economy is ever more exposed to sudden global changes. Responding to these challenges requires an engaged and adaptable citizenry. We all are at the mercy of recalcitrant minorities who fear change (when we ourselves are not members of such minorities).

Under these circumstances, the incentives of greed and fear are having perverse effects: Many Americans are resisting change, resorting, instead, to strategies of historic preservation. Lacking mechanisms for negotiating and ensuring the fairness of collective response, we are eschewing collaboration and seeking security and gain in schemes of paper entrepreneurialism and ploys of "beggar thy neighbor." We struggle to avoid sacrifices and burdens we believe others are successfully evading, and we refuse to support social services the direct beneficiaries of which are different from ourselves. And we seek to gain personal benefits at the expense of society at large, benefits like those we suspect others are already obtaining. The social fabric is slowly unraveling.

7.

The challenge of adapting to the era of human capital exemplifies the paradox of civic virtue. To the extent that people cooperate—willingly sharing their knowledge, skills, and resources with one another—each person is rendered better off than he would be without such cooperation. The collective power of everyone's talents and resources is greater than the mere sum of the individual talents and resources involved. But each person is aware that he can be even better off if everyone *but* himself acts with an eye to the common good, so that he can benefit from the result without bearing any part of the mutual burden. If each person follows this logic and rationally opts for personal gain at the expense of everyone else, there will be no cooperation. Everyone will be worse off. What is rational for the individual is tragically irrational for the society as a whole.

Any society that hopes to escape this grim logic—or the despairing solution of blunt coercion—must equip itself with ideals and institutions that inspire citizens to work together without fear of being victimized. The confidence that underpins cooperation depends on effective codes of fairness and on institutions that nurture a sense of economic citizenship —in short, on a potent concern with civic virtue. The notion that an atmosphere of civic membership and obligation is a requisite for prosperity may seem quaintly old-fashioned in an age of robots and microcomputers. But the logic is timeless: Civic virtue is not a matter of charity or ethics; it is the adhesive of social and economic life.

Civic virtue is not a new requisite, of course. History is filled with examples of societies whose economic decline paralleled the decay of their civic cultures. Their demises were caused not by shortages of resources but by outmoded forms of economic organization and a collective inability to change. The Italian city-states of the twelfth and thirteenth centuries, for example, were known for their public spirit and mutual cooperation. But these qualities were conspicuously lacking in the conservative, cynical, and economically stagnant Italy of the seventeenth century.

Italian manufacturers were progressively driven out of markets by new products and new systems of production from Holland. Italy was still a country of able businessmen and abundant capital. But its social structure had grown rigid; it could not adapt to the new economic conditions. The only consensus was against change.[10] By 1780 Naples had lost its commercial and industrial center, leaving behind, among its 500,000 inhabitants, some 100,000 beggars and homeless, an army of 20,000 soldiers, and more than 30,000 lawyers.[11]

The Dutch of the seventeenth century were vigorous economic and social innovators. But within 100 years they had been overtaken by the English. In the intervening period a conservative and fearful attitude had gradually settled over Holland. Those who had accumulated fortunes in the years of prosperity attended exclusively to keeping them. Politics turned ugly. Public spirit degenerated. The Dutch were slow to adopt new advances in shipbuilding, weaving, fishing, mapmaking, and navigation. The new ways of doing things—and the new talents, skills, and organizational arrangements they required—were too threatening to the established order.[12]

Britain's ascendancy spanned most of the nineteenth century. But its inability to adapt to changes in world markets or to adopt the new organization of economic and social life that such changes implied foreclosed its continued economic leadership. Industrialization brought with it new social problems that the nation largely ignored. The entrepreneurial manufacturers of the early part of the century came to adopt the accoutrements of the aristocracy they had supplanted. Their heirs settled into the comfortable professions of banking and finance. Modern Britain is racked by deep social schisms and class tensions which have all but blocked economic change.

In each of these historic periods the decay of civic virtue was only one aspect of a more general decline in social mobility and a consolidation of economic privilege. These social rigidities in turn undermined the capacity to adapt, and hence accelerated economic decline. Even in these early, simpler eras—when economic leadership was largely a matter of mustering physical resources and riding the slow waves of epoch-making innovations—the sense of citizenship was the foundation of prosperity. In the emerging era of human capital—when a nation's competitive vigor will depend much more immediately on its citizens' capacity to innovate, cooperate, and adapt together—the social adhesive of civic virtue will be an even more direct determinant of economic strength.

We will be able to conquer unemployment and inflation and enjoy enduring economic growth only to the extent that we harness the energy and ideals of all our citizens to the process—spreading the burdens and benefits equitably, making good the losses attendant upon economic change, and striving for justice and decency. A social organization based on greed and fear will fail because it cannot enlist the commitment of all Americans. The notion that social justice must be sacrificed for the sake of economic growth is simply wrong. Social justice is not a luxury bought at the expense of national economic health. It is the means for achieving and maintaining prosperity.

To put it simply, we need an economics that reaffirms our political life together and a politics that promotes our mutual prosperity. In an advanced industrial economy like ours this is the only economics, and the only politics, that make lasting sense. Either we will adapt to this new reality, or following our historical predecessors, the American ascendancy will needlessly come to a close.

NOTES

CHAPTER I: TWO CULTURES

1.   In the mid-1970's the distribution of income (after taxes) in advanced industrial nations looked like this:

	Japan	Sweden	Australia	Netherlands	W.Germany	Britain	Norway	Canada	U.S.	France
share of national income received by poorest 20 percent of families	7.9	6.6	6.6	6.5	6.5	6.3	6.3	5	4.5	4.3
share received by poorest 10 percent of families	3.2	2.9	2.8	2.7	2.5	2.4	2.1	1.5	1.5	1.4

See Malcolm Sawyer, "Income Distribution in OECD Countries," *OECD Economic Outlook* (Brussels: Organization for Economic Cooperation and Development, July 1976). Recent policy shifts in both France and the United States have now caused the United States to move into last place, with the poorest 20 percent and 10 percent receiving the smallest share of after-tax income of any major industrialized nation.

2.   See Chapter X for precise figures.

3.   The following table shows that the growth in American output (total, per capita, and per unit of labor input) has seriously lagged behind other industrial nations:

(percent)				
	Total		Per Capita	
	1960–1973 (1)	1973–1981 (2)	1960–1973 (3)	1973–1981 (4)
United States	4.2	2.3	3.0	1.2
Japan	10.5	3.8	9.3	2.9
Germany	4.8	1.9	3.9	2.0
France	5.7	2.5	4.6	2.2
United Kingdom	3.2	0.5	2.7	0.5
Italy	5.2	2.4	4.4	2.0
Canada	5.4	2.4	3.7	1.7

	Per Unit of Labor Input	
	1960–1973 (5)	1973–1981 (6)
United States	3.1	0.9
Japan	9.9	3.6
Germany	5.8	3.3
France	5.9	3.4
United Kingdom	3.8	1.8
Italy	7.8	1.4
Canada	4.2	0.4

Data for France, Italy, and the United Kingdom are based on gross domestic product. Data for the other countries are based on gross national product.

Source: Cols. 1, 2, 3, 4: International Monetary Fund, *International Financial Statistics* (various issues). Data for 1981 partly estimated by the American Enterprise Institute.

Col. 5 and col. 6, 1973–1979: John W. Kendrick, "International Comparisons of Recent Productivity Trends," in *Essays in Contemporary Economic Problems,* William Fellner, ed., 1981–1982 ed. (Washington, D.C.: American Enterprise Institute, 1981), p. 128.

Col. 6, 1979–1981: Organization for Economic Cooperation and Development, *Economic Outlook* (December 1981), p. 46.

4.   International comparisons of gross domestic product per capita are bedeviled by differences in official exchange rates and methods of measurement. Nevertheless, at least until 1979 the comparisons were useful for ascertaining relative competitiveness. Since many goods and services are not traded in international markets, such comparisons are not useful for measuring relative real standards of living. The Organization for Economic Cooperation and Development has devised the following comparisons, showing the ratio of gross domestic product per capita of selected countries to that of the United States:

	1960	1963	1970	1975	1979
Switzerland	57	66	70	118	139
Denmark	46	53	67	104	119
Sweden	67	75	86	118	115
Germany	46	53	64	95	116
Iceland	49	56	51	82	103
Norway	45	50	60	99	106
Belgium	44	47	55	90	107
Luxembourg	59	57	66	89	109
Netherlands	47	55	58	90	101
France	47	55	58	90	100
Canada	79	72	81	101	91
Japan	16	22	41	63	82
Finland	40	45	48	82	82
Britain	48	50	46	58	67

See OECD National Accounts Series, "Main Economic Indicators" (Brussels: Organization for Economic Cooperation and Development, relevant years).

Since 1981, with the dollar's artificial rise relative to other currencies, these sorts of comparisons have become less valid as proxies for competitiveness.

Another measure, based on the cost of a large uniform sample of goods and services in each country, shows the United States in a more favorable light, but even by this measure, other nations are gaining at a rapid clip. This measure also overstates the value of such intangibles as health care in America, considering that Americans' average life expectancy is shorter, and infant mortality higher, than in the other nations.

	1960	1970	1979 or 1980
United States	100.0	100.0	100.0
Germany	73.3	82.3	87.4 (1980)
France	61.6	75.9	80.0 (1979)
Japan	31.5	61.6	70.2 (1979)
United Kingdom	66.5	64.9	58.6 (1980)

Source: Irving Kravis, Alan Heston, and Robert Summers, "New Insights into the Structure of the World Economy," *Review of Income and Wealth* (December 1981), pp. 348–49.

5.   Unemployment in the United States has been worse than in many other industrialized nations, as the following table shows:

(percentage of total labor force unemployed) 1973–1981			
	Lowest Year	Highest Year	Average
United States	5.4	8.3	6.9
Japan	1.4	2.2	2.0
Germany	1.6	4.3	3.4
France	2.8	7.6	5.1
United Kingdom	2.9	11.0	6.1
Italy	5.3	8.1	6.8

NOTE: As standardized by the Organization for Economic Cooperation and Development.

Source: Organization for Economic Cooperation and Development, *Economic Outlook* (December 1981), p. 142; 1981 partly estimated.

In 1981 and 1982, the rate of unemployment in the United States was significantly higher than in Japan, West Germany, or France. Only Great Britain had a comparable rate.

6.   Life expectancy among American males (in 1975) was 68.7 years, but in Japan it was 72.2 years; in Sweden, 72.1; in West Germany, 68.8; and in France, 69.2. Life expectancy for American females also was lower than in most other

industrialized nations. See United Nations, *Demographic Yearbook* (New York: United Nations, 1979), pp. 402–14.

7.   See "The State of the Environment in OECD Member Countries" (Organization for Economic Cooperation and Development, 1980).

CHAPTER II: THE ERA OF MOBILIZATION

1.   See Simon Kuznets, *Economic Growth and Structure* (New York: W. W. Norton, 1965), pp. 305–27.

2.   On the central importance of timber resources to the speed of industrialization, see Heinrich Rubner, "Forstwirtschaft und Industrialisierung (besonders Frankreich)," in W. Fischer, ed., *Wirtschafts- und Sozialgeschichtliche Probleme der frühen Industrialisierung* (Berlin: Cologne, 1968).

3.   See Sidney Pollard, *Peaceful Conquest: The Industrialization of Europe 1760–1970* (Oxford: Oxford University Press, 1981), p. 26, and sources cited therein.

4.   Readers who wish to examine Britain's gradual economic demise, beginning in the middle decades of the nineteenth century, should see the now-classic J. H. Clapham, *An Economic History of Modern Britain II (1850–1880)* (London: Macmillan, 1932).

5.   From Thomas Edison's *Journal,* entry of February 1881.

6.   Cited in Elting Morison, *Men, Machines, and Modern Times* (Cambridge, Mass.: MIT Press, 1966), p. 40.

7.   See Adolf A. Berle, Jr., and Gardiner C. Means, *The Modern Corporation and Private Property* (New York: Macmillan, 1932), p. 56, Table VIII.

8.   Data from Paul Uselding, "Manufacturing," in Glenn Porter, ed., *Encyclopedia of American Economic History* (New York: Charles Scribner, 1980), pp. 409–11. See also Frederick C. Mills, *Economic Tendencies in the United States* (New York: National Bureau of Economic Research, 1932), pp. 4, 21–23.

9.   Data from U.S. Bureau of the Census, *Historical Statistics of the United States: Colonial Times to 1957* (Washington, D.C.: U.S. Government Printing Office, 1960). See also Colin Clark, *The Conditions of Economic Progress* (London: Macmillan, 1951), pp. 404, 408–09, 413.

10. U.S. Bureau of the Census, *op. cit.*

11. *Ibid.* See also Herbert Gutman, *Work, Culture, and Society in Industrializing America* (New York: Knopf, 1976).

12. This and other studies are cited in Jeremiah Jenks and Jeff Lauck, *The Immigration Problem,* 6th ed. (New York: Funk & Wagnalls, 1926), p. 148.

13. U.S. Bureau of the Census, *Historical Statistics of the United States: Colonial Times to 1970* (Washington, D.C.: U.S. Government Printing Office, 1975), Vol. 2, p. 731.

14. For a fuller account of the American gospel of success, see A. W. Griswold, "The American Gospel of Success," dissertation (Yale University, 1933), pp. 96–117; Irvin Wyllie, *The Self-Made Man in America* (New Brunswick, N.J.: Rutgers University Press, 1954), pp. 83–87.

15. See Kōzō Yamamura, *A Study of Samurai Income and Entrepreneurship* (Cambridge, Mass.: Harvard University Press, 1974), p. 152.

16. See Paul Uselding, *op. cit.,* pp. 409–13; U.S. Bureau of the Census, *Historical Statistics of the United States: Colonial Times to 1970,* Vol. 1, pp. 200–01, 224.

17. Data from Ralph Nelson, *Merger Movements in American History 1895–1956* (Princeton, N.J.: Princeton University Press, 1959).

18. Woodrow Wilson, *The New Freedom* (New York: Macmillan, 1913), pp. 57–58.

19. See R. Ozanne, *A Century of Labor-Management Relations at McCormick and International Harvester* (Madison, Wis.: University of Wisconsin Press, 1967), p. 3; S. Buder, *Pullman* (New York: Oxford University Press, 1967), pp. 10, 17.

20. U.S. Bureau of the Census, *Historical Statistics of the United States: Colonial Times to 1970,* Vol. 2, p. 153.

21. For a detailed account, see David Brody, *Steelworkers in America* (Cambridge, Mass.: Harvard University Press, 1960), pp. 50–58.

22. On the power and influence of factory foremen during this period, see Daniel Nelson, *Managers and Workers: Origins of the New Factory System in the United States, 1880–1920* (Madison, Wis.: University of Wisconsin Press, 1975), especially ch. 3.

23.   United States Commissioner of Labor, *21st Annual Report, 1906* (Washington, D.C.: U.S. Government Printing Office, 1907), p. 14–15.

24.   *Report of the Proceedings of the 14th Annual Convention of the American Federation of Labor,* held in Denver, Colo., December 1894 (Bloomington, Ill.: American Federation of Labor, 1905), p. 14.

25.   Richard Ely, "Pullman: A Social Study," *Harper's Monthly* (June 1885).

26.   See United States Bureau of Labor Statistics, *Welfare Work for Employees in Industrial Establishments in the United States* (Washington, D.C.: U.S. Government Printing Office, 1919), pp. 15, 73, 101–08. See also Stuart Brandes, *American Welfare Capitalism 1880–1940* (Chicago: University of Chicago Press, 1976), p. 20–31; and Machinery and Allied Products Institute, *The General Electric Approach to Industrial Relations* (Washington, D.C.: MAPI, 1962).

27.   United States Senate Committee on Labor and Education, *Investigation of the Strike in the U.S. Steel Industry,* Sixty-sixth Congress, First Session (Washington, D.C.: U.S. Government Printing Office, 1919), Vol. II, pp. 495, 524–25, 674–77. See also David Montgomery, "The 'New Unionism' and the Transformation of Workers' Consciousness in America, 1909–1922," *Journal of Social History* (Summer 1974).

28.   On the charity movement of this era, see George W. Corner, *A History of the Rockefeller Institu* (New York: Rockefeller Institute Press, 1964). See also Walter I. Trattner, *From Poor Law to Welfare State: A History of Social Welfare in America* (New York: Free Press, 1974), pp. 80–86.

29.   For a more detailed account, see Lawrence Goodwyn, *The Populist Moment* (New York: Oxford University Press, 1978), pp. 270–86.

CHAPTER III: THE MANAGERIAL IMAGINATION

1.   For empirical studies on growth and productivity in the United States during this period, see John Kendrick, *Productivity Trends in the United States* (Princeton, N.J.: Princeton University Press, 1961), pp. 70–71; Edward Denison, *Sources of Economic Growth in the United States* (New York: Macmillan, 1962); Robert M. Solow, "Technical Change and the Production Function," *Review of Economics and Statistics,* Vol. 39 (August 1957); United States Department of Commerce, *Long Term Economic Growth 1860–1965* (Washington, D.C.: U.S. Government Printing Office, 1966), pp. 101, 248, 251.

2.   On the stability of American manufacturing during this era, see United States Bureau of the Census, *Census of Manufacturers,* Special Rept. Series MC72-SR-2 (Washington, D.C.: U.S. Government Printing Office, 1975). See also Alfred D. Chandler, Jr., "The Structure of American Industry in the Twentieth Century: A Historical Overview," *Business History Review,* Vol. 43 (Autumn 1969), pp. 257, 283, 284; and Richard C. Edwards, "Stages in Corporate Stability and Corporate Growth," *Journal of Economic History,* Vol. 35 (July 1975), pp. 428–57.

3.   Data from Alfred D. Chandler, cited in Thomas K. McCraw, "Rethinking the Trust Question," in Thomas K. McCraw, ed., *Regulation in Perspective* (Cambridge, Mass.: Harvard University Press, 1981), p. 21.

4.   See Robert T. Averitt, *The Dual Economy: The Dynamics of American Industry Structure* (New York: Macmillan, 1968), pp. 38–44.

5.   Herbert Kaufman, *Are Government Organizations Immortal?* (Washington, D.C.: Brookings Institution, 1976), pp. 36–38.

6.   See David Montgomery, " 'Liberty and Union': Workers and Government in America," in R. Weible, ed., *Essays from the Lowell Conference on Industrial History* (Lowell, Mass.: Lowell Conference on Industrial History, 1981), p. 145, 148, 150.

7.   Wyona S. Coleman, " 'A Feeling of Security': The Iron and Coal Police —Armed Paternalism in the Coal Camps, 1926–1933," unpublished (1974), pp. 17–18.

8.   Robert and Helen M. Lynd, *Middletown: A Study in American Culture* (New York: Macmillan, 1929), pp. 75–79.

9.   U.S. Bureau of the Census, *Historical Statistics of the United States, Colonial Times to 1970,* Vol. 1, p. 114.

10.   See generally Morris Janowitz, *Social Control of the Welfare State* (New York: Elsevier, 1976), p. 30–38; and Raymond Callahan, *Education and the Cult of Efficiency* (Chicago: University of Chicago Press, 1962).

CHAPTER IV: THE PROFESSION OF MANAGEMENT

1.   Woodrow Wilson, "The Study of Administration," *Political Science Quarterly,* Vol. 2 (June 1887).

2.   *Ibid.*, pp. 212, 216, 218.

3.   Frederick Winslow Taylor, *The Principles of Scientific Management* (New York: Harper and Brothers, 1911), pp. 20–28.

4.   *Ibid.*, pp. 128–33.

5.   *Ibid.*, pp. 40–41.

6.   Samuel Lewisohn, *The New Leadership in Industry* (New York: Macmillan, 1926), p. 199.

7.   Taylor, *op. cit.*, p. 10.

8.   Louis Brandeis, *Letters* (New York: Doubleday, 1936), Vol. II, pp. 383–86, 543.

9.   *Evidence Taken by the Interstate Commerce Commission in the Matter of Proposed Advances in Freight Rates by Carriers,* Sixty-first Congress, Third Session, Ser. Vol. 5906 (1910), pp. 1152, 2620, 3723–24. See also Horace Bookwalter Drury, *Scientific Management: A History and Criticism,* 3d ed. (New York: Columbia University Press, 1922), pp. 36–38.

10.   On the popularity of scientific management during this era, see Samuel Haber, *Efficiency and Uplift: Scientific Management in the Progressive Era, 1890–1920* (Chicago: University of Chicago Press, 1964), pp. 51–74.

11.   L. Davis, R. Canter, J. Hoffman, "Current Job Design Criteria," *Journal of Industrial Engineering* (March–April 1955), pp. 5–8, 21–23.

12.   Taylor, *op. cit.*, pp. 31, 189, 211.

13.   Data from Joan Hoff Wilson, *Herbert Hoover, Forgotten Progressive* (Boston: Little, Brown, 1975), pp. 30–36.

14.   See Allan Nevins and E. F. Hill, *Ford: Decline and Rebirth 1933–1962* (New York: Charles Scribner, 1963), ch. 2–3.

15.   Robert J. Larner, "Ownership and Control in the 200 Largest Non-Financial Corporations, 1929 and 1963," *American Economic Review,* Vol. 56 (September 1966), pp. 777–87.

16.   Data from L. Corey, "The Middle Class," in R. Bendix and S. Lipset, *Class, Status, and Power* (New York: Macmillan, 1953); Seymour Melman, "The Rise of Administrative Overhead in the Manufacturing Industries in the United States, 1899–1947," *Oxford Economic Papers,* Vol. III (1951), p. 66; "Bringing Up the Boss," *Fortune* (June 1951), p. 119.

17.   Editorial, *Management Review,* Vol. xvii (February 1928), p. 48.

18.   Elton Mayo, *The Social Problems of an Industrial Civilization* (Boston: Harvard Business School, 1945), pp. 72–73.

19.   On "human-social" skills, see, for example, F. J. Ruethlisberger and W. J. Dickion, *Management and the Worker* (New York: Macmillan, 1939).

20.   Editorial, *Management Review,* Vol. xxvi (October 1937), p. 340; editorial, *Management Review,* Vol. xxvii (February 1938); Dale Carnegie, *How to Win Friends and Influence People,* originally *Public Speaking and Influencing Men in Business* (New York: Macmillan, 1926); National Association of Manufacturers, *Industry Believes* (New York: NAM, 1953), pp. 7–8.

21.   See William H. Allen, "Training Men and Women for Public Service," *Annual of the American Association of Political and Social Scientists,* Vol. XLI (May 1912), pp. 307–12.

22.   On the origins of the city manager movement, see Clarence E. Ridley and Orin Nolting, *The City Manager Profession* (Chicago: University of Chicago Press, 1934).

23.   *Speeches of President John F. Kennedy,* commencement address at Yale University, June 11, 1962 (Washington, D.C.: U.S. Government Printing Office, 1964).

24.   Kaufman, *op. cit.,* pp. 38–43.

CHAPTER V: THE SUPERSTRUCTURES OF MANAGEMENT

1.   R. P. Rumelt, "Strategy, Structure, and Economic Performance" (Division of Research, Harvard University Graduate School of Business Administration, 1974).

2.   For a detailed discussion on the evolution of the diversified American corporation, see Alfred C. Chandler, *The Visible Hand: The Managerial Revolution in American Business* (Cambridge, Mass.: Harvard University Press, 1977), pp. 469–83.

3.   *Hearings on the Promotion of Export Trade Before the House Judiciary Committee,* Sixty-fourth Congress, First Session (Washington, D.C.: U.S. Government Printing Office, 1916), p. 210.

4.   Estimates from F. M. Scherer, *Industrial Market Structure and Economic Performance*, 2d ed. (Boston: Houghton Mifflin, 1980), p. 68.

5.   Data on the automobile industry from Allan Nevins and Frank Hill, *Ford* (New York: Charles Scribner, 1934), Vol. 1, pp. 193–94, Vol. 2, p. 170; Ralph C. Epstein, *The Automobile Industry* (New York: A. W. Shaw, 1928), p. 48–52; Stanley Boyle and Thomas Hogarty, "Pricing Behavior in the American Automobile Industry, 1957–1971," *Journal of Industrial Economics*, Vol. 24 (December 1975), pp. 81–95; *Automobile Industries Annual Statistical Issues* (Detroit: R. L. Polk, 1927–1974).

6.   On the history of the U.S. steel industry, see Ida M. Tarbell, *The Life of Elbert H. Gary* (New York: D. Appleton, 1925), ch. 8; Grant McConnell, *Steel and the Presidency* (New York: W. W. Norton, 1963); Leonard W. Weiss, *Economics and American Industry* (New York: John Wiley, 1961), pp. 293–99.

7.   See Ira C. Magaziner and Robert B. Reich, *Minding America's Business: The Decline and Rise of the American Economy* (New York: Harcourt Brace Jovanovich, 1982), ch. 13.

8.   *Ibid.*, Exhibit 40, p. 82.

9.   The full account is found in Harwood L. Childs, *Labor and Capital in Politics* (Columbus, Ohio: State University Press, 1930), pp. 12–15.

10.   See Robert D. Cuff, "Business, the State, and World War I: The American Experience," in Jordan A. Schwartz, ed., *The Ordeal of Twentieth Century America, Interpretive Readings* (Boston: Little Brown, 1974); Robert F. Himmelberg, "The War Industries Board and the Antitrust Question in November, 1918," *Journal of American History*, Vol. LII (June 1965), pp. 59–74.

11.   Data from Richard Polenberg, *War and Society, the United States, 1941–1945* (Philadelphia: University of Pennsylvania Press, 1972), ch. 8.

12.   Arthur Jerome Eddy, *The New Competition* (Chicago: McClury, 1912). On the "open price" movement, see L. S. Lyon and Victor Abramson, *The Economics of Open Price Associations* (Washington, D.C.: Brookings Institution, 1936), pp. 15–23.

13.   Federated American Engineering Societies, *Waste in Industry* (New York: Federated American Engineering Societies, June 1921).

14.   On Hoover's activities at the Department of Commerce, see, for example, Ellis W. Hawley, "Herbert Hoover, the Commerce Secretariat, and the Vision of an Associative State," *Journal of American History*, Vol. LXI (June

1974), pp. 116–40; Joan Hoff Wilson, *Herbert Hoover: Forgotten Progressive* (Boston: Little, Brown, 1975), pp. 79–121.

15.   For a detailed history of the NRA and the underlying ideals of business-government organization that shaped it, see Ellis W. Hawley, *The New Deal and the Problem of Monopoly* (Princeton: Princeton University Press, 1966); Robert Himmelberg, *The Origins of the NRA: Business, Government, and the Trade Association Issue, 1921–1933* (New York: Fordham University Press, 1976), pp. 181–212.

16.   *Interim Report of the Antitrust Subcommittee of the Committee on the Judiciary on WOCs [Without Compensation] and Government Advisory Groups,* United States House of Representatives, Eighty-fourth Congress, Second Session (Washington, D.C.: U.S. Government Printing Office, 1956), pp. 7–8.

17.   *WOCs and Government Advisory Groups, Hearings Before the Antitrust Subcommittee of the Committee on the Judiciary,* U.S. House of Representatives, Eighty-fourth Congress, First Session, Part I (1955), p. 178.

18.   *Hearings Before the Committee on Government Operations on Amendments to the Administrative Expense Act of 1946,* United States House of Representatives, Eighty-fifth Congress, First Session (1957), p. 2.

19.   Data from E. Ginzberg et al., *The Economic Impact of Large Public Programs* (Salt Lake City: Olympus, 1976); U.S. Bureau of the Census, *Shipments to Federal Government Agencies* (Washington, D.C.: U.S. Government Printing Office, 1978).

20.   *National Patterns of R and D Resources, 1953–1972* (Washington, D.C.: National Science Foundation, 1972); National Science Board, *Science Indicators 1978* (Washington, D.C.: U.S. Government Printing Office, 1979).

21.   See Federal Trade Commission, *Staff Report on the Semiconductor Industry* (Washington, D.C.: U.S. Government Printing Office, 1977).

22.   See William Baldwin, Federal Trade Commission, Office of Policy Planning, *The Impact of Department of Defense Procurement on Competition in Commercial Markets* (Washington, D.C.: U.S. Government Printing Office, December 1980).

CHAPTER VI: THE NOVELTY OF MANAGEMENT

1.   See Kenji Okuda, "Management Evolution in Japan," *Management Japan,* Vol. 5, No. 4 (1972).

2.   See generally Arndt Sorge, "The Management Tradition: A Continental View," in M. Fores and I. Glover, eds., *Manufacturing and Management* (Oxford: Oxford University Press, 1967).

3.   Data from M. Fores and I. Glover, "Engineers in France," *The Chartered Mechanical Engineer* (April 1976); D. Monjardet, "Carrière des dirigeants et controle de l'entreprise," *Sociologie du travail,* Vol. 13 (avril–juin 1972); H. Hartmann and H. Weinold, *Universität und Unteinechmer* (Gutersloh: Bertelsmann, 1976); M. Fores and D. Clark, "Why Sweden Manages Better," *Management Today* (February 1975).

4.   Office of Foreign Economic Research, United States Department of Labor, *Report on U.S. Competitiveness* (Washington, D.C.: U.S. Government Printing Office, September 1980), Table V-27.

5.   See Lawrence G. Franko, "The Growth and Organization Efficiency of European Multinational Firms: Some Emerging Hypotheses," *Colloques International Aux C.N.R.S.,* No. 549 (1972), pp. 335–66; Okuda, *op. cit.*

6.   Leslie Hannah, "Visible and Invisible Hands in Great Britain," in Aldred D. Chandler, Jr., and Herman Deams, eds., *Managerial Hierarchies* (Cambridge, Mass.: Harvard University Press, 1980), p. 42; Leslie Hannah and J. A. Kay, *Concentration in Modern Industry* (London: Macmillan, 1977), ch. 5–6.

7.   See Solomon Levine and Hisashi Kawada, *Human Resources in Japanese Industrial Development* (Princeton: Princeton University Press, 1980), pp. 26–28.

CHAPTER VII: GLOBAL CHANGE

1.   See Chapter I, notes 3 and 4.

2.   See Chapter I, notes 5–7. See also Magaziner and Reich, *op. cit.,* ch. 1.

3.   Magaziner and Reich, *op. cit.,* p. 42.

4.   See Edward F. Denison, *Accounting for Slower Economic Growth: The United States in the 1970s* (Washington, D.C.: Brookings Institution, 1979), pp. 130–33.

5.   Using 1978 as a typical year, the U.S. government deficit was 0.6 percent of gross domestic product, while the Japanese government deficit was 6.1 percent of Japan's GDP, West Germany's deficit was 2.8 percent, France's was 2.3 percent, and Sweden's was 2.1 percent. See Organization for Economic Cooperation and Development, *National Accounts 1961–1978* (Paris: OECD, June 1980), Vol. II, pp. 240–252. See also Tax Foundation, *Facts and Figures on Government Finance* (Washington, D.C.: Washington Tax Foundation, 1979), 20th ed., p. 35.

The following table shows that the public share of total credit market funds raised by nonfinancial markets has also been lower in the United States than in other industrialized nations:

(percent)			
	1973	1979	1980
United States	12.3	15.9	32.1
Japan	18.6	48.1	46.8
Germany	12.9	22.7	31.9
France	9.9	21.4	N.A.
United Kingdom	19.0	25.4	44.6

NOTE: N.A. = not available.

Source: Organization for Economic Cooperation and Development, *Economic Outlook* (December 1981), p. 32.

6.   See Magaziner and Reich, *op. cit.,* pp. 45–51.

7.   United States Department of Commerce, *International Economic Indicators* (Washington, D.C.: U.S. Government Printing Office, various issues). The estimate of U.S. manufactured goods now exposed to international competition was calculated by adding up total production of U.S. goods in Standard Industrial Classification six-digit categories in which imports equal more than 10 percent of consumption or exports equal more than 10 percent of production.

8.   Calculated from United States Department of Commerce, *United States Industrial Outlook* (Washington, D.C.: U.S. Government Printing Office, 1982 and various issues).

9.   Calculated from Council of Economic Advisors, *Economic Report of the President* (Washington, D.C.: U.S. Government Printing Office, 1982), Tables

B-106 and B-107. See also Organization for Economic Cooperation and Development, *Main Economic Indicators: Historical Statistics 1960–1979* (Paris: OECD, 1980).

10.   United States data from National Research Council, *A Century of Doctorates* (Washington, D.C.: NRC, 1978), p. 47; European data from UNESCO, *Statistics of Students Abroad* (Paris: UNESCO, 1976), Table 6.

11.   For data on declining cargo freight costs, see Federal Aviation Administration, *Statistical Handbook of Aviation* (Washington, D.C.: U.S. Government Printing Office, various years); Air Transport Association, *Annual Report* (Washington, D.C.: ATA, various years); Organization for Economic Cooperation and Development, *Maritime Transport* (Paris: OECD, various years).

12.   Barend A. deVries and Willem Brakel, *Restructuring of Manufacturing Industry: The Case of the Textile Industry in Selected Developing Countries* (Washington, D.C.: World Bank, July 6, 1981), pp. 15–30.

13.   See Federal Trade Commission, *Staff Report on the United States Steel Industry and Its International Rivals* (Washington, D.C.: U.S. Government Printing Office, 1977), pp. 95–124.

14.   See Office of Technology Assessment, *Technology and Steel Industry Competitiveness* (Washington, D.C.: U.S. Government Printing Office, 1980), pp. 116–51; Comptroller General of the United States, General Accounting Office, *New Strategy Required for Aiding Distressed Steel Industry* (Washington, D.C.: U.S. Government Printing Office, 1981), ch. 2; U.S. House of Representatives, Committee on Energy and Commerce, staff report, *Crisis in the Steel Industry: An Introduction, and The Steel Industry in Transition* (Washington, D.C.: U.S. Government Printing Office, 1982), pp. 38–51.

15.   See Ira C. Magaziner and Thomas Hout, *Japanese Industrial Policy* (London: Policy Studies Institute, 1980), pp. 45–54.

16.   See Report of the Independent Commission on International Development Issues, *North: South: A Programme for Survival* (Cambridge, Mass.: MIT Press, 1981), pp. 172–86; Deepak Ial, *Market Access for Semi-Manufacturers from Developing Countries* (Geneva: Graduate Institute of International Studies, 1979); International Labor Organization, *Yearbook of Labor Statistics* (Geneva: ILO, 1975).

17.   Steve Lohr, "South Korea Betting on Ships," *The New York Times* (June 6, 1982), p. D 1.

18.   See Chen Kao-tang, ed. *China Yearbook 1980* (Taipei: China Publishing Co., 1981), pp. 266–74.

19.   International Labor Organization, *op. cit.*

20.   See Magaziner and Reich, *op. cit.*, pp. 99–101.

21.   In a study undertaken by the National Science Board a panel of international experts on science and technology were asked to select 400 inventions developed between 1953 and 1973 which in their opinion were most important to world technological and economic advance. Of this list, the proportion of inventions that derived from Great Britain was significantly greater than from any other nation. See National Science Board, *Science Indicators 1974, 1976* (Washington, D.C.: NSB, 1975, 1977).

22.   Magaziner and Reich, *op. cit.*, pp. 77–85.

23.   *Ibid.*, pp. 72–77.

24.   Data on services from United States Department of Commerce, International Trade Administration, *Current Developments in U.S. International Service Industries* (Washington, D.C.: U.S. Government Printing Office, 1980); United States Department of Commerce, Bureau of Economic Analysis, *Survey of Current Business* (Washington, D.C.: U.S. Government Printing Office, March 1980), p. 50.

CHAPTER VIII: PAPER ENTREPRENEURIALISM

1.   Data on ratio of staff positions to production workers from United States Department of Labor, Bureau of Labor Statistics, *Employment and Earnings* (Washington, D.C.: U.S. Government Printing Office, 1976), Table B–2. See also George Delehanty, *Non-Production Workers in U.S. Manufacturing* (Amsterdam: North Holland, 1968), p. 149. Data also gleaned from interviews with personnel officers at various companies.

2.   Jeremy Main, "How to Battle Your Own Bureaucracy," *Fortune* (June 29, 1981), pp. 54–58. See also "Look Who's Covered in Red Tape," *Fortune* (May 4, 1981), pp. 357–62.

3.   There exists a vast literature on communications distortions within organizations. See, for example, Donald Campbell, "Systematic Error on the Part

of Human Links in Communications Systems," *Information and Control,* Vol. 1 (1958), pp. 334–69; and Kenneth J. Arrow, *The Limits of Organization* (New York: W. W. Norton, 1974), pp. 53–54.

4.   Data from W. T. Grimm and Company, *Mergers Summary* (Chicago: W. J. Grimm, annual issues); Federal Trade Commission, *Statistical Report on Mergers and Acquisitions* (Washington, D.C.: U.S. Government Printing Office, various issues).

5.   Data compiled by Mark Kaplan, "High, Necessary Cost of the Take-over Game," *Financier* (June 1981), p. 44–48. Data also gathered from interviews.

6.   See, generally, "Should Companies Pay Takeover Ransom?" *Dun's Review* (May 1981), pp. 103–06; Paul Blustein, "More Firms Paying Premium Prices to Wrest Shares from Antagonists," *Wall Street Journal* (January 8, 1981), p. 22.

7.   See Geoffrey Colvin, "The Smart Taxophobe at Baldwin United," *Fortune* (March 8, 1982), pp. 52–59.

8.   See George Getschow, "Slick Accounting Ploys Help Many Companies Improve Their Incomes," *Wall Street Journal* (June 20, 1980), pp. 1, 34. Examples also gleaned from interviews.

9.   For a detailed look at these and other ploys, see Abraham Briloff, *The Truth About Corporate Accounting* (New York: Harper & Row, 1981).

10.   Thomas Garbett, "When to Advertise Your Company," *Harvard Business Review* (March–April 1982), p. 100.

11.   "Annual Reports Grow More Lavish at Many Companies," *Wall Street Journal* (January 6, 1982), p. 1.

12.   Jonathan Rowe, "Firms Keep Auditors at Arm's Length," *Multinational Monitor* (August 1980), pp. 18–20.

13.   Commodity Future Trading Commission, *Annual Report* (Washington, D.C.: U.S. Government Printing Office, 1981), p. 126.

14.   Estimate derived from data in S. Flanders, *1979 District Court Time Study* (Washington, D.C.: Federal Judicial Center, 1980); American Bar Association, *Annual Membership Report* and *Section and Division Membership Report* (Chicago: ABA, various years); Director of the Administrative Office of the

U.S. Courts, *Annual Report* (Washington, D.C.: U.S. Government Printing Office, various years).

15.   As but one example, consider the experience of B. Charles Ames, who resigned in 1981 as president of the Reliance Electric Company, eighteen months after the firm had been acquired by Exxon. "[O]ur corporate staff grew enormously after the acquisition," he explained. "We went from about 12 to 25 or 30 auditors, and everyone had a lot more paperwork. . . . Also, after the acquisition, we never had any specific objectives. It was a very mushy, bureaucratic decision-making environment." Quoted in *The New York Times* (May 31, 1982), p. D 7. Soon thereafter Exxon sold Reliance. The author's interviews with various executives of smaller businesses that had been acquired by larger ones also bears this out.

16.   See periodic surveys of the backgrounds of chief executive officers undertaken by Golightly and Company and by Heidrick and Struggles. See also John A. Sussman, "Making It to the Top: A Career Profile of the Senior Executive," *Management Review,* Vol. 68, No. 7 (July 1979), pp. 14–21; and Henry Beam, "The New Route to the Top," *Advanced Management Journal,* Vol. 44, No. 2 (Spring 1979), pp. 55–62.

17.   Estimate based on United States Department of Labor, Bureau of Labor Statistics, *Employment and Earnings* (Washington, D.C.: U.S. Government Printing Office, various issues).

18.   For Harvard survey data, see Diana Zuckerman, "Career and Life Goals of Freshmen and Seniors," *Radcliffe Quarterly* (September 1982); on legal fees, see Annual Survey of Legal Fees, Costs, and Remuneration, *Legal Times of Washington* (Washington, D.C.: Law and Business, various issues). See also Price Waterhouse Annual Survey of Lawyers.

19.   Japan data from "Science and Technological Manpower and Expenditures for Research and Experimental Development," *United Nations Statistical Yearbook, 1977* (New York: UN, 1978), p. 922; *Census of Japan* (Tokyo) 1975, Vol. 5, Part I, Div. I, p. 282. United States data from United States Department of Labor, "Employed Persons by Detailed Occupation, 1972–1977," *Handbook of Labor Statistics* (Washington, D.C.: U.S. Government Printing Office, 1978), p. 82; National Science Foundation, *National Patterns of R and D Resources: Funds and Manpower in the United States, 1953–1974* (Washington, D.C.: U.S. Government Printing Office, 1974), NSF 74–304.

20.   See G. C. Allen, "Industrial Policy and Innovation in Japan," in C. Carter, ed., *Industrial Policy and Innovation* (London: Heineman, 1981), p. 80.

21.   Survey by LaMalie Associates of 260 executives who were involved in takeover transactions involving $300 million or more. Cited in *Wall Street Journal* (August 18, 1981), p. 1.

22.   Survey by Michael Maccoby and associates, *The Gamesman: Winning and Losing the Career Game* (New York: Simon & Schuster, 1976), pp. 200–01.

23.   Surveys undertaken by National Personnel Associates (1980) and *Personnel Journal* (1980), cited in *The New York Times* (November 30, 1980), p. D 1.

24.   "Coup at AM," *Fortune* (March 23, 1981), p. 16.

25.   See "RCA: Still Another Master," *Business Week* (August 17, 1981), pp. 80–86.

26.   See Charles G. Burck, "A Group Profile of the Fortune 500 Chief Executive," *Fortune* (May 1976), pp. 173–77, 308–12.

27.   "Did Main Characters in Big Takeover Saga Let Egos Sway Them?" *Wall Street Journal* (September 24, 1982), pp. 1, 22; see generally Ann Morrison, "Job-Hopping at the Top," *Fortune* (May 4, 1981), pp. 127–30.

28.   Survey by Ward Howell International, reported in "Takeovers Spur More Parachutes," *The New York Times* (September 28, 1982) p. D 3; see also Roger Ricklefs, "Top Bosses More Likely to Get Axed, and Large Settlements When They Do," *Wall Street Journal* (July 14, 1980), p. 17; N. R. Kleinfield, " 'Golden Parachutes' for Ousted," *The New York Times* (April 6, 1982), p. D 1; "Bendix Safeguards Executive Benefits," *The New York Times* (September 12, 1982), p. D 3.

29.   Data from Robert E. Hall, *The Importance of Lifetime Jobs in the U.S. Economy* (Washington, D.C.: National Bureau of Economic Research, Working Paper No. 560, 1980); Robert C. Cole, *Work, Mobility, and Participation: A Comparative Study of American and Japanese Industry* (Berkeley, Calif.: University of California Press, 1979), pp. 60–91.

30.   See Peter Nulty, "A Peacemaker Comes to RCA," *Fortune* (May 4, 1981), pp. 140–53; "RCA: Still Another Master," *op. cit.,* pp. 80–86.

31.   See "Can Semiconductors Survive Big Business?" *Business Week* (December 3, 1979), p. 66–85. Data also based on interviews with executives in several companies that manufacture semiconductors.

32.   See, for example, the study of the stock prices of acquiring companies undertaken by Robert A. Schmitz for McKinsey and Co., cited in *The New York Times* (May 31, 1982), p. D 7. A recent study of executive compensation in 140 large companies showed no correlation between compensation paid to chief executives and return on shareholders' equity, but a relatively high correlation between executive compensation and company size. Cited in Carol Loomis, "The Madness of Executive Compensation," *Fortune* (July 12, 1982), pp. 42–52.

The phenomenon of increased pay for increased size is easiest to see when two companies merge. In 1979 Dart Industries paid its chief executive $500,000 and Kraft paid its chief executive $460,000; in 1980, when the companies merged, the compensation of the chief executive of the combined enterprise shot up to $700,000. In 1981 he was paid $750,000. But that year Dart and Kraft's return on equity was only 12.8 percent, well below the returns that Dart and Kraft were earning before the merger. *Ibid.,* p. 44.

33.   "RCA: Still Another Master," *op. cit.*

34.   Data from survey by Sibson and Co., cited in *The New York Times* (December 16, 1981), p. D 2.

35.   Data from Loomis, *op. cit.;* "Business Perks That Rile the White House," *U.S. News and World Report* (March 27, 1979), pp. 33–34.

36.   Interview with official of enforcement division of Securities and Exchange Commission, May 18, 1982.

37.   Tim Metz, "Outside Professionals Play an Increasing Role in Corporate Takeovers," *Wall Street Journal* (December 2, 1980), p. 1; Tim Carrington, "Merger Advisers Say the Big Fees They're Charging Are Warranted," *Wall Street Journal* (July 17, 1981), p. 29; Robert Cole, "End of Marathon Battle Prompts Little Glee," *International Herald Tribune* (January 9–10, 1982), p. 11; Jim Drinkhall, "Fees Charged by Itel's Overseers Suggest Bankruptcy Can Be Enriching Experience," *Wall Street Journal* (June 5, 1981), p. 27; Larry Lempert, "Plaintiffs' Camp Torn Asunder by Fees," *Legal Times of Washington* (June 15, 1981), p. 1.

38.   Data from Carol Gilmore, "To Catch a Corporate Thief," *Advanced Management Journal* (Winter 1982), p. 35.

39.   Thomas O'Toole, "Banks Are Being Robbed, Embezzled at a Record Rate," Washington *Post* (March 2, 1981), p. A 8.

40.   Thomas Friedman, "Silicon Valley's Underworld," *The New York Times* (December 3, 1981), p. D 1; "The Spreading Danger of Computer Crime," *Business Week* (April 20, 1981), pp. 86–92; "Semiconductor Thefts, Mostly by Employees, Plague the Industry," *Wall Street Journal* (January 8, 1981), p. 1.

41.   John P. Clark and Richard Hollinger, *Theft by Employees in Work Organizations* (Minneapolis, Minn.: University of Minnesota, 1982), pp. 41–51.

42.   Harbour and Associates, *Comparison and Analysis of Automobile Manufacturing Productivity in the Japanese and North American Automotive Industry for the Manufacture of Subcompact and Compact Cars* (Berkeley, Mich.: Harbour, 1981), p. 41.

43.   United States Department of Labor, Bureau of International Labor Affairs, *Labor Disputes in Selected Countries* (Washington, D.C.: U.S. Government Printing Office, 1979).

44.   See Louis Harris, "The Steelcase National Survey of Office Environments: Do They Work?" (New York: Steelcase, 1978). See also United States Chamber of Commerce, *Workers Attitudes Toward Productivity* (Washington, D.C.: Chamber of Commerce, 1980).

CHAPTER IX: HISTORIC PRESERVATION

1.   See, generally, Federal Trade Commission, *Staff Report on the United States Steel Industry and Its International Rivals* (Washington, D.C.: U.S. Government Printing Office, 1977).

2.   On the recent history of the U.S. automobile industry, see Robert Leone, William Abernathy, Stephen Bradley, and Jeffrey Hunker, *Regulation and Technological Innovation in the Automobile Industry,* report prepared for the Office of Technological Assessment (Cambridge, Mass.: Harvard Business School, July 1981).

3.   On the recent history of the U.S. television receiver industry, see James E. Millstein, "The Problem of Consumer Electronics: The Case of the U.S. Television Receiver Industry," in L. Tyson and J. Zysman, eds., *American Industry in International Competition* (Berkeley, Calif.: University of California Press, 1982). See also Magaziner and Reich, *op. cit.,* ch. 14.

4.   On the recent history of the videocassette industry, see "The Giants in Japanese Electronics," *The Economist* (February 20, 1982), pp. 80–81.

5.   See, generally, Office of Technology Assessment, *U.S. Industrial Competitiveness: A Comparison of Steel, Electronics, Automobiles* (Washington, D.C.: U.S. Government Printing Office, July 1981).

6.   Magaziner and Reich, *op. cit.,* ch. 13.

7.   See United States International Trade Commission, *Annual Report* (Washington, D.C.: U.S. Government Printing Office, various issues).

8.   For a fuller description of these subsidies, see Magaziner and Reich, *op. cit.,* ch. 19.

9.   *Ibid.,* pp. 248–54.

10.   Interviews with officials in the Office of Management and Budget.

11.   See Federal Trade Commission, *Staff Report on the United States Steel Industry and Its International Rivals,* p. 74; Office of Technology Assessment, *Technology and Steel Industry Competitiveness* (Washington, D.C.: U.S. Government Printing Office, 1980), pp. 340–59.

12.   Office of Technology Assessment, *Technology and Steel Industry Competitiveness,* p. 68.

13.   *Ibid.* See also General Accounting Office, Comptroller General of the United States, *New Strategy Required for Aiding the Distressed Steel Industry* (Washington, D.C.: U.S. Government Printing Office, 1980), pp. 5–7.

14.   *The New York Times* (January 31, 1982), p. F 26.

15.   See Lydia Chavez, "The Year the Bottom Fell Out for Steel," *The New York Times* (June 20, 1982), p. F 1; "U.S. Steelmakers Slim Down for Survival," *Business Week* (May 31, 1982), pp. 88–89.

16.   See United States International Trade Commission, *The History and Current Status of the Multifiber Agreement* (Washington, D.C.: U.S. Government Printing Office, 1978); Vinod Aggarwal and Stephan Haggard, "The Domestic and International Politics of Protection in the U.S. Textile and Apparel Industries," unpublished (1981).

17.   See David Yoffie, "Orderly Marketing Agreements as an Industrial Policy: The Case of the Footwear Industry," *Public Policy,* Vol. 29, No. 1 (Winter 1981).

18.   Millstein, *op. cit.*

19.   National Labor Relations Board, *Annual Report* (Washington, D.C.: U.S. Government Printing Office, various issues).

20.   *The New York Times* (April 27, 1982), p. D 5.

21.   Japanese Ministry of International Trade and Industry, *The Vision of MITI Policies in the 1980s* (Tokyo: MITI, March 17, 1980).

22.   William Baldwin, Federal Trade Commission, Office of Policy Planning, *The Impact of Department of Defense Procurement on Competition in Commercial Markets* (Washington, D.C.: U.S. Government Printing Office, December 1980), pp. 92–95.

23.   Japanese Ministry of International Trade and Industry, *op. cit.*

24.   *Computer Aided Engineering* (January 1981), pp. 25–30.

25.   *Fiberoptics Report* (June 15, 1981), pp. 1–3. See also Marc Aaron Cohen, "The U.S. Fiber Optics Industry: The Japanese Challenge, International Competitiveness, and Public Policy," unpublished master's thesis, (John F. Kennedy School of Government, April 1982).

26.   *Laser Report* (August 10, 1981), p. 2.

27.   See Michael Borrus, James Millstein, and John Zysman, "International Competition in Advanced Industrial Sectors: Trade and Development in the Semiconductor Industry," study prepared for the Joint Economic Committee, Congress of the United States, February 18, 1982. See also Charles River Associates, "Innovation, Competition, and Government Policy in the Semiconductor Industry," unpublished report (March 1980), pp. 3–48.

28.   Baldwin, *op. cit.*, p. 13, Table II-1.

29.   *Ibid.*, p. 53.

30.   William J. Perry, undersecretary of defense for research and engineering, testimony in "Department of Defense Authorization for Appropriations for Fiscal Year 1980," *Hearings Before the Committee on Armed Services,* U.S. Senate, Ninety-sixth Congress, First Session (Washington, D.C.: United States Government Printing Office, April 6, 9, 10, 11, and 23, 1979).

31.   Estimates from Data Resources, Inc., reported in *Business Week* (February 8, 1982), p. 94.

32.   See Robert Reich, "Regulation by Confrontation or Negotiation?" *Harvard Business Review* (May–June 1981), pp. 82–91.

33.   See Robert W. Crandall, *The U.S. Steel Industry in Recurrent Crisis* (Washington, D.C.: Brookings Institution, 1981), p. 106, Table 5-3; Federal Trade Commission, *Effects of Restrictions on United States Imports: Five Case Studies and Theory* (Washington, D.C.: U.S. Government Printing Office, June 1980).

34.   See Federal Trade Commission, *Staff Report on the United States Steel Industry and Its International Rivals,* pp. 94–129.

CHAPTER X: DEAD-END LABOR

1.   James Medoff, "Labor Markets in Imbalance," unpublished (1983).

2.   United States Department of Commerce, Bureau of the Census, *Census of Population 1980* (Washington, D.C.: U.S. Government Printing Office, 1981).

3.   See Harvey Brenner, Joint Economic Committee of the U.S. Congress, *Estimating the Social Costs of National Economic Policy: Implications for Mental and Physical Health and Clinical Aggression* (Washington, D.C.: U.S. Government Printing Office, 1976).

4.   See United States Department of Commerce, United States Department of Labor, *Sharpening Government's Response to Plant Closings: A Two-Year Report on the Commerce-Labor Adjustment Action Committee* (Washington, D.C.: U.S. Government Printing Office, 1979).

5.   Estimates from Kim Clark and Lawrence Summers, "Unemployment Reconsidered," *Harvard Business Review* (November–December 1980), p. 171; Frank de Leeuw et al., "The High-Employment Budget: New Estimates 1955–1980," *Survey of Current Business,* Vol. 60, No. 11 (November 1980).

6.   National Committee on Employment and Unemployment Statistics, *Counting the Labor Force,* preliminary draft (Washington, D.C.: NCEUS, 1979), p. 65; United States Department of Labor, Bureau of Labor Statistics, *Employment and Earnings* (Washington, D.C.: U.S. Government Printing Office, June 1982, July 1983).

7.   Estimates from U.S. Department of Labor, Bureau of Labor Statistics, *Employment Projections for the 1980s* (Washington, D.C.: U.S. Government Printing Office, 1979), Bulletin No. 2030, pp. 30–32. See also BLS "Occupational Matrix" (January 1980).

8.   _Ibid._

9.   Irene A. King, U.S. Department of Health, Education, and Welfare, _Bond Sales for Public School Purposes_ (Washington, D.C.: U.S. Government Printing Office, 1975).

10.   Estimated from United States Department of Labor, Bureau of Labor Statistics, _Employment and Earnings_ (Washington, D.C.: U.S. Government Printing Office, various issues).

11.   Estimated from United States Department of Labor, Bureau of Labor Statistics, _Employment and Earnings,_ (March 1980).

12.   See Robert Howard, "Second Class in Silicon Valley," _Working Papers for a New Society_ (September–October 1981), pp. 21–26; Martin Charnoy and R. Rumberger, _Segmented Labor Markets: Some Empirical Forays_ (Palo Alto, Calif.: Center for Economic Studies, 1975), pp. 40–41.

13.   United States Department of Labor, Bureau of Labor Statistics, "Unemployment Compensation in Eight Industrial Nations," _Monthly Labor Review_ (Washington, D.C.: U.S. Government Printing Office, July 1976).

14.   For a critique of the public service job program, see James O'Toole, _Making America Work: Productivity and Responsibility_ (New York: Continuum, 1981), ch. 8.

15.   Estimates of private-sector training expenditures from the American Society for Training and Development, "Employers' Educational Systems" (June 20, 1980); data on private-sector training per employee from Medoff, _op. cit._

16.   On the trade adjustment program, see General Accounting Office, Comptroller General of the United States, _Considerations for Adjustment Under the 1974 Trade Act: A Summary of Techniques Used in Other Countries_ (Washington, D.C.: U.S. Government Printing Office, January 18, 1979); U.S. Department of Labor, Bureau of International Labor Affairs, _The Impact of International Trade and Investment on Employment_ (Washington, D.C.: U.S. Government Printing Office, 1978); General Accounting Office, Comptroller General of the United States, _Restricting Trade Act Benefits to Import-Affected Workers Who Cannot Find a Job Can Save Millions_ (Washington, D.C.: U.S. Government Printing Office, 1980).

17.   U.S. Office of Education, _Digest of Educational Statistics_ (Washington, D.C.: U.S. Government Printing Office, 1966).

18. Report of the New York City Youth Literacy Task Force, reported in *The New York Times* (April 7, 1982), p. A 1.

19. Educational Testing Service, *Annual Report* (Princeton: ETS, various issues).

20. Report of the National Assessment of Education Progress, cited in *The New York Times* (November 12, 1981), p. A 19.

21. Survey data from U.S. Office of Education, *Digest of Educational Statistics* (Washington, D.C.: U.S. Government Printing Office, 1980); National Educational Association and National Science Foundation, cited in *Economist* (October 10, 1981), p. 104; additional survey data from Educational Testing Service, cited in *The New York Times* (May 27, 1982), p. A 7; American Assn. for the Advancement of Science, *Education in the Sciences: A Developing Crisis* (Washington, D.C.: AAAS, 1982).

22. Data from Allan D. Bromley, survey of education, *Science* (July 10, 1981).

23. Cited in *Wall Street Journal* (August 20, 1981), p. 52.

24. See Fred Hechinger, "Graduate Schools' Decline Leads to Wide Concern," *The New York Times* (July 28, 1981), p. C 5; Roger Lowenstein, "Surge in Engineering Enrollments Begins to Ease Industry's Shortages but Stirs Trouble at Colleges," *Wall Street Journal* (August 20, 1981), p. 52.

25. See United States Department of Commerce, Bureau of the Census, Office of Federal Statistical Policy and Standards, *Social Indicators 1976* (Washington, D.C.: U.S. Government Printing Office, 1977), Chart 362, p. 393; United States Department of Labor, Bureau of Labor Statistics, "International Comparisons of Unemployment," unpublished (April 1980).

26. See Richard E. Peterson et al., Educational Testing Service, *Adult Education Opportunities in Nine Industrialized Countries* (Princeton: ETS, September 1980), Vol. 1, pp. 98–147, 234–66.

27. See Klaus von Dohnanyi, *Education and Youth Employment in the Federal Republic of Germany* (Washington, D.C.: Carnegie Council on Policy Studies in Higher Education, 1978); Peterson et al., *op. cit.*, Vol. 2, pp. 65–77; P. Andrews et al., *The German Vocational System: Comparative Papers in Further Education* (Bristol, England: The Further Education Staff College, 1979).

28. Interview with Takeshi Isayama, deputy special representative, Japanese Ministry of International Trade and Industry, December 9, 1981.

29.　　See Magaziner and Reich, *op. cit.*, p. 144, Exhibit 51.

30.　　Data from Organization for Economic Cooperation and Development, *Unemployment Compensation and Related Employment Policy Measures* (Paris: OECD, 1979); *Japan Statistical Yearbook* (Tokyo) 1980, Table 351, pp. 519–21; United States Department of Labor, Bureau of Labor Statistics, "Unemployment Compensation in Eight Industrial Nations," *Monthly Labor Review* (July 1976), updated in interviews.

31.　　Data from survey by World Priorities, *World Military and Social Expenditures* (New York: World Priorities, 1981).

32.　　*United Nations Demographic Yearbook 1978* (New York: UN, 1979), pp. 286–89, 402–14.

33.　　See Magaziner and Reich, *op. cit.*, p. 16, Exhibit 5.

34.　　Organization for Economic Cooperation and Development, *Educational Statistics in OECD Countries* (Paris: OECD, 1981).

CHAPTER XI: SOCIAL CHANGE

1.　　See Herbert Striner, *Retraining as a National Capital Investment* (Washington, D.C.: American Productivity Center, February 1982); Daniel Hamermesh, "Subsidies for Jobs in the Private Sector," in John Palmer, ed., *Creating Jobs* (Washington, D.C.: Brookings Institution, 1979), pp. 106, 110; J. Bishop, *Vouchers for Creating Jobs, Education, and Training: VOC JET, An Employment-Oriented Strategy for Reducing Poverty* (Madison, Wis.: Institute for Research on Poverty, July 1977).

2.　　See Magaziner and Reich, *op. cit.*, p. 248, Exhibit 78.

3.　　These data are based on a large number of surveys, news reports, and interviews with corporate personnel officers. See, for example, Earl Gottschalk, Jr., " 'Company Housing' on the Rise in California as Schools and Firms Try to Lure Employees," *Wall Street Journal* (October 26, 1981), p. 29; "When Companies Help Pay for Adoption," *Business Week* (November 2, 1981); Earl Gottschalk, Jr., "Firms Increasingly Help Spouses of Transferred Employees to Find Jobs," *Wall Street Journal* (January 21, 1982); "Child Care Grows as a Benefit," *Business Week* (December 21, 1981); Common Cause, *The Untouchables* (Washington, D.C.: Common Cause, September 1981).

4.   Estimates based on data in Martin Rein and Lee Rainwater, "From Welfare State to Welfare Society" (Joint Center for Urban Studies, 1980); United States Chamber of Commerce, *Employee Benefits* (Washington, D.C.: Chamber of Commerce, 1979).

5.   See R. Piscale, "Personnel Practices and Employees' Attitudes: A Study of Japanese and American Managed Firms in the U.S.," *Human Relations*, Vol. 31, No. 7 (1978), pp. 597–615.

6.   West German data from *Les Comptes de la protection sociale: Méthodes et Séries 1959–1978* (Paris: INSEE, 1979); U.S. data from Rein and Rainwater, *op. cit.;* see also United States Department of Commerce, Bureau of Economic Analysis, *The National Income and Product Accounts of the United States, 1929–1974* (Washington, D.C.: U.S. Government Printing Office, 1977), Statistical Tables; United States Department of Commerce, Bureau of Economic Analysis, *Survey of Current Business* (Washington, D.C.: U.S. Government Printing Office, July 1976), Vol. 56.

7.   Estimate derived from data in Rein and Rainwater, *op. cit.*

CHAPTER XII: POLITICAL CHOICE

1.   For more detailed discussions of these systems of participation, see Japan Federation of Employees Association (Nikkeiren), *Report of the Committee for the Study of Labor Questions* (Tokyo, March 1981); Benjamin C. Roberts, Hideaki Okamoto, and George Lodge, *Collective Bargaining and Employee Participation in Western Europe, North America, and Japan* (New York: Trilateral Commission, 1979); Beat Hotz, "Productivity Differences and Industrial Relations Structures," unpublished (1982).

2.   See United States Department of Commerce, Bureau of Industry Analysis, *Survey of Current Business* (Washington, D.C.: U.S. Government Printing Office, various issues); see also Organization for Economic Cooperation and Development, *International Investment and Multinational Enterprises* (Paris: OECD, 1981).

3.   See Kazushi Ohkawa and Shinohara, *Patterns of Japanese Economic Development* (New Haven: Yale University Press, 1979); Kiyohiko Fukushima, "Memo on the Transfer of Technology from Japan to the LDCs" (Nomura Research Institute, April 1979); Eleanor M. Hadley, *Japan's Export Competitive-*

ness in Third World Markets (Washington, D.C.: Georgetown University Center for Strategic and International Studies, 1981).

4.   Interviews with Volvo executives, January 1982.

5.   See A. Premchad, "Government and Public Enterprises—The Budget Link," *Finance and Development* (December 1979), pp. 27–30; Kenneth Walters and R. Joseph Monsen, "State-Owned Business Abroad: The New Competitive Threat," *Harvard Business Review* (March–April 1979), pp. 160–70.

6.   For case studies on investment strategies of pure multinationals, see Jack Baranson, *Technology and the Multinationals* (Lexington, Mass.: D.C. Heath, 1978).

7.   Estimate based on United States Department of Commerce, Bureau of Industry Analysis, *Survey of Current Business* (February 1982).

8.   Survey conducted by *Japan Economic Journal.* See "Foreign-Capitalized Firms Show Keen Interest in Plant Building," *Japan Economic Journal* (September 21, 1982), p. 3.

9.   See Raymond Ahearn et al., "Wage and Price Policies in Australia, Austria, Canada, Japan, the Netherlands, and West Germany," Joint Economic Committee, Congress of the United States (Washington, D.C.: U.S. Government Printing Office, June 24, 1982).

10.   Carlo M. Cipolla, "The Economic Decline of Italy," in C. Cipolla, ed., *The Economic Decline of Empires* (London: Methuen, 1970).

11.   Fernand Braudel, *Capitalism and Material Life 1400–1800* (New York: Macmillan, 1973), p. 417; Sidney Pollard, *Peaceful Conquest: The Industrialization of Europe* (Oxford: Oxford University Press, 1981), p. 211.

12.   C. R. Boxer, "The Dutch Economic Decline," in Cipolla, *op. cit.*

INDEX